# François Rabelais

# FRANÇOIS RABELAIS

## *Critical Assessments*

*Edited by*
*Jean-Claude Carron*

THE JOHNS HOPKINS UNIVERSITY PRESS

Baltimore and London

© 1995 The Johns Hopkins University Press
All rights reserved. Published 1995
Printed in the United States of America on acid-free paper
04  03  02  01  00  99  98  97  96  95        5  4  3  2  1

The Johns Hopkins University Press
2715 North Charles Street
Baltimore, Maryland 21218-4319
The Johns Hopkins Press Ltd., London

Library of Congress Cataloging-in-Publication Data

François Rabelais : critical assessments / edited by Jean-Claude Carron.
    p.   cm.
    Selected and revised papers delivered at a 1991 symposium at the
University of California, Los Angeles.
    Includes bibliographical references.
    ISBN 0-8018-5028-2 (alk. paper)
    1. Rabelais, François, ca. 1490–1553? — Criticism and interpretation —
Congresses.   I. Carron, Jean-Claude.
PQ1694.F73   1995
843'.3 — dc20                                        94-37222
                                                        CIP

# Contents

# Jean-Claude Carron

# Introduction

FRANÇOIS RABELAIS: CRITICAL ASSESSMENTS comprises selected and revised papers delivered at a 1991 UCLA symposium that brought together internationally preeminent
Renaissance scholars and Rabelais specialists.[1] The contributors' own work is situated at the cutting edge of interdisciplinary research that defines Rabelaisian studies today. With the passage
of time, it has become clear that the symposium represented an
important collective effort at a strategic moment in the study of
Rabelais's comic work. The original essays, published here for the
first time,[2] document the dialogue that emerged around innovative
readings informed by new critical methodologies. Beyond providing
a fresh insight into the ongoing scholarly debate, this volume, taken
as a whole, signals a reorientation of Rabelais studies and a provi-
sional culmination of long-standing scholarly disputes in a newfound consensus among the various ideological and intellectual
points of views that constitute recent Rabelais criticism.

Two interrelated questions seem to drive the entire collection. The
first relates to historical distancing and to the conditions of reception
of Rabelais's texts: "Who were Rabelais's readers and what did Rabelais's contemporaries read in his text?" The second stems from the
debate on textual production, hermeneutic closure, and interpretative opening: "When, how, and why does a textual sign mean?" Both
questions function as analytical leitmotifs, problematizing specific
topics that lie at the heart of Rabelais and Renaissance studies today:
interpretative strategies (Michel Jeanneret, Michael J. B. Allen); textual self-reflexivity (Richard Regosin, Raymond La Charité, Edwin Duval); priority of "text/form" or "thought/content" (Terence
Cave, Gérard Defaux, Jean-Claude Margolin); evangelical message
and biblical references in the Rabelaisian text (François Rigolot,

Defaux, Margolin); compositional design and framing of Rabelais's individual books (Duval, La Charité, Regosin); Rabelais's "annoying" ambiguities and often scandalous contradictions (Cave, Marc Bensimon, Defaux, Thomas Greene, Rigolot); Rabelais's misogyny (Carla Freccero, Rigolot).

The historicization of the sociocultural context is the common ground from which each essay tries to deal with the central questions raised by both the status of the reader and the strategies of interpretation and textual production. The same questions allow scholars to reexamine the now-familiar concepts of textual difference and unity and of historical alienation, familiarization, and defamiliarization as essential critical tools for the study of the early modern period. Traditional comparative reader-response expectations are reexamined in terms of contemporary historical distanciation.

Most essays variously address the question of the modern reader's alienation from the context necessary for a "correct" textual interpretation: Rabelais's contemporaneous reader, the explicit historical addressee able to recognize and evaluate intertextual references obvious to him, is opposed to the modern reader, anachronistically blind to lost intertextuality and cultural or historical references, scandalized by obscene and sacrilegious jokes, or in need of becoming aware of historical generic or rhetorical principles. Reading from Rabelais's contemporaries' point of view allows Rigolot, among others, to discover unsuspected biblical intertextuality in the Rabelaisian text. Defaux's identification of Rabelais's geographical and autobiographical neorealism derives from the reconstructed reaction of contemporaneous readers. The contemporary reception of the text also motivates Cave's analysis of the sixteenth-century use of the unfamiliar, Greene's classification of cursing, Jeanneret's inquiry into the way unusual signs signify, when they signify, and for whom they signify, or Duval's effort at understanding the compositional anarchy of the problematic *Tiers livre*, as well as La Charité's and Regosin's interpretations of textual framing based on historically defined generic realities. If nearly everyone recognizes the need for contextualization in order to read the partially unfamiliar text of the premodern era, Freccero's feminist point of view exposes the need for a different awareness: male modern readers are not alienated enough from Rabelais's ideological and textual "realism." Having underscored Rabelais's textual misogyny, she denounces the same misogynous practice in Rabelais's critics by refusing to become a silent accomplice.

Contradiction and ambiguities that seem to permeate every aspect of Rabelais's comic work are another aspect of defamiliarization imposed by the text, and few readers have been able to avoid the question of how to assess the epistemological dimension of Rabelais's constant use of opposition, paradox, and antithesis. Greene argues for maintaining the simultaneously positive and negative power of words in his examination of cursing. Speaking of Rabelais's appositive thinking, which always works in reaction to an opposite rather than on its own ground, Defaux calls for "a fair balance between the comic and the serious." Like Greene, he finds simultaneity and coexistence of nonexclusive opposites, which are neither successive nor synthetic; this leads him to denounce the concept of serious laughter suggested by Bakhtin.

Yet others generalize this conclusion in the broader context of the Renaissance. Contrasting Rabelais and Erasmus, Margolin underscores the latter's ambiguity and reactionary stance as a totality of *ir*reconciliation. Bensimon shows how an ideal of perfection is subverted by the irruption of Panurge in *Pantagruel*. And instead of the coexistence or simultaneity of irreconcilable dichotomies, Cave concludes his study of familiarity and distanciation with the concept of inclusion and connection.

Rabelais's work belongs to a relatively familiar and continuous universe for the modern reader, which enables him to grasp the otherwise alien text. According to Cave, the inclusion of both high and low culture makes of the Rabelaisian text an early modern text. Thus even when, for example, the Christian message is destabilized, contextualization and a sense of historicity should help guide the modern reader not to extrapolate from his own point of view. The disruption of an essentially positive, Christian evangelism by an overwhelming textuality does not necessarily annul the religious aspect of the text, which is still present, even if parodied or maligned and thus never truly contradicted. For most critics, the coexistence of traditional medieval mockery and of modern evangelical message is but one aspect of early sixteenth-century culture. In the eyes of his contemporaries, Rabelais's parody of religion is not incompatible with the Christian message of evangelism.

His apparent ambiguous treatment of the evangelical message — of all serious subjects, for that matter — and his paradoxical use of cursing or of laughter might be scandalous today, but the reader of the time would have been familiar with it. Against the unbalanced views of readers who select exclusively one position over another, the essays presented here refuse to privilege either side of the numerous opposition. And by not imposing a one-sided ideological reduction of the multivalent text, they allow Rabelais's comic work to belong to the early modern era. For all, the Rabelaisian text is a puzzling mixture of old and new, of high and low, of familiar and alien.

Surprising, but confirming the general view, is the post-Bakhtinian tendency that universally asserts itself for the first time with such vigor in these essays. It arises from a new understanding of the opposition between high and low culture, made possible by debates initiated in the mid-eighties over Bakhtin's influential but too exclusive vision of an overwhelmingly popular dimension in Rabelais's work.[3]

This collection, which finds its unity in a remarkable confluence of interest among specialists close to one another, is also unique as the first effort to bring together the main proponents of an ongoing quarrel among ancients and moderns on interpretative strategies for the Rabelaisian text. It is a milestone insofar as the parties involved, the essential core of Rabelais specialists, and all well acquainted with one another both personally and professionally, arrived at an unexpected rapprochement at the Los Angeles symposium after years of ideological and methodological contention. The debate became acute on the occasion of the 1984 quincentennial celebrations (Tours, Lexington). Since the publication of the proceedings of the Lexington (La Charité 1986) and Tours (Céard and

Margolin 1988) symposia, the quarrel has marked most of the critical debate on Rabelais on both sides of the Atlantic. While still emphatically marked by individual points of view, the conference presentations in Los Angeles acknowledged the limits of a given position and allowed space for exchange and dialogue.

Scholars like Cave, Jeanneret, La Charité, and Regosin, who are among the main representatives of modern or postmodern critical currents, prudently distance themselves from unwanted extremes that had tended to corner them up to now. Emblematic of the new critical fairness, Cave, correcting his hard-edged, deconstructivist stance based on the concept of interpretative indetermination, writes that "the notion that Rabelais's text can mean anything one wants it to is absolutely untenable," immediately adding that "the opposite view of unitary meanings is equally untenable." Denouncing some of the attacks on his deconstructive approach, Cave affirms that there is "not a single interpretative frame." Responding to this statement, Defaux rejects the positivist stance frequently identified with him and goes out of his way to accommodate the notion of semantic polyvalence of the text. Even a non-Rabelaisian specialist like Allen finds himself drawn into the debate. Bringing together both approaches, the English historian of philosophy shows that the modern notion of an open and individually determined textual meaning could find an early modern model in sixteenth-century Ficinian Neoplatonism. Meanwhile, Jeanneret reviews the contentious question of open literary interpretation in the most modern sense of the word and finds in Allen's philosophical analysis of Neoplatonist hermeneutics the strongest support for his apparently ahistorical view of interpretative indeterminacy. Rigolot, another central figure in this debate on literary interpretation, avoids raising that specter again and, in a move destined to correct the impression of having abandoned historical contextualization, begins to "[reconstruct] a Christian humanist horizon" in order to uncover intertextual parody hidden from the modern reader. At the same time, we are reminded that "contextual fluency is only a prerequisite for a fuller textual understanding of humanist fiction."

Similar critical reassessments and methodological reminders were made necessary by the recent debate opposing modern criticism, accused of privileging textual self-referentiality while willfully ignoring history, and traditional criticism, seen as privileging extratextual references while ignoring the specificity of the text as object. Regosin and La Charité, both strong defenders of self-reflexive textuality, take great care in relativizing their current readings, opening the field to less formal approaches. La Charité calls upon the authority of traditional rhetoric, of Plato and the Bible, to read through the self-referential Rabelaisian text. Regosin, while revisiting a critical comment of the self-reflexive character of writing in the prologues, concedes that the *Tiers livre* "is not primarily about writing but includes a number of referential values." Toning down what some have claimed his stand to be, Regosin recognizes here that not all writing is exclusively about writing. In this collection, however, the poetic function of the text and its linguistic surface are unanimously privileged over the intellectual, philosophical, or religious referential message in all papers addressing the question. At the same time Duval, while analyzing the composition of the *Tiers livre* according to traditional references, shows how two episodes of the same book play precisely on textual self-referentiality.

Formalists and literary theorists systematically call for historical and contextual grounding of their interpretative strategies, while critics traditionally interested in philosophical and historical content or in semantic control widen and multiply their analysis by recognizing the unsettling dominance of the text in Rabelais's project and through a more active and explicit textual grounding. To consider only the main figures of the recent debate, Cave, Jeanneret, and Rigolot invest their discourse with a strong referential and historical dimension, while Defaux and Duval focus on poetic and textual realities for their interpretative strategies. Defaux privileges the poetic aspect of the text, even though the biblical intertext and evangelical propaganda are inseparable from it. Margolin, on the other hand, proposes that a comic treatment often overwhelms the same undeniable evangelist message. Greene, exploring Rabelais's internal contradictions, underscores the vituperative verbal excesses of the text that underlie the therapeutic comedy that he knows so well.

Obviously, "coming together" does not have to mean, nor can it really mean, a full reconciliation in which individuals relinquish deeply held intellectual and ideological convictions. Different theoretical and critical preferences strongly color the essays. The right to differ inevitably results in the recognition of the other's critical integrity and, in our case, constitutes a reopening of the closed, exclusionist discourses of the recent past. Cross-fertilization is the key word, for these essays announce the possibility of a new critical dialogue based on a newfound direction of study. In fact, it would be a mistake to expect a unified approach to the complexities of the Rabelaisian text. In spite of their diversity, each essay, while offering its own answer to the question of how to read the Rabelaisian text (or any historical text, for that matter), recognizes that a single, "correct" reading is simply not possible. As this collection exemplifies, Rabelais criticism comprises all readings, including that of major outsiders. Feminist studies, conspicuously absent at the Tours quincentennial conference, is still struggling to assert its place and its voice within or against the current male-dominated scholarship.[4]

It is precisely from that open-ended reassessment of individual approaches that the lectures were transformed into the essays collected here. A strong sense of critical awareness and intellectual fairness was the main result of this convergence. Unlike the partisan, clannish quarrels that preceded it, here a consensus was built on the recognition by each party of the validity of other methodological or ideological claims and of the need to include rather than exclude unexpected and unfamiliar points of view. The call for historical and critical defamiliarization allows and justifies new readings that are often scandalous to other modern readers, who must acquiesce in this alienation in order to participate in modern textual interpretation. Defaux, Cave, Rigolot, and Freccero take an additional step in this process of alienating distanciation by historicizing their approach. Their readings thematize the need to shock the modern reader with an unexpected interpretation of a text believed to be quite familiar. Such critical practices offer the possibility of recreating a puzzling situation similar to the one lived by the same readers confronted with the early modern text. The alienation felt by other readers confronted with an unfamiliar reading is the price they pay for their own reading.

The following record of this encounter offers a positive and constructive reorientation of Rabelais studies in several new directions, stemming primarily from the cross-fertilization of a number of critical tendencies. This collection allows a diversity of critical approaches to combine into a single dialogue that invites others to share in a rare, totalizing glimpse of general critical self-reassessment.

Following the introductory essay, the collection is divided into three parts, with the studies grouped around textual or contextual realities. Textuality, the writing process, and the debate surrounding current interpretative strategies are the focus of the first section, "Bones of Contention." The second section, "Marrows of Discontent," comprises two papers dealing with current literary and historical alienation, the treatment of women and feminism. In the last section, "Médullaires," interdisciplinary content studies on linguistic, rhetorical, religious, ethical, and philosophical references are brought together.

The compositional concept of framing individual books is central to the essays of Regosin and La Charité. Following a thematic of "writerly process and rhetoric of reading" formulated in the prologue, La Charité's essay on compositional framing is devoted to the undecipherable introductory chapter and the final prophetic riddle of *Gargantua*, which together frame the narrative text. La Charité shows that this entry/exit framing is a "deliberate choice," and the "particular manipulation of fictional space" underscores its submission to structural rules of composition. A number of themes present in this frame — digging and unearthing, for example — are shown to be emblems themselves for the creative activities of writing and reading, which are seen as spatial unearthing and discovery.

Regosin's paper, more directly related to the prologue of the *Tiers Livre*, can be found in the third part of the collection in relation to Duval's reading of the same book.

In a move that appears to be a concession to the tenets of textual priorities, Defaux claims that, for Rabelais, textual gaming is more important than historical reality; the poet dominates the thinker or the evangelical apologist. Defaux centrally considers the writing process, and the excesses in *Gargantua* become part of the overall textual message. Yet we are immediately warned that the two dimensions are not separable and that the self-referential writing process is constantly informed by extratextual realities. From this view, Rabelais's realism does not stem from a traditional positivist presentation of the text as a straightforward mirror of the contemporary world or of the author's thought. The true novelty of Defaux's view is that Rabelais's realism has strong autobiographical overtones, rooted in a specific local and personal universe that serves as background to his comic narrative. Defaux calls for the need to consider this undeniable "presence of the world and self of Rabelais within his own text" in order to discover the text's process of signification.

Cave, situated in the wake of post-Foucaldian and post-Bakhtinian critical practices, problematizes the traditional Renaissance opposition of past and present, old and new, denying that they are merely a simple set of contradictions or a sudden revolution. In the same text, connections, rather than contradictions or successions, operate between high and low culture. For example, to convey a sense of cultural mix, Cave refers to the early modern period rather than to the Renaissance per se, which is too exclusively defined by high culture. The reperiodization of the early modern, already practiced by cultural historians, has the additional advantage of disalienating the concept for the modern reader. While early modern maintains the distance necessary to justify the thesis that the Rabelaisian text is in fact alien to us, it still allows modern readers to recognize antecedents of their own thought, even though no univocal appropriation is possible. Cave points to the exemplary treatment of vernacular languages, an aspect of the opposition between high and low culture. The polyglot Panurge not only speaks several "low" vernacular languages learned while traveling, but his modern use of Greek and Latin, among other languages, in the episode of the first encounter with Pantagruel is also characteristic of the transformation of the old into a pleasurable mixture of high and low, rather than a strict opposition. Cave proposes that Rabelais's work is a restructuring of the entire familiar past, by which the alien is initially little more than a veiled or masked double, such as Panurge or the cabbage planter (only in the *Quart livre* does Rabelais deal more directly with "truer" aliens). The Rabelaisian text is said to be partially alien to us, functioning like a distorting mirror in which we are nonetheless able to recognize ourselves.

In a new phase of his ongoing problematization of interpretative strategies, Jeanneret opposes an old allegorical reading of stable signs having fixed and predetermined meanings to a modern semiotic reading in which the new sign is open to an uncertain, polysemic meaning yet to be found. For Jeanneret, the new interpretative strategy must revolve around questions about how, when, and what to read, now that the security of medieval hermeneutics is abandoned, in a world in which words are incapable of conveying stable truth and left to the uncertainty of individual interpretation. The new relationship between sign and meaning is examined in the specific treatment of monsters as signs in the *Quart livre*. With its buildup of uncontrollable signs, the *Quart livre*, already the locus of Cave's alienation, is the ideal field of experimentation for the new conditions of meaning in a universe where the stability of hermeneutics has given way to signs gone wild. Drawing on Allen's Neoplatonic view of the inadequacy and insufficiency of language, and apparently close to the Erasmian ideal of silence addressed elsewhere by Defaux, Jeanneret's interpretative strategy requires a prospective and creative reading in which meaning emerges only at the end of the process engaged by a trusting, generous, and well-prepared reader.

Carla Freccero repositions herself vis-à-vis her long-standing denunciation of the predominantly male genealogy of Rabelais critics by showing how our modern, liberal, male-dominated society is in too many ways still scandalously similar to that of Panurge and Pantagruel with their cruel treatment of women. The traditional eagerness to laugh and to find textual value at the expense of women is an uncomfortably familiar and misogynist reaction. Freccero reconsiders what might be called the "Wayne Booth incident," suggesting that it exemplifies the irrepressible male laugh at the humiliated woman harassed by Panurge with Pantagruel's approval. According to Freccero, Rabelais's antifeminism, like that of some modern male critics, is fueled by the same repressive, reactionary principles that led to the Hill/Thomas hearings. This situation draws attention to the reversal of alienation proposed by the general call for historical distanciation as the point of departure at the Los Angeles symposium. Instead of finding themselves alienated from the texts studied, modern male readers find themselves, where misogyny is concerned, dangerously close to Rabelais's antifeminism, as Wayne Booth's laughter, though reluctant, makes clear. Here women are the true outsiders, unable to accept this laughter as a purely textual pleasure. According to Freccero the advent of a feminist Rabelais criticism is doubly significant, for the exclusion of women from Rabelais's world parallels that experienced by women in modern, male-dominated society. Freccero's call for a new Rabelais criticism demonstrates what Barbara Johnson has called an "alternative evolved in struggle."

For Rigolot, the modern male critic's experience of the alien might well be that of current feminist discourse. His essay uncovers a biblical intertext in one of the least-expected episodes of the text and builds a scandalous, even blasphematory parallel between the three temptations of Christ and one of the misogynist episodes, made up of three successive scenes of sexual harassment in which Panurge would be Satan and the lady a Christlike figure in *Pantagruel* (21–24). Aware of both the constraints on the historically contemporary reader and the current evolution of sociocultural reality, Rigolot is interested in the apparent contradiction between the stated evangelical message of *caritas* in the text and the humiliation of the woman. Today's readers, called upon to read Rabelais's texts according to the historicization of ideological and new sociocultural values, can only be scandalized by the antifeminist dimension of the text. Rabelais's contemporaries seem to have been more tolerant toward a puzzling mixture of paradoxical realities.

In his lexical and ethical study of cursing within the Rabelaisian text, Greene reveals a deep-rooted contradiction similar to that of Rigolot's paradoxical mixture. He examines the same juxtaposition of the *caritas*-like content of Rabelais's evangelical message with the therapeutic claim of the text on one hand and the insistent recourse to the malevolent and dangerous practice of cursing on the other. Rabelais's writing project seems positive and constructive. Silene, marrow, and wine are therapeutic, and the book, like laughter, has healing powers. In reality, however, the power of cursing, which can dispel or undo danger and thereby cleanse, can also unleash malevolent forces in order to destroy. If we want to understand Rabelais, we must keep alive the contradiction of a medical writer's therapy, which claims to use the power of words and laughter to heal, even though they can be used equally well to wound.

For Duval, Rabelais is willing to assume responsibility for the inherent contradictions in the composition of an entire book, thus playing on the reader's expectations. Extending the conclusion in his latest book on the composition of *Pantagruel* (1991), Duval shows how the antiepic and anticompositional character of the problematic *Tiers livre* is in fact fully known and accepted by the author, for whom it becomes a compositional process. As the sequel to *Pantagruel*, the *Tiers livre* ignores the rules of writing good history and makes fun of the medieval chronicler Monstrelet, who does the same without being aware of it. Based on a telling intertextuality that includes Lucian, Horace, and the rhetoric of historiography, Duval's analysis of Rabelais's "compositional monster" applies the generic rules of history writing to the most disturbing of Rabelais's texts. As an example of textual self-reflexivity, Duval shows how Diogenes's aimless tub-rolling activity in the prologue to the *Tiers livre* is emblematic of a deliberate refusal to conform to the literary models of writing history — a model of what it should not be.

Regosin, examining Rabelais's opening strategies, demonstrates how prologues, specifically the prologue of the *Tiers livre*, function as a beginning for writer and reader alike. For the writer, they serve as a prewriting activity through which anxiety can be overcome by allowing the writing process to start. This logocentric activity, mirroring the whole writing process, is also directly linked with reader control and reception. Reading is shown to be an interpretative activity.

In their related analysis of compositional framing, both Regosin and La Charité conclude their respective readings by recognizing a strong sense of original compositional structure in Rabelais's unusual textual framing. But while neither La Charité's nor Regosin's analyses are narratological, unrelated as they are to the hero's tale, Duval's essay focuses precisely on the absence of conventional narrative structure in the *Tiers livre*, concluding that it was Rabelais's deliberate decision not to follow the rules of generic composition he knew so well.

Margolin's essay shows how Rabelais distances himself from the intellectual and ideological father figure of Erasmus through playful treatment of the most serious aspects of the Erasmian intellectual and religous message. Margolin compares their treatment of language and writing. While in Erasmus the teacher prevails, in Rabelais the poet dominates, with words often used for their creative and comic power. While both humanists are on the same side in the fight against the dogmatic spirit, the message is ideologic for Erasmus and fictionalized for Rabelais. While textual *varietas* and abundance may be present in both cases, in Erasmus they are present essentially as teaching tools and, in Rabelais, as signs of creative genius and sources of comic excess. In Rabelais, the undeniable biblical references are "overwhelmed by huge waves of comic," and the parodic effects are often missed by modern readers. In Rabelais, self-reflection and poetic function often take over and become aporetic and reactive, with no need for true dialectics or explicit evangelical propaganda, the latter of which merely plays a background function.

Margolin's call to militancy emerges from his own autobiographical reading of Rabelais and is not far thematically from Defaux's premises. The latter identifies the main differences between Rabelais and Erasmus, his intellectual father, in textuality and personal investment. For Defaux and Margolin, the Lucianesque influence in Erasmus seems to have caught Rabelais's attention. But whereas Margolin sees in Rabelais's folly the source of a strong sense of self-expression and comic creativity or the intrusion of an ego disturbing the Erasmian message, Defaux sees in it an undecidable aspect of the Rabelaisian transmission of reality through personal and autobiographical investment. For both critics, nothing in the Rabelaisian text refutes the possibility of an evangelical message. For most of the contributors to this volume, the message survives even when coexisting with the most excessive textuality and the appearance of a heretical parody.

Marc Bensimon shows how the narrative in *Pantagruel* questions the seriousness of the model of perfection proposed by Gargantua in his letter to his son. The letter's quest for perfection through knowledge is subverted when, forgetting the father figure, Pantagruel whimsically teams up with Panurge, liberating himself from Gargantua's expectation for a "like father, like son" model of seminal propagation and androgynous resemblance.

Finally, in an authoritative confirmation by an outsider of the coming together of insiders, Michael J. B. Allen shows that the central interpretative question raised by modernists had already been raised by Ficino, namely, how to determine where the hidden meaning lies when it is "scattered about here and there" or how and when to decide that there is no mystery behind the veil. Preferring the *Parmenides* to the *Banquet* as a tool for understanding the philosophical background of the current debate on interpretation, Allen invokes the recent modernist and postmodernist position vis-à-vis the inadequacy of language as an echo of the Neoplatonic conception of the interpretative act and of truth. Taking the *Cinquième livre* as Rabelais's own, Allen squarely positions Rabelais—or at least Alcofribas's notion of reading and interpretation as theorized by the modernists—on the side of an early modern exercise in personal, interpretative choice. For Allen as for Jeanneret, truth has a new value; it is no longer a preestablished and fixed given, lying in its entirety behind the medieval figure of allegory and ready to be disclosed and fully comprehended. On the contrary, it is a series of mysteries (nine, according to the *Parmenides*) escaping the limits of language and open to intuitive apprehension. The new interpretative act is aimed against the fixity of meaning and for the liberty of intellect, as is characteristic of the evangelical message.

As demonstrated by the brief survey of the contributions in this collection, interdisciplinary dimension, along with assessment of contemporary theories of interpretation and their historical applicability, make *François Rabelais: Critical Assessments* essential reading not only for the international community of Rabelais specialists but also more generally for Renaissance students and scholars. This volume of critical essays complements the recent publication of two new English translations of Rabelais by Donald Frame and by Burton Raffel.[5]

# I Bones of Contention

Raymond La Charité

# The Framing of Rabelais's *Gargantua*

*Naturally, a manuscript*

—Umberto Eco, *The Name of the Rose*

Toward the end of the prologue to *Gargantua,* the narrator makes light of the possible resonances of his enterprise and confides that "à *la composition de ce livre seigneurial,* je ne perdiz ne emploiay oncques plus, ny aultre temps que celluy qui estoit estably à prendre ma refection corporelle, sçavoir est beuvant et mangeant" (1:9, my emphasis) [in *the composition of this lordly book,* I neither wasted nor ever employed any more or other time than that which was established for taking my bodily refection, that is to say eating and drinking (5)]. While readers of this brilliant prologue have long since shown the care with which Alcofribas orchestrates his thematics of reading and interpretation, the phrase "la composition de ce livre seigneurial," applicable to the fiction in its entirety, has remained more or less unnoticed. And yet it appears that it points directly, not only to the matter of authorial control but also to the central question of structure and of the overall configuration of the fiction. Alcofribas may downplay his commitment to the work at hand, but the text Rabelais concocts displays a deliberate choice and manipulation of fictional space that far surpasses that of *Pantagruel* and perhaps even that of the *Tiers livre* and *Quart livre.*

For *Gargantua* is indeed "composed" — not merely written — and "put together," its parts conjoined and placed strategically to create an architectural whole that is doubly *seigneurial,* both the tale of a

3

prince and a magnificent, noble monument. In *A Dictionarie of the French and English Tongues*, Randle Cotgrave glosses *composition* as "a composition; making, framing; a confection, compositure; compounding, also, a worke, or booke, or the writing of a worke or booke." In *Gargantua*, Rabelais erects a solid, visual "framing" within whose form the fiction is fashioned. Accordingly the text takes on the appearance of an architectural, spatial configuration (with a precise point of entry and a clearly marked exit), in essence a kind of "outside" of the text that is in keeping with the thematics of the prologue and the memorial construct described as "le manoir des Thelemites" (1:198) [the manor of the Thélémites (123)].

The framing of *Gargantua* rests, of course, on two seemingly undecipherable poems — "Les Fanfreluches antidotées, trouvées en un monument antique" [The Antidoted Frigglefraggles, found in an ancient monument (ch. 2)], which launches the history and story of Gargantua, and the "Enigme en prophetie" [A Prophetic Riddle (ch. 58)], which brings the fiction to an abrupt conclusion. While it is true that these poems continue to resist our interpretive efforts, my purpose in this essay is to show that both of these textual barriers function nevertheless as indicators of enclosed space, as markers of containment, and that the fiction they embed is therefore not only the tale of Gargantua but also the story of textuality inasmuch as the framing device is the product of chance excavation. Hence, to the extent that both the "Fanfreluches antidotées" and the "Enigme en prophetie" are unearthed fragments, a sort of reliquary, their intertext being the transmission and survival of texts, *Gargantua* can be seen to emerge as fundamentally emblematic of the act and art of reading in all of its parts, not just in the opening prologue.

## Space and Place

*Gargantua* is both a playful and serious fiction about reading and interpretation, which seeks to account for the phenomenon of interpretation itself. Through the various formal devices Rabelais uses and the rhetorical strategies he deploys, he attempts to control and channel our reading and thus our reception and interpretation of his work. From the prologue to the "Enigme en prophetie," the reader is treated to an incomparable display of artifice and legerdemain, and the duplicitous text reminds him constantly that its production and completion rest ultimately in his hands. Reader competence and complicity are the name of the game, and, as a result, countless episodes are constructed in essence as tests.

The prologue remains the principal repository of Rabelais's problematics of reading. In the main, Rabelais thematizes narration as a secretive act and reading as an act of discovery, of unearthing. Whereas the prologue to *Pantagruel* is defensive in that, intertextually, Alcofribas draws upon narrative authority derived from the "*Grandes et inestimables Chronicques de l'enorme geant Gargantua*" (1:215) [*Great and Inestimable Chronicles of the Enormous Giant Gargantua* (133)], the prologue to *Gargantua* abandons the handling of an intertext as an antimodel.[1] Instead, Alcofribas foregrounds his quest for narrative authority by claiming that he has a secret, that he has enclosed it within the fiction, and that, like the dog with its bone, "de quelle devotion il le guette, de quel soing il le guarde, de quel ferveur il le tient, de quelle prudence il l'entomme, de quelle affection il le brise, et de quelle diligence il le sugce" (1:7) [with what devotion he watches it, with what care he guards it, with what fervor he holds it, with what prudence he starts on it, with what affection he breaks it, with what diligence he sucks it (4)], the patient and hardworking reader can extricate it.[2]

The originality of this narrative strategy lies in its manipulation of space and visual metaphorics. For, just as the reader is asked whether he has seen the dog with its bone ("veistes vous oncques chien rencontrant quelque os medulare? . . . Si veu l'avez, vous avez peu noter . . ." (1:7) [Did you ever see a dog coming upon some marrow bone? . . . If seen one you have, you were able to note . . . (4)]), he is also called upon to imagine the book as a bone, a body, and a box, metaphoric containers whose goods must be revealed, released, and absorbed. Untold wealth has been hidden and buried within the space of the book-as-depository, and the Silenic reader must be able to open and close the text, both withdraw its cache and, by manipulating it and becoming one with it, contribute to its process of accrual. Tom Conley suggests that "Rabelais exige une lecture visuelle des mots" (Conley, 97).[3] In fact, Rabelais forces the reader to conceive of the book as matter, as an object to be seen, as a treasure trove to be broken into, not as an abstract and auditory entity. The metaphors endow the book with a palpable, tactile quality that the reader cannot suppress. In the prologue to *Pantagruel*, books play a substitutive role, "une espèce de remplaçant" (La Charité 1985, 262), and its narratees are essentially depicted as listeners, as passive recipients. In the prologue to *Gargantua*, by contrast, narratees and ideal reader are diggers, interacting bodily, so to speak, with the find at hand. Indeed, the dog not only wrestles with his bone, he also eats it.

Irony and guffaw aside, the prologue does far more than spoof and play with reading and interpretive models as it aligns and juggles reversible topoi of surface versus depth, insides versus outsides.[4] It also conjures up the notion of the book as space and, by playing with space and creating space, establishes and expands the space of the text, a vertical and horizontal expanse, anchored terrestrially, built from the ground up, by accretion and accumulation, culminating in the bursting and rising of Thélème, a creation of textual space, both verbal and visual, without parallel.

The prologue metaphorizes textuality as latent power and energy whose pent-up forces must be unleashed and made to rise and break surface through the process of reading. Reading is release, the creation of opening and expansion, and the prologue performs the process in that its unfolding as performance is engineered in such a way that it seems to progress dynamically and analogically from layer to layer by means of repetition and accretion.

The dense metaphorical articulation the reader encounters at the outset parallels the inner-to-outer mechanism. At this juncture, the prologue is tightly coiled — metaphorical layers compressed as in a spring — but as the text flows the rhythm distends little by little, progressively faster until it virtually bursts into the final invective. The movement is one-dimensional in the sense that it is forever expanding in girth and distance as its potential for meaning seeks release and surface. Moreover, the openness that the prologue posits through the tensile quality of its early stages corresponds to the multiplicity of meaning it will encounter in time. While the early scaffolding draws the reader's eye toward constriction, toward restriction in terms of an interpretive model, the outer-expansion-driven movement ultimately engulfs all.[5]

The essential principle upon which the organization of space rests in *Gargantua* is opening, the burst toward openness and, artistically, freedom. The prologue and the book deny closure. Rather, they extol the dynamics of intertextuality, the ongoingness and openness of meaning. The expanse and space of the Abbey of Thélème episode, for example, coming as it does at the culminating point of the fiction, attest to the energetics of the principle. In its manifestation of artistic freedom, it subverts reader expectations. Yet this created space stands for the preeminence of form. The accumulation of words on the page may not lead the reader to further understanding, but the rising architectural form does. If necessary, as Mallarmé put it so well, "Rien n'aura eu lieu que le lieu" (Mallarmé, 474–75). With Thélème as with the prologue, Rabelais exhibits a keen sense of creative space. He has an eye for pictorial representation, which goes well beyond mere narrative art. The figural contours that the prologue bandies about — insides and outsides — are immediately implemented upon its close, as text begins to flow from it and inscribe itself within graphic margins, the "Fanfreluches antidotées" and the "Enigme en prophetie."

## Framing

One cannot read *Gargantua* without realizing that the "Fanfreluches antidotées" and the "Enigme en prophetie" jut out from the page, so to speak, and give it an alluring contour, a satisfying symmetry, albeit puzzling. Many readers have alluded to the structural relationship. Early on, Jean Plattard remarked that "le livre de *Gargantua*, qui s'est ouvert sur un poème énigmatique, les 'Fanfreluches antidotées,' se clôt sur une composition du même genre" (Rabelais 1912–55, 2:441 n. 47). Others have since noted that the episodes "encompass the bulk of the book" (Tetel, 32) or "encircle the narrative" (Berry, 55) or give it a "belle ordonnance" (Paris, 158).[6] And while M. A. Screech faults Rabelais's abrupt announcement of the "Enigme en prophetie" ("Did ever a major author more crudely stick another bit on the end?" [Screech 1969, 112]), he does suggest that, taken together, "these two enigmas give to *Gargantua* an aesthetic balance" (Screech 1979b, 131). But in general, commentary has been cautious and has not gone beyond recognizing the existence of the polarity.

More recently, Guy Demerson has outlined a promising view of the episodes in that he is able to relate their relative positioning to that of other episodes in *Gargantua* by means of a structuring principle he calls "composition en inclusion":

> Maintes correspondances thématiques suggèrent cependant que Rabelais a eu recours à un procédé de disposition bien connu de l'Antiquité et de la Bible et fréquemment utilisé à la Renaissance, l'*inclusion*: ce qui apparaît comme un kaléidoscope de motifs apparentés mais désunis, d'éléments analogues éparpillés, pour un oeil myope ou indolent, est en fait une mise en ordre par symétrie concentrique (A.B.C.D.E.D'.C'.B'.A'.), appelant l'attention du lecteur éveillé et éduqué sur l'élément central (E), et lui faisant désirer la surgie des éléments finaux. (Demerson 1986, 136)

The virtue of this schema is that it calls for alert and active reading and justifies the placement of the "Fanfreluches antidotées" and the "Enigme en prophetie" as a required and integral component of the whole. They are not mere afterthoughts, playful obscurities, or satisfying adornments, but crucial signposts. Hence, Demerson is able to see that these markers develop the writerly process and rhetoric of reading formulated in the prologue (139).

That these two episodes not only energize the configurative system of the fiction but also function as its strategic areas is made abundantly clear through the symmetry of their inclusion. Indeed, the fiction draws attention to their association by stressing the similarity of their respective discoveries:

> Et fut trouvée [l'antiquité et geneallogie de Gargantua] par Jean Audeau en un pré qu'il avoit près l'arceau Gualeau, au dessoubz de l'Olive, tirant à Narsay, duquel faisant lever les fossez, toucherent les piocheurs de

leurs marres un grand tombeau de bronze, long sans mesure, car oncques
n'en trouverent le bout par ce qu'il entroit trop avant les excluses de
Vienne. Icelluy ouvrans en certain lieu, signé, au dessus, d'un goubelet à
l'entour duquel estoit escript en lettres Ethrusques: HIC BIBITUR,
trouverent neuf flaccons en tel ordre qu'on assiet les quilles en
Guascoigne, desquelz celluy qui au mylieu estoit couvroit un gros, gras,
grand, gris, joly, petit, moisy livret, plus, mais non mieulx sentent que
roses.

En icelluy fut ladicte geneallogie trouvée, escripte au long de lettres
cancelleresques, non en papier, non en parchemin, non en cere, mais en
escorce d'ulmeau. . . .

A la fin du livre estoit un petit traicté intitulé: *Les Fanfreluches
antidotées.* (1:12–13).[7]

[And it (the genealogy and antiquity of Gargantua) was found by Jean
Audeau in a field he owned near the Gualeau Arch, below the *Olive*, as
you head for Narsay; in having its ditches cleaned, the diggers with their
picks struck a great bronze tomb, immeasurably long, for they never
found the end of it because it went too far into the mill-dams of the
Vienne. Opening this in a certain place stamped on the outside with a
goblet around which was written in Etruscan the letters HIC BIBITUR
(HERE YOU DRINK), they found nine flagons in the order in which they
put ninepins in Gascony, of which the one in the middle covered a huge,
stout, big, gray, pretty little moldy little book smelling more but not
better than roses.

In this was the said genealogy found, written out at great length in
chancery letters, not on paper, not on parchment, but on elm bark. . . .

At the end of the book was a little treatise entitled *The Antidoted
Frigglefraggles.* (8)]

What the narrator presents here in great detail is reduced to short-
hand for the concluding episode, but it is no mere coincidence, for
it clearly mirrors the first: "Je ne veulx oublier vous descripre un
enigme qui fut trouvé aux fondemens de l'abbaye en une grande
lame de bronze" (1:205) [I do not want to forget to set down for you
a riddle which was found in the foundations of the abbey on a great
bronze plate (127)]. The "Je ne veulx oublier" is patently a signal for
which the reader has been waiting. Both writings are discovered
unexpectedly by chance in the ground, the first within a bronze
tomb, the second written on a bronze plate or tombstone. Both are
reproduced in the fiction. The one significant difference is that the

"Fanfreluches antidotées" are inscribed on elm bark, hence truly ancient, undoubtedly from the dawn of writing since their bed of inscription predates in logical order the use of paper, parchment, and wax.

Whatever else might be said about this elaborate encoding of the framing, it appears that there would not be all that much to say about *Gargantua* beyond the prologue if Rabelais had not taken the trouble to position this frame. After all, Gargantua's saga is fairly straightforward, delineating in even greater detail what is already latently present in *Pantagruel*. On its own, the saga does not play on or reflect the great hidden secrets promised in the prologue. Indeed, without the frame, the vibrant ambiguity of the book in its entirety would be greatly diminished, and *Gargantua*, although hardly hollow, would not be the accomplished work of art that it is.

Not the least of the many feats of this book is the way in which the reading model of the prologue is subverted so totally that the reader is forced to seek hidden meaning in the frame, in the outside, rather than within; this is again a major example of the way in which the fiction plays out and plays off the prologue as it multiplies instances of reversibility and misdirection. Consequently, the interpretive construct is no more reliable than the manipulative narrator, whose penchant for confusion dictates the narrative structure of the work.[8]

The greatest irony of all, of course, is that the ease with which one is led to believe outsides can be penetrated if one will only work at it is confounded by these two impenetrable barriers, solid Silenic configurations whose insides and outsides are but mirror images. And yet to the extent that these markers continue to attract our eye and attention, their solidity is readable. In drawing the gaze of the reader inward and onward on the path of the writing they themselves are — and on the writing that authorizes their emergence in the fiction — they stand for that special blend of Rabelaisian textuality whose goal is to invite the reader to share writing as process, as dynamic plurality, while simultaneously resisting the reader's grasp and his eagerness to appropriate and petrify meaning. They are both "pinctures contrefaictes" (1:5) [paintings imagined (3)] and "choses precieuses" (1:5) [valuables (3)], neither inside nor outside, but creative space glossing the prologue and signaling ultimately that the hidden secret the prologue harbors is nothing more than the symbiotic intertwining of writerly seduction and interpretive quest.

But what of the specifics of the discoveries? What does their near standardized ritualistic unearthing imply? At the very least, their presence in the fiction stresses concretely the overarching importance of texts and texutal analysis as the glue of the fiction. Without texts, the fiction could not get under way and could not initiate closure; they provide the history upon which the narrator bases and extracts his story. As hidden narratives, they embed the principal narrative and they direct our reading. As unearthed texts, "de l'écrit dans l'écrit" [writing within writing],[9] requiring deciphering, they function as fictional intertexts for the proliferation of intertextuality and interpretation.

The prologue develops an aesthetic of depth, an archaeology of reading in which excavated layers ultimately reveal the *trouvaille*, the artifact that justifies the enterprise. In chapter 1, for example, "un grand tombeau de bronze" is found within the earth. Within the tomb the "piocheurs" find "un gros, gras, grand, gris, joly, petit, moisy livret." And within the "livret" rest "ladicte geneallogie" and "un petit traicté." With the "Fanfreluches antidotées" and the "Enigme en prophetie," the fiction literally enacts the program.

## Manuscripts

At the close of Umberto Eco's *The Name of the Rose*, Adso, the narrator and pupil of Brother William of Baskerville, the novel's medieval sleuth, reveals that the mysterious text that fascinated its many keepers and led to the death of so many monks was none other than the long-lost second volume of Aristotle's *Poetics* on the subject of comedy. Ironically, the loss and absence of the text are made irrevocably permanent by the fire that engulfs the library and the abbey and brings the search to an end. Fittingly, Eco encapsulates the whole of his creation in the epigraph, "Naturally, a manuscript" (xi).

Likewise, as though the origin of all things were a text, the fiction that is *Gargantua* rests on manuscripts and is the product of what was an absence, but in this instance the mysterious texts, "Ghosts of books" (Eco, 609), resurface, nurture the narrative, and kindle a search for meaning. The "lost" intertexts, metaphors for the issue of origins and for writing and reading, remind us not only of absent texts and of the ways in which the past impinges upon the present but also of the need for active manipulation, confrontation, and reclamation of meaning, as indeed will both the narrator with his "petit traicté" and Gargantua and Frère Jean with their monument (1:209).

The two manuscripts included in the fiction are anterior to the experience of the narration. Referring to the "Fanfreluches anti-dotées," John Porter Houston remarks that "this poem written on elm bark shows Rabelais's increasing sense of the possibilities of the document, in the form of language taken from life or lying outside the limits of narrative style" (Houston, 25). As documents, the two manuscripts bear witness to the present as heir to the past and authenticate as well as authorize the narrative.

Even more important is the manner in which these manuscripts are discovered, for it serves to heighten their significance as authorizing subtexts. In both cases, the ground is disturbed, first for a ditching operation, then for the foundations of the Abbey. In each case — and all the more so because of the discoveries — the digging alerts the reader to the central act of writing and to the fact that the fiction is about to engage in an important piece of writing. For behind the digging lurks the well-known association, going all the way back to Plato, between ploughing, the dressing of a field, and writing.

Moreover, by means of the buried manuscripts, Rabelais historicizes the narrative, grounds it in the earth and in history, so to speak, as we move from grave to grave. The text thus vivifies the memory and knowledge of origins and the past and proceeds to a degree as a memorial narration. While the unearthed manuscripts give life to the fiction, they are also testimony to the discontinuity of history and are emblematic of an ending, hence the precarious and ambiguous nature of the Abbey of Thélème, built on a Janus-faced manuscript.

Thomas M. Greene points out that Renaissance writers as a breed displayed their veneration of antiquity and their sense of loss through the use of "necromantic metaphors of disinterment, rebirth, and resuscitation" (1982, 32). To be sure, Rabelais is of his time, but what is particularly interesting about his resurrection of the past is the way in which he uses it as the structuring principle of his fiction. Whereas he rewrites the past in *Pantagruel* through his reenactment of Creation, in *Gargantua* he is more intent upon preservation, restoration, and transmission — certainly of manuscripts (Alcofribas is paleographer, scrivener, and editor) — and Rabelais focuses this preoccupation on activations of reading, hence the manuscripts retrieved from the past and inscribed in the fiction in order to replenish the present.

The manuscripts resonate in other ways. As resurfaced fragments emblematic of rise and fall, birth and death, loss and recovery, they are reread, so to speak, and echoed in Gallet's forceful "harangue" (1:117) [speech (73)] to Picrochole ("Ainsi ont toutes choses leur fin et periode" [1:119] [Thus all things have their end and their period (74)]) and Gargantua's eloquent "contion" (1:182) [speech (112)] to Picrochole's defeated followers ("car le temps, qui toutes choses ronge et diminue" [1:184] [for time, which erodes and diminishes everything (my translation)]). Fittingly, in a narrative in which politics in war and peace play such a crucial role and in which Gargantua is not unlike Aeneas, whose greatness rests on moral virtue as well as strength, the ploughed-up manuscripts remind us of Virgil's call in the *Georgics* (1:493–97) for a return to the simple virtues: "Yea, and a time shall come when in those lands, as the farmer toils at the soil with crooked plough, he shall find javelins eaten up with rusty mould, or with his heavy hoes shall strike on empty helms, and marvel at the giant bones in the upturned graves" (Virgil, 114–115). Clearly, *Gargantua* is writing over writing, a kind of palimpsest, and it is thus most appropriate that its footing reside by means of these manuscripts within the earth as reliquary and textual archive. As in *Pantagruel*, the earth bears fruit, and the history of books and reading is the history of rediscovery.

An additional, biblical resonance imposes itself. In 2 Kings 22–23, during the reign of Josiah, the high priest discovers in the Temple, which is still under renovation, a lost Book of the Law. He gives it to the royal scribe, who reads it and then reads it again out loud for the king. Upon hearing these words, Josiah is filled with sorrow ("he rent his clothes" [22:11]) because he learns how miserably they are following God's commandments ("our fathers have not hearkened unto the words of this book, to do according unto all that is written concerning us" [22:13]). To launch his reform, he gathers all the people about him in the Temple and he reads "in their ears all the words of the book of the covenant which was found in the house of the Lord" (23:2).

In a seminal article, "Joseph's Bones and the Resurrection of the Text: Remembering in the Bible," Regina M. Schwartz shows how pervasive the thematization of loss and recovery is in the Bible. It is "so frequently depicted in the text and enacted by the text that it informs each of the 'scenes of writing' the Bible offers" (117). Clearly, Rabelais's "scenes of writing" in *Gargantua* stem from a combination of writerly and sacred considerations. Out of the depths of the earth, Rabelais's lost manuscripts, restored by the fiction and read out loud in the case of the "Enigme en prophetie," attain their full import in the last scene of the book.

## Reading

"Restoit seulement le moyne à pourvoir" (1:188) [There remained only the monk to provide for (116)]. With these words, Rabelais begins the penultimate episode of the book, the six-chapter rhetorical exercise that, like a panegyrical poem, praises the site, building, governance, and inhabitants of the Abbey of Thélème. It is a kind of covenant between king and subjects, a celebration and promise of peace, plenitude, and personhood, raised on the debris of war, a fitting monument, as uplifting as its imposing architecture — a new beginning. For the writer, it is also a literary haven. Abandoning narrative discourse for description, Rabelais demonstrates his mastery of the rule of medieval *descriptio*, bedazzling the reader with his accumulation and storage of words within the space of the Abbey. Because *descriptio* relies on previous description, Thélème is literally an exercise not only in construction but also in recovery, in resurrection. It is essentially an architectural and pictorial reflection of the entire narrative act and interpretive program. As a result, it is not surprising to find deep within its walls, in its innermost recesses, indeed at the origin of its creation, the enigmatic manuscript, miraculously preserved for posterity, that provides the closing panel of the frame — once again a reversal in that the beautiful and harmonious Abbey of Thélème harbors a disquieting and deceptive inside.[10] At the very end of the book, the object of consideration, the final inside, is a text, which is exactly what the reader was told to search for in the prologue. And its very nature as poetic form rests on the coexistence of an inside and an outside, a truth couched in deceptive language. *Gargantua* thus closes on a resounding *mise en abîme* of the entire narrative.[11]

At no point in *Gargantua* is Rabelais more in control of his fiction than at the end. Neither a "pirouette pour dire adieu au lecteur" (Morçay, 63 n. 2) nor an indication that "visiblement, Rabelais est au bout de son rouleau" (Desonay, 102 n. 3), the "Enigme en prophetie" plays off the Abbey of Thélème in a dazzling display of the intricacies of enclosure and closure. While the abbey as construction and building renews the thematics of beginning and opening, the "Enigme en prophetie" heralds the thematics of closure by its apocalyptic references to catastrophe, death, the end of the world, and its repeated use of *fin* in the last verses: ". . . le temps bon et propice / De mettre *fin* à ce long exercice," "Pour mettre à *fin* les eaulx et l'entreprise," "les aultres en la *fin* / Soient denuez," "Cil qui en *fin* pourra perseverer!" (1:208, my emphasis) [". . . the good and proper day / This exercise to end and put away," "On finishing these floods and the event," "finally, let the others go / Stripped and denuded," "Whoever to the end can persevere!" (129–30)].

Paradoxically, because the "Enigme en prophetie" is a discovered manuscript — a new, hitherto unknown, unpublished text — it also thematizes beginning and therefore defers closure. Or rather it is both inaugural and closural, a duality played out by its interpreters, as they in turn are made to prolong the acrobatics.

From the beginning of the Abbey of Thélème episode (ch. 52) to the end of the book (ch. 58), the narrator slowly but surely slips from view until at the last he is totally eclipsed by Gargantua and Frère Jean, two readers engaged in dialogue over the manuscript that has just been read ("La lecture de cestuy monument parachevée" [1:209] [The reading of this document completed (130)]).[12] In other words, Alcofribas progressively loses the text as his narrative voice is supplanted by internal readers. Indeed, the brilliance of this finale lies in the inscription of two conflicting internal readings that are not resolved within the fiction, thereby further complicating the task of the reader to whom the whole of the work is addressed.

Although critics may differ as to how these contrastive interpretations should be viewed, it seems to me crucial that the text comes to a close with an interpretive act, itself inconclusive. Its purpose, of course, is to valorize the role of the reader, to entice him inward, into the process.[13] Neither the narrator nor the other readers or listeners who are present for the reading and exchange ("es assistans" [1:209] [to the company (130)]) make a choice or attempt to resolve the issue. Using the words of Stanley E. Fish, one can say that the concluding dialogue makes of *Gargantua* "an *event*, something that *happens* to, and with the participation of, the reader" (386). In *Gargantua*, the reader is given a choice of ending; while it is a game worth playing, it is one he cannot win. Still, the game is worth the candle, and Frère Jean's "exposition" (1:209) on "le jeu" (1:210) is not inappropriate with regard to the active contest that pits reader against text.

Rabelais's text resists completion for the very reason that reading and interpretation are its core, and interpretation is an ongoing and never-ending process. The fiction comes to an end; reading and interpretation do not. In essence, *Gargantua* calls for reading and completion beyond its limitations as text. To open this book is to be never able to close it again.

Rabelais has wrought this infinite opening throughout the book, but it receives its greatest attention at the end as the writer fabricates a fiction of the end. He purposefully thwarts the reader's desire for completion, not only by leaving internal readings in suspension but also by introducing pensiveness, dialogue, and silence. At the conclusion of the reading of the "Enigme en prophetie,"[14] Gargantua is

made to speak twice: first, by means of an unsolicited and contextualizing reflection on the persecution of evangelicals, and second, where Frère Jean steps in abruptly and asks him point blank to
address the question, "Que pensez vous, en vostre entendement,
estre par cest enigme designé et signifié?" (1:209) [What, in your
understanding, do you think is designated by this riddle? (130)].
"Quoy? . . . Le decours et maintien de verité divine" (1:209) [How's
that? . . . The continuance and upholding of divine truth (130)] are
Gargantua's reply and last words in the text. Frère Jean immediately
and vigorously rejects Gargantua's explanation — "Par sainct Goderan (dist le moyne), telle n'est mon exposition" (1:209) [By Saint
Goderan, said the monk, such is not my explanation (130)] — and
delivers himself of the truth of the enigma, while decrying the effort to interpret in terms of "allegories et intelligences tant graves"
(1:209) [allegories and interpretations as ponderous (130)]. But
Gargantua's emotional muteness speaks volumes. It is the sign of
pensiveness, his attitude throughout the reading of the "Enigme en
prophetie," since, when it is over, we are told that he "souspira
profondement" (1:209) [sighed deeply (130)]. His pensiveness and
then his silence envelop Frère Jean's commentary — and therefore the
last words of the text — and become the silence unto which ends of
texts open, the silence of reading and the silence of thought.

And of pleasure, as Frère Jean in his last words summons us to
cheer the players: "Après le jeu, on se refraischit devant un clair feu,
et change l'on de chemise, et voluntiers bancquete l'on, mais plus joy-
eusement ceulx qui ont guaigné. Et grand chere!" (1:210) [After the
game, the players refresh themselves before a bright fire and change
their shirts, and gladly they feast, but most joyfully the winners. And
so good cheer! (130)]. His explanation is no less emblematic of the
reader's stance than that of Gargantua, and, since he has the last
word, his are the words that ensure that the reader will not be able to
marginalize the fictional construct. Thus, within *Gargantua* as work
of art, two kinds of texts struggle to be heard, the writerly and the
scriptural. They are not at variance. Gargantua, "l'homme de la
prophétie," and Frère Jean, "l'homme de l'énigme,"[15] are united in
the same way that the "Fanfreluches antidotées" and the "Enigme en

prophetie" are linked beneath the surface of the text, the unrecover-
able end of the first find ("long sans mesure, car oncques n'en trouverent le bout" [1:13] [immeasurably long, for they never found the
end of it (8)]) undoubtedly surfacing toward the "fondemens de
l'abbaye" (1:205) [foundations of the abbey (127)]. For they are
readers, one reading spiritually, the other literarily, each seeking the
life-giving properties of his text. Gargantua sees Holy Scripture ("Le
decours et maintien de verité divine" [1:209] [The continuance and
upholding of divine truth (130)]), Frère Jean sees "le jeu." Both
are sustained by their readings and interpretation. "In their ears"
(2 Kings 23:2) their texts are retrieved and renewed. The unearthed
text is indeed promise of salvation.

# Gérard Defaux

# Rabelais's Realism, Again

*Ainsi demeurera le tonneau inexpuisible.*
*Il a source vive et veine perpetuelle.*

—Rabelais, *Le Tiers livre*

Contrary to what my title may suggest, I do not intend to revive the long-dead quarrel between Leo Spitzer and the so-called Rabelaisants grouped behind the towering figure of Abel Lefranc. I have always believed that their quarrel was without real substance, initiated by a scholar who had many talents but whose bad temper and polemical stance were such that, in Rabelais's case, they finally blurred his critical intelligence. I hope I am not the only one today who sees that the Manichean distribution of roles imposed upon us, the scholars of the next generation, was fundamentally unfair, did not make much sense, and ultimately had more damaging than soothing consequences for Rabelais scholarship. To oppose "historisme" and "poésie," as Spitzer did, to pretend that attention paid to historical data or details necessarily blinds the critic's eye to considerations of a more linguistic, formal, and literary nature is simply wrong and leads nowhere. It brings to mind the comment made some time ago by Horace in one of his satires: "In avoiding a vice, fools run into its opposite. . . . There is no middle course" (I,2:20) [Dum vitant stulti vitia, in contraria currunt. . . . Nil medium est]. In his desire to rescue Rabelais studies from the impasse of positivism, to show that there was more in the Picrocholine war than a legal battle between Rabelais's father and Gaucher de Sainte-Marthe, Spitzer jumped to the other extreme and locked himself in. His strategy of exclusion and his reductionism were certainly of a different nature than Lefranc's, but they were still

19

for him what they had been for the school of his predecessor. The same spirit prevailed, and the same blindness. Everything had been reversed, but nothing had changed.

With this new *querelle des Anciens et des Modernes* in mind, I would like to comment on how we have been reading *Gargantua* in the last two decades, with the hope of showing, first, how the text successfully resists all one-sided interpretations à la Lefranc or à la Spitzer, and, second, our need to adopt a critical stance that respects every major component of the text — including its obvious and, in my opinion, overly neglected realism.

I shall take as my point of departure Michael A. Screech's 1970 edition of *Gargantua*. In this remarkable work, Screech walks in Lefranc's footsteps, but he goes much farther than his predecessor by offering us what might legitimately be called the traditional interpretation of *Gargantua*. According to him and his collaborator V. L. Saulnier, Rabelais's second book, unlike the blundering and imperfect *Pantagruel*, that "ours mal léché," is a real masterpiece, a work controlled by a craftsman in which its master has inscribed the quintessence of his thought and philosophy on all the important issues of his age. In this view, Rabelais, acting as a zealous admirer and disciple of Erasmus and using his book as a pulpit, truly preaches a series of sermons: in favor of an enlightened, humanist, and liberal education against the obsolete, stultifying, and barbaric methods of Scholasticism; for the Peace of Christ against war and its violence; for the king as philosopher and philosopher as king against the tyrant forsaken by God and bereft of reason; and for a world freed by Christian *libertas* against a world ruled and enslaved by the Law, the Gloss, and all forms of "institutions humaines." Since every sermon, every "leçon" of this sort, by its nature, implicitly requires the absolute transparency of the medium in which it is expressed, it consequently follows that the language of *Gargantua* must scrupulously avoid any ambivalence or ambiguity, that it is doomed to univocity, constrained and forced into it. Contrary to the oracle, whose authority is based on the mystery of an ambiguous formulation, the propagandist and the pedagogue — that is, the preacher — whose primary concern is to teach and convince, cannot afford to be ambiguous, unclear, or sibylline. He must, to the best of his rhetorical abilities, use a simple, immediately accessible, and transparent language; he must turn the language he is using into a tool of exchange and unequivocal communication.

As I tried to suggest in my study of the comic mask in *Gargantua* (Defaux 1974), this is but one part of the story. There is much more in Rabelais's book than this traditional reading claims. First there is the narrator, whose presence dismantles all certainties. We all know that irony, word-play, equivocation and ambiguity, and parody and sophistry are maistre Alcofribas's main raison d'être. He loves playing with words and meanings as much as Gargantua's *gouvernantes* love playing with his "petite andoille vermeille" (1:50) [his little red sausage (31)] and seeing how it raised its ears (31).[1] His pleasure sometimes consists in letting words play by themselves, in recognizing their autonomy and abandoning himself joyfully to it. For him, words are nothing but an enticing and empty form, open to a wide range of possible meanings, uses, and metamorphoses. When it comes to language, everything for him depends on circumstances and motivations, on the impression he wants or has to make. He is the perfect incarnation of the Sophist, of Callicles or Gorgias, and the reincarnation of Panurge.[2]

As a consequence, the reader in *Gargantua* is not at all confronted with Rabelais's thought or philosophy, as Screech would like us to believe, but with the thought or philosophy of a persona, of a fictitious character who sometimes speaks his own mind and sometimes the author's and whose diffuse and always palpable presence and comic density represent a subtle and formidable obstacle to any attempt at interpretation, an obstacle that not only cannot be cleared away but also cannot even be, most of the time, properly outlined and evaluated. The reader of *Gargantua* is thus left with the impossible task of distinguishing the indistinguishable, of unmasking an author whose face and mask are so strangely similar that it is quite difficult in most instances to know exactly what he wears and when he wears it. He or she is left with the responsibility of disposing of this cumbersome, obtrusive, festive, and protean mediation and with the urge to establish, if they exist, the text's serious perspectives, evidently distorted by the presence and relentless sophistic play of this comic persona. Hence the existence of numberless difficulties. There is nothing more elusive and disconcerting than the thought of a writer who not only refuses to take himself seriously but also refuses to distinguish between the laughable and the serious. Nothing more ambiguous, also, than his writing. And the perplexed reader, wondering if the writing can ever be taken at face value, tries to draw a line between the serious and the nonserious and takes refuge in a worn-out but comforting paradox, asking whether laughter itself is not after all *Gargantua*'s most serious matter.

The quandary is easy to define at first sight. It has its origin in the uncanny juxtaposition of the book — not only the book *tel qu'en lui-même*, such as it is, but such as it is traditionally presented — and the fictitious character who is said to have written it. It would be difficult to imagine an odder couple than this one. It is a marriage of opposites, the perfect oxymoron. The incompatibility is so tangible that it could safely be compared to that which, since Plato, exists between Socrates, the philosopher and seeker-of-truth, and Protagoras or Gorgias, the Sophist, logographer, and doxosophos, the sucker-for-glory. In the first instance, we have a book with dogmatic and pedagogical overtones, a book which from time to time takes on the look of a sermon and offers us, often at the expense of fiction itself, a formal exposé of evangelical and humanist propaganda. In the second, we have a parody of the preposterous historiographer, a caricature of the omniscient scholastic debater, of the Sophist as professional jester. All in all, a creation totally at odds with its proclaimed creator.

If this juxtaposition is striking, it is far from being uncommon. It is traditional among the writers considered the major proponents of comic wisdom, to whom maistre Alcofribas alludes in his prologue, those who find inspiration not in sweat and lamp oil, but in the "dive" bottle and its "purée septembrale." From the very beginning, truth has been taught under the guise of folly and farce. Democritus never declined gravity or excluded depth. A worthy disciple of Lucian, Erasmus reminds us of this at the threshold of his *Encomium moriae*: "Nothing, says he, is more witty and more felicitous (*fes-*

*tivius*) than to propose serious matters through frivolities (*nugas*)."[3] He uses the same argument in his letter to Martin Dorpius, relying on Horace's example and authority: "Et Flaccus existimat jocosam quoque admonitionem non minus atque seriam conducere: ridentem (inquit) dicere verum/qui vetat?" (Erasmus 1979, 143) [Horace also believes that a humorous admonition may be just as profitable as a serious one: There is nothing, he says, to prevent you from telling the truth with laughter in your heart and a smile on your face!]. Since the wisest men of ancient times were well aware that truth penetrates more readily into the minds of mortals when it comes on the wings of pleasure, we should not be surprised at the juxtaposition of a book that was apparently written to teach us serious and important matters with a fictive narrator whose verbal and scholastic intemperance indicate that, side by side with Ortuinus Gratius, he might have appeared among the Obscure Men of Cologne.

The coexistence in the same narrative space of a kind of handbook of Erasmian propaganda, the author of which is anything but serious and, in many instances, seems eager to remind his readers that he had too much to drink, is so essential to Rabelais's purpose that it is clearly stated at a theoretical level in the prologue and repeated at the practical level in the fifty-sixth and last chapter of the book, in which Gargantua and Frère Jean propose two totally different readings of the text of the "Enigme en prophetie."[4] The first sees it as a scriptural call to resist persecution for the Gospel unto the end, and the second finds no allegorical meaning, only the plain and simple description of a tennis game wrapped in "obscures parolles." Thus properly framed, it is in the end the entire text of *Gargantua* that proclaims again and again its silenic nature as expressed in the prologue (1:5–9) [3–5]: surprising nature, even monstrous and unnatural in its novelty, in which coexist a *sensus literalis*, a literal meaning made of "mocqueries, folateries et menteries joyeuses" [mockeries, tomfooleries, and merry falsehoods], and an *altior sensus*, a higher meaning that Alcofribas, aroused by the prospect of making some money, successively describes as "celeste et impreciable drogue" [heavenly drug beyond price], "substantificque mouelle" [substantific marrow], and "doctrine plus absconce" [more abstruse doctrine] fraught

23

with revelations, "très haultz sacremens et mysteres horrificques" [very lofty sacraments and horrific mysteries] concerning the three classical domains of moral philosophy as they were deemed to exist since Aristotle and Cicero: ethics, here present as "nostre religion," "vie oeconomicque" [domestic life], and "estat politicq" [political state]. Serious matters indeed and quite unexpected in a book whose "enseigne exteriore" [outward sign] and style can only elicit smiles of derision. If anything can be taken as true in this masterpiece of self-serving rhetoric, it is that "l'habit ne faict poinct le moyne" (1:6) [the robe does not make the monk (4)].

Once this monstrous juxtaposition of meanings, this new *concordia discors*, has been defined and properly understood, it becomes increasingly impossible to think of *Gargantua* as a book exclusively serious or exclusively comic and grotesque and of its real or fictitious author either as a stern schoolmaster whose main task is to define the ideal humanist curriculum in every detail or as a writer who writes "pour ne rien dire" [to say nothing] and whose only real ambition is to give free rein to the signifier as it plays its own fascinating game.

The text stubbornly refuses this kind of mutilation. Time and again, it posits itself as both thought and play, comic and serious, useful and delectable. At every level, from sentence to chapter and chapter to book, the text owes its existence to the juxtaposition of these opposites and to the puzzling tension they generate. It is an easy and perfectly legitimate task to extract from *Gargantua* a "substantificque mouelle," to isolate all of its ideological utterances, those fragments of thought borrowed mainly from such Christian humanists as Guillaume Budé, Jacques Lefèvre d'Etaples, Juan-Luis Vives, and Erasmus. It is equally easy and legitimate to read *Gargantua* as a dialogic play of languages, as a sophistic and carnavalesque "bricolage" in which the reader moves from perplexity to perplexity, unable to bring to a satisfactory conclusion his pursuit of a forever deferred meaning. Too often, however, and in spite of the hardship implied, the reader chooses only one of these aspects of the text and completely ignores the other. In the crucial domain of poetics and style, in the domain of the voice heard in *Gargantua* offering, after the "propos des bien yvres" (1:25–29) [the palaver of the potted (15–18)], Grandgousier's Paulinian sermon to the pilgrims gone astray, it is never for Rabelais one or the other, but always, as with Trouillogan, one and the other, never one without the other, and both at the same time.

Faced with such a text, the reader who decides not to simplify things, who wishes to strike a fair balance between the comic and serious aspects of the book — between what Rabelais, referring to Lucian in his prologue to the *Tiers livre* (1:402) [259], calls Aristophanesque comedy and Platonic dialogue — finds himself at a loss, totally frustrated in his desire for integration and coherence, unable to reach a firm ground, to rest as Plato's philosophical dog rests when he has finally found what he was looking for.

The reader may believe at first that the coexistence of the most serious content with the most buffoonish and extravagant delivery does not in any way affect the corrosive and liberating power of laughter or the forceful univocity and urgency of the message inscribed in it — each of these elements preserving the purity and specificity of its original being. In fact, some textual unities, more than the sentences, the adages, and other apophthegmata, seem to lend themselves to a kind of selective reading process. They look like gems waiting to be separated from their surrounding matrix. For example, the moving piece of advice given by Grandgousier to the pilgrims: "Entretenez voz familles, travaillez, chascun en sa vocation, instruez voz enfans, et vivez comme vous enseigne le bon apostre sainct Paoul" (1:169) [Look after your families, each man work in his vocation, bring up your children, and live as the good Apostle Saint Paul teaches you to do (104)]. Or the violent denunciations of the caphars and false prophets who, by holding the holy saints of God responsible for the miseries that strike people on this earth, make them look like devils; of the so-called servants of the Word of God, those impostors whose scandalous doctrines poison the soul of poor and simple folks; or of those kings who call themselves Christian and Catholicus, but rule over their kingdom as frivolous, unscrupulous, childish, and bloodthirsty tyrants, who believe they are entitled to emulate the "anciens Hercules, Alexandres, Hannibalz,

Scipions, Cesars et aultres telz" (1:171) [ancient Herculeses, Alexanders, Hannibals, Scipios, Caesars, and others like them (105)] and who dream of wars and conquests in a world that should be a world of peace and "dilection mutuelle"; or again, the humanitarian and pacifist declarations; the resounding evangelical professions of faith heard in almost every chapter of the Picrocholine war; the determination, expressed so many times, to buy peace at any cost and to wage war only when all other possible means of resolving the dispute have failed; the willingness, if one finally goes to war, to spare bloodshed as much as possible, to use "engins" and "cauteles" (1:116) [expedient devices (71)], to resort to all imaginable stratagems of war rather than pure violence with the hope "[de sauver] toutes les ames et les [envoyer] joyeux à leurs domiciles" (1:116) [(to save) all the souls and (send) them back joyfully to their homes (71)].⁵ Rabelais repeatedly takes an unequivocal stand: he uses every opportunity to spread the word; when his fiction does not give him the opportunity he needs, he does not hesitate to create it. Since "le propos le veult" [the story requires it], fiction follows.

But these fragments of concretized meaning are not always as unambiguous as they seem at first sight. They have not always successfully resisted the ludic contagion of the text that surrounds them and in which we would like them to be set like closed, transparent, and motionless units. Even though the writing praxis in *Gargantua* seems from time to time subservient to the dictates of ideology, in truth it respects nothing. It obeys only its own imperatives, which have nothing in common with those that govern the "plus hault sens" and its "doctrine plus absconce." For example, when Grandgousier is presented to us as the embodiment of the King as Christian and Philosopher, of the Prince "adorner of the People," whose only ambition is the well-being of his subjects and the consolidation of peace, of the father-figure whose main concern is to avoid the fatal irruption of violence, the text offers with Frère Jean a formidable show of Homeric massacres, an unparalleled celebration of the magic of language, in which the most graphic details, the most furious and deadly blows, the most atrocious incidents repeatedly pummel the reader. The latter's only reasonable conclusion is that he is dealing with a book in which the most authentic pacifism coexists with "le plus horrible spectacle qu'on veit oncques" (1:110) [the most horrible sight you ever saw (68)], with a book that feels no shame in flatly contradicting itself. After having sung the praise of Christian love and peace, it gives way to the destructive raptures of war, the monk deciding to put an end to the killing only when he is tired and when his "bracquemart," his sword, breaks in two and when the chapter (*Gargantua* 44), breathless and exhausted, can do nothing else but end. Everything in this devious and deceptive book happens as if truth and value, all those things Rabelais is apparently fighting for, were swept away by the exhilarating music and rattling of words, the sheer ecstasy of their accumulation and coming together, as if it were finally less important to propagate the philosophy of Christ than to emulate or ape Homer and Virgil, Plutarch and Lucian, to be the burlesque imitator of these great masters.

The reader who gets a clear picture of these inconsistencies is led to believe that the writer in Rabelais takes precedence over the pedagogue and the thinker.[6] Of the two tasks that seem to have mobilized Rabelais's energy in *Gargantua* — that of the religious, social, and political reformer and that of the artist in love with his medium, of the poet master of words and creator of fiction — the latter undoubtedly seems to prevail. If need be, we can imagine a Rabelais solely interested in the art of telling tales and careless about the rest. But the reverse — that is, the idea of a Rabelais solely interested in the dissemination of ideology and totally oblivious to storytelling, impervious to fiction — is, in my opinion, utterly inconceivable. Ideology exists for him only insofar as it can be translated into fiction, expressed in narrative terms.[7]

Rabelais seems so skeptical when it comes to ideas, he seems to harbor such a distrust of the purely intellectual, speculative, discursive, and theoretical, that he never bothers to probe the logical aporias he might encounter. He is content with reproducing these aporias just as he found them in the treatises, diatribes, and other profound writings of his contemporaries. Thus the wide-ranging quarrel between Luther and Erasmus over the issue of free will takes in *Gargantua* the form of two declarations, both of which are absolute and neither of which can be reconciled with the other. The first, made by Grandgousier on the matter of Picrochole, is resolutely Lutheran: "Dieu eternel l'a laissé au gouvernail de son franc arbitre et propre sens, *qui ne peult estre que meschant sy par grâce divine n'est continuellement guidé*" (1:115–16, my emphasis) [Eternal God has abandoned him to the rudder of his own free will and sense, which cannot but be wicked if it is not continually guided by divine Grace (71)]. The second, on the other hand, appears in the utopian and courtly context of Thélème. It reflects the theological optimism of Erasmus, as found, for example, in his interminable *Hyperaspistes* of 1526: "En leur reigle n'estoit que ceste clause: FAY CE QUE VOULDRAS, parce que gens liberes, bien nez, bien instruictz, conversans en compaignies honnestes, *ont par nature un instinct et aguillon, qui tousjours les poulse à faictz vertueux et retire de vice, lequel ilz nommoient honneur*" (1:204, my emphasis) [In their rule was only this clause: DO WHAT YOU WILL, because people who are free, well born, well bred, moving in honorable social circles, have by nature an instinct and goad which always impels them to virtuous deeds and holds them back from vice, which they call honor (126)]. Many worthy efforts have been undertaken to account for these two passages and to persuade us they are not contradictory. The argument is usually that Picrochole does not belong to the Elect, that he is neither free, well-born, nor well-bred, and that he is certainly not moving in honorable social circles. I prefer to think that, in these two declarations, Rabelais wanted to recognize the limits of the human spirit, that he quite knowingly juxtaposed two incompatible theses in order to suggest that the truth, if it is discussed too much, gets lost, and that nothing certain can ever emerge from the quarrels and distinguos of theologians, even if they are Erasmus and Luther.

Towards the end of 1524, Marguerite d'Angoulême asked the same kind of questions in her *Dialogue en forme de vision nocturne*. The spirit of the little princess Charlotte de France replied that no Christian soul had any business getting mixed up in such sterile disputes. It was far better to not try too hard to penetrate God's secrets and not add to the confusion created by Erasmus and Luther. Lefèvre d'Etaples had taken the same attitude in his *Epistres et evan-*

*giles pour les cinquante et deux dimenches de l'an* (1525). When people went to him shortly before his death in 1536 to ask whether Luther or Erasmus was right, the old scholar invariably replied, "I have no idea" [Hoc ego ignoro]. In *Gargantua*, Rabelais seems to profess the same kind of modesty. To a certain extent, he believes in the ideas and discourses engendered by the intellect, but he never forgets the dangers of *cuyder*. The spirit exists for him only when it is incarnate, preferably in a fiction. Reduced to itself alone, floating around at the level of forms, of paradigms and ideas, of exemplars of Plato, the spirit is nothing but a sophism. It embraces only the wind.

So, in Rabelais, the poet, the artist of language, predominates over the militant evangelist and humanist. This explains why the main episodes of the book are structured by the Sophistic practice of logical opposition, of what we might call the opposition of opposites.[8] This procedure goes back through the medieval logicians to the *Categoriae* of Aristotle: "Opposita, juxta se posita, magis elucescunt." "Et les opposez," as Pierre de La Ramée translates in his *Dialectique* (1555), "sont de leur nature entre soy esgallement notoires . . . et néantmoins l'un mis devant l'autre est plus clairement apperçeu" [And opposites are, by their very nature, equally plain, one to the other. But nevertheless, one placed next to the other is more clearly perceived].[9] What else is *Gargantua* proposing to us than the Manichean opposition of two worlds, one hateful and the other hoped for? The entire book rests upon a constant play of antitheses and contrasts, "bien et mal, vertu et vice, froid et chauld, blanc et noir, volupté et doleur, joye et dueil" (1:43) [good and evil, virtue and vice, cold and hot, white and black, pleasure and pain, joy and sorrow (27)], being and appearance, *sensus literalis* and *altior sensus*, God and Satan. This play informs the text not only at the lexical level but also at the level of its images, styles, chapters, themes, characters, and situations. The world of Picrochole is the inverse of that of Grandgousier, the education of Ponocrates is the opposite of that of maistre Thubal, and Thélème, given by Gargantua to Frère Jean, the anti-monk, is nothing other than an anti-monastery.

To extend the demonstration to textual details and stylistic analysis would be easy to do. Once we have seen how it works, nothing is more obvious and more predictable. I would rather point out here how difficult and dangerous it is in this context to attempt to define too narrowly what we usually call the thought of Rabelais, that is, his ideal of education, government, society, and religion. The reason is that the play of opposites that structures *Gargantua*, and which will reappear in the *Tiers livre*, frequently substitutes its own imperatives, the laws of its own operation, for those imperatives and laws that ideological considerations would impose if they were the only ones in the book. As we have seen, this is far from the case. Frequently, one detail of this contrasted picture justifies its existence only by its role in the system of oppositions. It is not there to illuminate the spirit of any program or to define any ideal, but rather because the rules of the game that govern the writing require it to be there — out of concern for an aesthetic principle, as Jean Plattard understood many years ago (Plattard, 79). In this way, everything at Thélème — the rule, the architecture, the way of life, clothing, daily activities, participants — can be explained by the desire of Frère Jean and Gargantua to institute a religious community "au contraire de toutes aultres" (1:189) [in the opposite way from all the others (116)]. Accordingly, in this place there will be no "murailles au circuit, car toutes aultres abbayes sont fierement murées" (1:189) [there must never be walls built around it, for all other abbeys are proudly walled (116)]; nor will there be a clock, "parce que es religions de ce monde tout est compassé, limité et reiglé par heures" (1:189) [because in the monasteries of this world everything is compassed, limited, and regulated by hours (116)]; "Item, parce que ordinairement les religieux faisoient troys veuz, sçavoir est de chasteté, pauvreté, et obedience" (1:190) [because ordinarily the religious made three vows, to wit of chastity, poverty, and obedience (117)], it is decided that "là honorablement on peult estre marié" (1:190) [they could honorably be married (117)]; and that each one will be rich and live in liberty without having to answer to anyone for his acts.

From one item to the next, right up to the "DO WHAT YOU WILL," the abbey is founded on and rests on the opposition of contraries. The education offered by Ponocrates is less a minute, detailed ex-

pression of the Rabelaisian ideal of pedagogy — his own *De pueris
instituendis* — than it is the exact contrary of the pedagogical praxis
of the Sorbonne's old wheezers, which praxis is itself a function of its
opposite and in no way a reflection, representation, or mirror of any
historical reality. Gargantua gets up at four in the morning to pursue
a course of study in which "il ne perdoit heure quelconques du jour"
(1:88) [he didn't waste any hour whatever of the day (55)], to the
point at which his teacher takes advantage of the moment when
Gargantua goes "es lieux secretz faire excretion des digestions natu-
relles" (1:88–89) [to the private places to make an excretion of
natural digestions (55)] to expound upon "les poinctz plus obscurs
et difficiles" (1:89) [the most obscure and difficult points (55)] of
the previous day's lesson. But this is not because Rabelais perceives
some ideal in this unbounded obsession with the utilization of time.
Quite the reverse: we know that it was at Montaigu, this "colliege de
pouillerie" (1:140) [that louse-ridden school (86)], which both Erasmus and Rabelais detested, that this kind of schedule was imposed.
Frère Jean will put it this way: "les heures sont faictez pour l'homme,
et non l'homme pour les heures" (1:156) [hours are made for man,
not man for hours (96)]. Gargantua will banish clocks and quad-
rants from Thélème while affirming that "la plus vraye perte du
temps qu'il sceust estoit de compter les heures" (1:189) [the greatest
waste of time he knew of was to count the hours (117)].

No, Gargantua gets up early because, under the rod of maistre
Thubal, he got up quite late indeed, "entre huyt et neuf heures"
(1:80). In a whole day, he never put in more than "quelque mes-
chante demye heure" (1:82) [some paltry half hour (50)] of study.
Truth and historical reality, the so-called referent, are here sacrificed
to the joys of antithesis and the imperatives of satire. In going from
Thubal Holofernes to Ponocrates, the reader does not go from bad
education to good, as they might have existed in any real sense at the
time Rabelais was writing. Rather, the reader goes from extreme
laziness to extreme mental and physical strain. These two forms of
"institution," although they are antithetical, meet in the same excess
by means of a writing prone to hyperbole. Gargantua plays "au flux,
à la condemnade, à la prime, à la charte virade, à la vole, au maucon-

tent, à la pille, au lansquenet, à la triumphe" (1:83) [Flush, Primiera, Grand slam, Robber, Trump, Prick and spare not, One hundred, The spinet, Poor Moll (50–51)]. He hunts "le cerf, le chevreuil, l'ours, le dain, le sanglier, le lievre, la perdrys, le faisant, l'otarde" (1:93) [the stag, the roebuck, the bear, the fallow deer, the wild boar, the hare, the partridge, the pheasant, the bustard (58)]. He throws "le dart, la barre, la pierre, la javeline, l'espieu, la halebarde" (1:94) [the dart, the put, the stone, the javelin, the boar-spear, the halberd (58)]. There is no difference at all. We can clearly see the exaggerations, simplifications, deformations, and alterations that Rabelais imposes upon reality, and we understand as well that they eliminate any documentary value that the episode may have and that has all too often been attributed to it. In *Gargantua*, Rabelais is far less concerned with reality and historical accuracy than he is with gaming, laughter, and the creation of a universe by means of language. It is exactly this game, laughter, and creation that Alcofribas's presence in the book symbolizes.

This does not mean, however, that *Gargantua* lacks commitment. Quite the reverse; Rabelais laughs and makes us laugh. But he is all the while faithful to Horace and to his utilitarian concept of art. He never forgets to instruct and educate us. Looking at the utopian triumphs of Ponocrates and Grandgousier over Janotus and Picrochole, it is easy to pick up on his hatreds and sympathies. His hatreds are especially clear and unambiguous. In the first place, Rabelais is no lover of the Sorbonne; no one could argue with this. He hates everything about it: the politics it supports, the scholastic culture it cheapens, its narrow, formalistic, and tyrannical definition of religion and faith, of which it professes itself the orthodox and vigilant rampart. But it seems equally clear that Rabelais, like the Christian humanists of his generation, hoped that the spirit of the Gospel would return the world to a state of love, reason, and peace. *Gargantua* thus would constitute a call to action and militancy, particularly in the character of Frère Jean with his symbolically broad shoulders and his "baston de la croix." In its unbounded optimism — 1533, after all, is the year of great expectations for the evangelical movement — *Gargantua* generates, in the most utopian of spaces, the new world that humanism longed for. Rabelais shares these views. But to go beyond these fundamental positions would be to forget Rabelais the artist, the gamesman, the master of language. It would be to suggest an impoverished image of the book.

It would be a mistake, however, to conclude that *Gargantua* is nothing but a kind of closed system in which writing, which is mostly writing about writing, is ultimately specular and folds back on itself. Historical reality is much too present to be discarded that easily. We cannot simply say that Rabelais, in his desire to create a story and play with it, to abandon himself to the laws of language and let words do as they please, dreams only of forgetting the world in which he lives. Although *Gargantua* presents itself as a mirrored play of writing, it nevertheless remains loaded with allusions to the most burning religious and political topics of the day. The book also feeds on memories, characters, and events from the daily life of François Rabelais. This book is accordingly his book in a double sense: not only is he the author but he also seems to have wanted to inscribe in it vast tracts of himself and his past. It would be difficult to imagine, much before the example of Proust, such an undisguised return to the self.[10] As I have already pointed out, chapters nine and ten of *Gargantua*, on the significance of white and blue, refer to Lyons (Defaux 1974, 114–23). They cannot be completely understood except in relation to the milieu of the printers — Seb. Gryphius, F. Juste, O. Arnoullet, etc. — that Rabelais frequented in Lyons from 1532 to 1535. Similarly, the Picrocholine war is rooted with absolutely accurate topographical precision in a half acre or so of the county of Chinon, in Touraine, near La Deviniere, Rabelais's birthplace. In spite of the use of myth and folklore, the episodes of the bells of Notre Dame and the "sergents du guet" martyred by Panurge in *Pantagruel* reveal an intimate knowledge of Paris, its buildings and monuments, its streets, lanes, and back alleys. Although the fiction of *Gargantua* imposes its laws and defines the rules of the game, reality refuses to be forgotten. This occurs to such an extent that we may end up asking whether the childhood of Gargantua and the festivities that accompany his birth, up to and including the "mirifical" asswipe, are taken from personal experience.

It is the presence of a personal experience in *Gargantua* that has caused Rabelais to be called "the greatest realist" and his work "a mirror of the life and times of its author" or "a mirror of his life" (Lefranc, 7). Painstaking research in the archives, records, and registers of the region of Chinon has established that the names of people and places in the episode of the Picrocholine war are quite real. They are the names of places that really existed and are for the most part still there and of people that Rabelais knew. All are indisputably documented. Forgier, Marquet, and Gallet really existed. Picrochole is Gaucher de Sainte-Marthe, the seigneur of Lerné and personal physician to the abbess of Fontevrault. Evidence from the period or soon after confirms the identification. An uproarious trial over fisheries took place between Gaucher de Sainte-Marthe, a hothead if ever there was one, and the boatmen of the Loire and the Vienne, who were defended by Antoine Rabelais and his colleague Jean Gallet. It is completely possible with a detailed map of the region to follow the military confrontation as it spreads out over the landscape between the legions of Gargantua and the ruffians of the Picrocholine army. There is no element of fantasy in this, only absolute realism.

Given the mood of our times, however, these facts were quickly forgotten. One has only to say that Pichrochole exists in a more important sense than does Gaucher de Sainte-Marthe (which is certainly true). Or that the Pichrocholine war exceeds by far the rural frame of Chinon, and some scuffle among shepherds over "fouaces" (which is undeniable). Or to bring up the clown of Banville, who jumps onto the "springboard of the real" only in order to "fly off to the stars," and to "the unreal of poetry" (Spitzer 1960), in order to put an end to all speculations and reflections of this kind.

What we have here is an error that we must correct, although not by returning to the narrow positivism of archivists and literary historians. Rather, we should reflect on the possible significance of this undeniable presence of the world and self of Rabelais in his own text. Why did Rabelais so obviously invest himself in his fiction? Why did he construct its frame and its unfolding according to his own experiences and memories? How shall we come to terms with the dimension of *Gargantua* that, for lack of a better word, we may call autobiographical? Or with the fact that it seems difficult for Rabelais to extract himself from his fiction and to let us forget that he is right in the middle of it? In my opinion, this is the kind of question we should be asking today, if we are ever to escape from the polemical oversimplifications and the too-easy oppositions of Leo Spitzer, and if we wish to make more progress in understanding the text than did the Rabelaisians. Rabelais was certainly a "poet," an incomparable artist of language. He was also, to a great extent, a historian and witness of his time, as well as his own historiographer.

It is quite impossible in this paper for me to go back over the whole ontotheology that, in this devout and hyperreligious century, defined not only the subject but also the relationship between the subject and language.[11] A preliminary answer may be found in the will to represent, which seemed at that time to motivate the writer, and in the principles of pleasure and enjoyment of self, which also seemed, in a general but clearly visible way, to preside over his activity. In taking up residence within his own writing, Rabelais gave himself pleasure above all. What he offers is his own version of the remembrance of things past. In his book, he sketches out a symbolic itinerary from childhood to adulthood, from the most basic and material physiological drives — "eat, drink, sleep; sleep, drink, eat" — to those pure, disincarnate, and wholly spiritual drives toward self-will and self-mastery — "DO WHAT YOU WILL." This symbolic itinerary is, more than anything else, a reveling in the ego and its past, driving deep into the ego's history and acculturation. It is the birth and affirmation in writing of one subjectivity and the blossoming out of this subjectivity in a place — that is, language — which, although exterior to the ego, is nevertheless its true place where it is most astonishingly alive and present, intact and miraculously preserved.

In *Gargantua*, Rabelais expresses in his own way the great humanist and classical credo of Plato, Horace, and Quintilian, according to which the written and spoken word is always necessarily the word of someone, the "truchement de son ame," or its mirror, the faithful expression and representation of the self. At the same time, Rabelais demonstrates that this self-evident presence of the self in writing is also a presence for and to another; it is the desire to engage in dialogue in order to communicate, to have someone to talk to. In the end, if Rabelais/Alcofribas says "I," it is because he is driven by the desire to be able to say "you." Even today, he never stops reminding us that his first two books (because what is true of *Gargantua* is equally true of *Pantagruel*) were written for a regional and even local public. This public did not consist solely of potential or anonymous readers. They were quite real, they frequented the places that Rabelais did, and they may even have known him personally. They were thus in a better position than anyone else to appreciate his allusions and jokes. How could Forgier, Marquet, and Gallet not have read *Gargantua*, since it had to some extent been written for them and was addressed to them?

From the perspective of the book as dialogue, the reading of the local public would necessarily differ from that of the reading by the public from Paris or Lyons. At the same time, the two readings would have had similarities, since both publics would have found themselves in familiar territory, in a text that spoke to them in a well-known language, that never stopped signaling to them, and that produced familiar echoes in their ears. In this way, there is established and defined before our eyes what we might call a network of readings that are properly and authentically Pantagruelian. It is by means of this network that Rabelais hopes to be recognized and understood. He counts upon it to establish the communion and dialogue, the complicitous and genuine exchange, the heart-to-heart talk, the conviviality and *festivitas* that, according to Pantagruel and his apostles, constitute the very essence of Pantagruelism.

Beyond the circle of neighbors, relatives, friends, and acquaintances, it is the humanist who takes up the baton: the lover of "antiquaille" and *bonae litterae*, the jurist, physician, or theologian, whose attention is attracted by the erudite allusions that Rabelais scatters throughout his text and by the game of parody that he plays with classical epic and the lives of the saints. And beyond that are the joker, the buffoon, the fool, and the wag, all those who delight in the fantasies and obscenities of this gigantic folklore, in the laughter of farces and tomfooleries. . . .

Briefly defined in this manner, Rabelais's book becomes a kind of feast open to all appetites, a great banquet where the wine flows for all men of good will and where all palates and all tastes find satisfaction. In his desire to be "bien venu en toutes bonnes compaignies de Pantagruelistes" (1:9) [welcome in all good companies of Pantagruelists (5)], Rabelais seems to have multiplied himself into as many copies of Rabelais as there are readers. He is a new Father One-for-all, betraying a concept of the book and reading that is not our own, but that reappears in Montaigne at the end of the century. At the same time, he is so concerned about his public that he takes care to make out the guest list himself and to prepare a special menu for each one. In spite of this *convivium dispar*, he so wants to preserve the harmony and esprit de corps of his drinking buddies, that he carefully excludes all party poopers, parasites, hypocrites, "cagotz, matagotz, escargotz," and other professional *agelastes*. It is as though he does everything to keep the book from drifting away, as though it is necessary at all costs and by means of all kinds of winks and nods to control all possible ports of call and to keep it from coming to rest on unknown shores.

This is a special kind of dialogue, in which the author dictates both the questions and the answers and keeps the reader, so to speak, on a leash. There is nonetheless a will to dialogue, demonstrated in *Gargantua* by the allegorical and completely reflexive chapter consecrated to the "propos des bien yvres." In the prologue to the *Tiers livre*, Rabelais, transformed into an omnipresent and omniscient, though silent, wine steward and cupbearer, presents his book as a "tonneau inexpuisible" (1:402) [inexhaustible . . . barrel (259)], a "vray Cornucopie de joyeuseté et raillerie" (1:402) [a real cornucopia of joyfulness and jesting (259)], in which one has only to drink "franchement, librement, hardiment" (1:402) [freely, frankly, boldly (259)] without paying or sparing anything. In a completely different register, this will to dialogue is demonstrated by the inscription over the great door of Thélème, which speaks to Rabelais's anxiety about the Pantagruelian community that he is creating, and by the care he uses in distinguishing the elect from the rest, opposing those who enter to those who will not: "Notez bien ce que j'ay dict, et quelle maniere de gens je invite." (1:402) [Mark well what I have said, and what manner of people I invite (259)]. For Rabelais, "reader" is never a catchall word, a convenient etiquette covering up some undefined reality. Rather, the reader is a familiar character, possibly not really known, but nonetheless a specific someone whom the text creates and whom Rabelais awaits.

The bond woven here between author and reader through the text looks much like the one of which Rabelais offers a metaphorical illustration in his prologue. When correctly read, as Edwin Duval has recently taught us to read it, the prologue reveals itself to be motivated by a deep concern for the reader, by the visible and almost palpable desire to interest and seduce him.[12] It leads us, by a brilliantly orchestrated hermeneutic progression, from the title, "l'enseigne exteriore," to the literal meaning; from the literal meaning to the highest meaning; from the highest meaning to the compositional procedure of the text, the question of the poetics of inspiration; and from this question to the person of the author surprised in the act of creation, in the process of writing down his text while eating and drinking and prey to a bacchic furor. In other words, the progression leads not only from the exterior to the interior of the text, but also from the finished, printed text to its author, the "party-hearty guy and boon companion" who wants to share his riches, both those he is conscious of possessing and those he does not know he has. When all is said and done, it is as if the text existed only to lead to its author and then to disappear behind his back, as if it had always existed only to give birth to something else, to create a voice, a presence, to generate this profound communion of hearts and minds that goes by the name of Pantagruelism and that, for Rabelais, is the most important reality of all.

*Terence Cave*

# Travelers and Others: Cultural Connections in the Works of Rabelais

B y way of prologue, I begin on familiar terrain with what is probably the best-known example of an encounter with the alien in the works of Rabelais: the dialogue between the narrator Alcofribas and the planter of cabbages whom he finds on his journey into Pantagruel's mouth in *Pantagruel* 32. It is particularly well known, no doubt, because Auerbach made it the point of departure of his chapter on Rabelais in *Mimesis*. I want to look first at Auerbach's response not only because it continues to be a powerful and influential reading but also because it poses in a particularly striking way the question of the relationship between different types and levels of culture.

Auerbach suggests that this episode comprises at least three different categories of experience. The first is "the grotesque theme of gigantic dimensions," which arrives in Rabelais via the late medieval French chapbook *Les Chronicques gargantuines* and Lucian's *True History* (we may already note, as Auerbach does not, that these texts belong to very different cultural domains). The second category is provided by the "Renaissance" theme of the discovery of a new world, which opens up the possibility of a relativistic outlook; this theme will be developed in the following two centuries, acquiring, as Auerbach puts it, "a revolutionary force which shakes the established order" (236). The third category is embodied in the theme "tout comme chez nous": in the interstices of his comic fantasy and his new-world themes, Rabelais describes the familiar, local French world, the world seen from the Touraine, as it is. Auerbach further claims that this third level is entirely incompatible with the other levels (237).

It is clear that this analysis is designed to serve Auerbach's theme of mimesis, a literary history of forms and of ways of perceiving the world. It also tends to separate the historical, represented here by the reference to the Renaissance, from the literary or literary-historical.

It is not difficult to show that the historically "new" insight of the second level is dependent on the other levels and cannot operate without them. The encounter with the cabbage planter sets in motion a reflexive movement in which the alien and the familiar are transposed. It is this movement — and not merely the new-world theme, as Auerbach suggests — that will be traced further by Montaigne in *Des cannibales* and eventually turned into a full-scale satirical instrument by the eighteenth-century philosophes. Furthermore, the placing of the cabbage planter in the scenario of a popular legend is far from accidental; after all, the legend belongs in its own way to the realm of the familiar and the everyday. The imaginative momentum that begins to make the conception of a new world possible emerges from that conjunction. One might add that the role played by Lucian's *True History*, a text available in Rabelais's day only to the learned, is ancillary here.[1] There is thus no reason to assign priority or privilege to the so-called Renaissance theme.

What is interesting in this episode is thus rather the *connection* that Rabelais's text establishes between the three levels: it is this connection that makes the text uniquely suggestive both as literature and as history. Auerbach himself appears to grasp this point elsewhere in his analysis. He speaks of the "promiscuous intermingling of the categories of event, experience and knowledge, as well as of dimensions and styles," that characterizes Rabelais's "manner of seeing and comprehending the world" (238); but in the passage referred to above, he asserts that Rabelais "only lets the [new-world] theme begin to sound," that he "immediately buries [it] under grotesque jokes" (236, 237). These jokes appear in his account to be a synecdoche for the "old," for an out-of-date world view we must necessarily regard as inferior. Or perhaps for him they are not even old, not historically marked at all. They are just jokes, a category situated in some limbo of the intellectual hierarchy.[2] It is true that the strategy of cultural reversal that looks so familiar to us in retrospect only surfaces momentarily and that it shades back into quite different, even alien structures of imaginative thought. But it is crucial to avoid turning that flicker effect into a value-laden antithesis.

In a recent article on this and other episodes, Frank Lestringant has clarified and refined the same nexus of themes. He is not dismissive of the imaginative role played, for example, by the gigantic body of Pantagruel and Gargantua, but, on the threshold of his argument, even he slips into a value judgment not unlike Auerbach's in claiming that, in *Pantagruel* 32, the Renaissance spirit brings new life and meaning to a rather banal theme of folklore (Lestringant, 44).[3]

Essential questions of scholarly method and aesthetic judgment are at issue here. I wish to raise them simply in the form of a question mark at this point: What is the historical specificity of a given segment of Rabelais's writings and, in the end, of his work as a whole? How far does a decision on that point determine our reading of Rabelais's work as a text we would classify as "literary"?

The central part of this paper will explore further the representations of travel and of encounters with the other in *Pantagruel* and *Gargantua*, with a briefer glance at the later books. What will be at stake here is the dialectical connection between different levels or types of culture (the high and the low, the learned and the practical, the exotic and the everyday) and between the old and the new. The value of this group of representations as a paradigm is precisely that it does not belong a priori to any one cultural or historical category.

One may reasonably suppose that, forty years after the Columbian voyage, the sense of an enlarged geographical space had become part of the popular imagination. By this I mean, quite simply (and without reifying "the people" or "the popular"), that everyone had heard a version of this new-world story. Rabelais was well informed on most of the central issues of his day and exceptionally capable of giving them imaginative form. Yet *Pantagruel* bears no obvious signs of a preoccupation with new-world narratives; *Gargantua*, even less. The one exception is the announcement by the narrator in the final chapter of *Pantagruel* that he will subsequently recount the story of Pantagruel's voyages to fabulous lands, including those beyond the Atlantic where "cannibales" dwell. It belongs very clearly, as the reference to Prester John indicates, to a long-standing tradition of legendary travel stories, with no modification of perspective other than the burlesque tone.

The only long journey in the first two books is the voyage of Pantagruel and his friends to Utopia (*Pantagruel* 24). Here, the route visibly shifts into the domain of the unknown and the fantastic after the Cape of Good Hope, as if Rabelais's text were charting a limit or frontier in the imagination of space in 1532. Almost a hundred years later, Hieronymus Megiser will claim that Madagascar counts as a new-world territory because, despite vague references in classical texts, it was properly "discovered" in the early sixteenth century (Megiser, 1–5). That remark historicizes with some precision the shifting frontier between the old world and the new. The fact that Pantagruel's voyage is also mediated by a high-culture text — Sir Thomas More's description of the route to Utopia — makes little difference here. The gesture of placing a marvelous new territory at or just beyond a perceived geographical limit marks that limit as part of a wider early sixteenth-century imagination of which the learned Utopia is just one variant.

Another parallel instance is the plan of global conquest sketched out by Picrochole's advisers (*Gargantua* 33). It covers the whole of the Mediterranean basin, Asia Minor, the European continent, the Baltic, and northwest to the confines of the then familiar world.[4] In this way, it repeats the territorial ambitions of ancient potentates such as Darius and Alexander, and of the crusaders (the Holy Land is annexed en passant), and probably satirizes those of Charles V. But there is no question of a voyage west or of a circumnavigation of the globe. One need only imagine what this episode would have been like if it had been written fifty years later to see the limits which, in 1532, Rabelais takes for granted. Montaigne's *Des cannibales* and *Des coches* are still a long way off.

These remarks are not meant to be disparaging. The sense of a historical moment is delivered not by some brilliant novelty —

by Rabelais's supposed participation in every aspect of a legendary Renaissance — but by a series of reflexes that reveal a habit of mind neither progressive nor reactionary. Precisely because Rabelais is not trying to foreground the question of geographical space, he shows us, by accident as it were, the shape of that space as an informed participant in early sixteenth-century culture perceived it. It is telling that, in the very episode where the new-world theme is specifically sounded, there is no exotic voyage, no sea, no archipelagoes or landfalls; also no cannibals. The points of reference and comparison are European,[5] the religion is Christian, the cabbage planter a good imitation of a French peasant, not least because he speaks French and therefore requires no interpreter.

This is not to say that shifts are not perceptible in the way in which traveling is imagined in *Pantagruel* and *Gargantua*. Lestringant has sketched out some of these, stressing especially the replacement of *pérégrination* by *itinérance* (Michel Korinman's terms): the eschatological allegory of pilgrimage, tracing its route and purpose by reference to Biblical texts, is satirized in the story of the pilgrims in Gargantua's mouth (*Gargantua* 38), while the narrator's tour of the world in Pantagruel's mouth is free of both anxiety and anagogical significance.[6]

In *Gargantua*, Rabelais himself gives prominence to reflection on the nature of journeys by stage-managing a convergence between the adventure of the pilgrims in Gargantua's mouth and Picrochole's plan of conquest. The pilgrims are somewhat implausibly brought back into the narrative so that they can receive a harangue from Grandgousier in chapter 45 that exactly parallels his homily against imperial conquest, delivered to Toucquedillon at the beginning of chapter 46. The homily makes explicit a sense of changing times and changing political and ethical geography:

> Le temps n'est plus d'ainsi conquester les royaulmes avecques dommaige de son prochain frere christian. Ceste imitation des anciens Hercules, Alexandres, Hannibalz, Scipions, Cesars et aultres telz, est contraire à la profession de l'Evangile, par lequel nous est commandé guarder, saulver, regir et administrer chascun ses pays et terres, non hostilement envahir les aultres, et, ce que les Sarazins et Barbares jadis appelloient prouesses,

maintenant nous appellons briguanderies et meschansetez. Mieul eust il faict soy contenir en sa maison, royallement la gouvernant, que insulter en la mienne, hostillement la pillant. (1:171)

[It is no longer the time to conquer kingdoms thus with damage to our own Christian neighbor and brother. This imitation of the ancient Herculeses, Alexanders, Hannibals, Scipios, Caesars, and others like them is contrary to the Gospel's profession, by which we are commanded to guard, save, rule, and administer each man his own lands and countries, not hostilely to invade the others; and what the Saracens and barbarians once called exploits are now called brigandages and wicked deeds. He would have done better to restrain himself within his own house, governing it royally, than to come invading in mine, hostilely pillaging it. (105)][7]

Lestringant has argued that this pious injunction has little to do with the complex imaginative reflections on the experience of travel embodied in the giant's mouth episodes (Lestringant, 33–34). One might rather say that it represents a translation into axiological terms of the analysis carried out at an imaginative level in these episodes. It is an integral element in a complex group of reflections, and the structure of the group, rather than any one of its component parts, is what provides us with a sense of what it was possible to think and say about journeys in the early 1530s. Thus, for example, the emphasis of these books is arguably better represented by Grandgousier's theme of a return to the familiar and domestic than by any heady evocation of Renaissance new-world voyages.

The structure of the group is of course always subject to reorganization and expansion, both by Rabelais and by ourselves. Other groupings produce other — although presumably not *historically* incompatible — senses. Grandgousier's anti-imperialist speech ought to be looked at in relation to the opening sequence of the *Tiers livre*, where a benevolent colonial enterprise is imagined. The cabbage planter of *Pantagruel* 32 could also be juxtaposed with Panurge's speech in mid-ocean on the happiness of cabbage planters.[8] Relations, as Henry James famously said, end nowhere: he was talking of the real world, as opposed to fiction, but the frontier between the two, the frontier where relations supposedly end, is impossible to determine in the case we are considering.

I propose now to take one other point of reference in *Pantagruel* that greatly augments the implications of the group so far discussed, while at the same time displaying to a remarkable degree an intrinsic complexity of structure. This is *Pantagruel* 9 and 14: the arrival of a polyglot stranger who proves to be a Frenchman just returned, somewhat the worse for wear, from the eastern Mediterranean.[9]

This episode is often and for good reasons contrasted with the "écolier limousin" episode of *Pantagruel* 6. But it begins at once to take on a different coloring if it is read as one of a series of recurrent episodes featuring travel and the figure of the traveler. Its theme and structure already announce the cabbage planter episode; the analogy is indeed self-evident as soon as it is pointed out. Both episodes represent an encounter with a disconcerting stranger, an alien, who proves by a reversal of perspective to be reassuringly familiar. In each case, at the crucial moment when familiarity supervenes, gardens are evoked. When Panurge finally speaks French, he says that he comes from the Touraine, the garden of France. The cabbage planter, by definition, is cultivating his garden; planting cabbages is virtually a proverbial expression connoting the everyday and the domestic. The garden is the sign of the homely and the natural, discovered unexpectedly here amidst the alien. The episodes are also alike in their relation to other texts. Both draw on Greek narrative models (Homer, Lucian) where such encounters are treated according to a set formula.[10] Both use a frame of reference derived from a late medieval French work, the farce of *Maître Pierre Pathelin*, the *Chronicques gargantuines.*

It is true that the positions of the characters are reversed. *Pantagruel* 9 is set on home ground, on the outskirts of Paris, at the point where journeys begin; *Pantagruel* 32 takes place in the alien world of Pantagruel's mouth, a kind of unthreatening heart of darkness. Panurge talks like a foreigner but proves not to be one; the cabbage planter evidently is an alien but neither behaves nor speaks like one (the elision of the language problem is indeed striking when the episodes are juxtaposed). The paradigm jointly constituted by these mirror images remains fundamentally the same: they are, precisely, mirror images, scenes that stage a recognition of the familiar in the alien.

The arrival of Panurge in the narrative is connected to several other episodes in the first two books, especially those concerning pilgrimages and imperial conquest.[11] It transpires that, when Panurge was captured by the Turks, he had been taking part in a kind of latter-day crusade (1:270 [166]).[12] In his more detailed account in *Pantagruel* 14, he goes on to tell how the Turks nearly roasted him alive and how the roasting miraculously cured him of a long-standing sciatica, just as one of the pilgrims in *Gargantua* is providentially cured of a "brosse chancreuze" (1:292 and 144 [181 and 89]). Panurge's journey then is in some sense a burlesque crusade and pilgrimage.

The language map sketched out by Panurge's polyglot replies is also comparable to the geographical configurations represented in the first two books. Of the thirteen languages that figure in the expanded version of the chapter, seven are modern European languages, three are the consecrated ancient languages (Hebrew, Greek, and Latin) familiar to humanists, and three others (Antipodean, Lanternois, and Utopian) are invented. The map then is predominantly European, while gesturing towards places beyond the margins: a language of the Antipodes, a language apparently not spoken by Christians,[13] and the language of Utopia. Interestingly, Turkish and Arabic are not represented, while the languages of the North Sea and the Baltic (Scottish, Danish, Dutch, German) are prominent. There is no doubt an aleatory factor here (the availability to Rabelais of linguistic informants), but even that has a certain historical weight.

As a traveler, Panurge is less carefree and detached, less of a tourist, than Alcofribas. His adventures with the Turks may be regarded in this sense as *pérégrination* rather than *itinérance*. On the other hand, his engagement with crusade and pilgrimage seem marginal; he doesn't allegorize his journey, as the pilgrims in *Gargantua* do, and he appears rather as an opportunistic adventurer.[14] He is already Panurge *polytropos*; he belongs to all categories and to none and thus enables connections to be made between different kinds and levels of experience.

The mark of his versatility in this inaugural episode is his skills as a polyglot. These skills are often regarded as being in some sense erudite,[15] and it is true that his Hebrew is "bien rhétoriquement prononcé," his Greek classical in form, and his Latin Ciceronian. However, there is nothing in the narrative that suggests he has scholarly aims or interests. The learning of modern languages was not in the main regarded as a scholarly pursuit in the sixteenth century, and Panurge may be assumed to have acquired them en route or from fellow travelers, with the help of the practical word lists being published at that time in increasing numbers.[16] Since Greek and Hebrew were major living languages of the eastern Mediterranean, his knowledge even of these takes on a practical aspect: his pronunciation of Greek is modern, and it is far from absurd that Carpalim should ask him whether he has lived in Greece.[17]

It is of course not necessary to assume that he speaks all or indeed any of these languages comprehensively. Perhaps, like Thomas Mann's Felix Krull, he has the con-artist or trickster's ability to speak a few sentences of a language as if he knew it perfectly. Perhaps, like latter-day hitchhikers, he has learned to say politely just what he needs to say: "I've no money, no food, can you help?" His performance is in fact comparable with that of the polyglot language manuals, which present the same words or phrases in the different languages in parallel columns. Panurge's speeches are not identical, but they are similar enough to suggest a multilingual repertory of useful phrases.

This is the positive aspect of the polyglot's skills. A recurrent prefatory topos of contemporary language manuals and travel diaries is that a knowledge of languages brings the peoples of the world together in mutual friendship and charity. But the same prefaces often also carry a counter-topos: if you don't learn languages, you will have to put yourself in the hands of an interpreter who may well cheat you.[18] In this light, the polyglot is a dangerous trickster. When Nicolas de Nicolay, speaking of the skills of Jews living in Turkey as financiers, merchants, and polyglots, fulminates against them as cheats and liars, he is projecting onto the figure of the Jew the universal anxiety of the traveler.[19] Travelers to Turkey like Nicolay and Pierre Belon dwell at length on the variety of languages spoken there: Constantinople becomes in their account the modern, practical equivalent of Babel — multicultural, bewildering, disturbing, potentially dangerous.

Panurge has often been associated by critics with Babel and with the arbitrary difference of conventional languages.[20] The view sketched above is not incompatible with this high-culture reading, and it is clear that the structure of the episode partly depends on high-culture elements — the Hebrew-Greek-Utopian-Latin sequence, for example, and the references to the *Odyssey* and the *Aeneid*. But among the many things that seem to be happening in *Pantagruel* 9/14, one of the most central must surely be a mediation between learned culture and practical culture. This is true at several levels. Panurge the modern traveler is also an avatar of Ulysses; the Greek hospitality ethic still proves valid, transposed now into a Christian language and invoked in a practical situation that enacts the most fundamental of human duties toward the Other. The modern Babel of the journey eastward, of which Panurge has picked up some of the voices, echoes the ancient Babel.

The most complex mediation, however, occurs in the sequence of foreign languages spoken by Panurge, where a contrastive opposition — modern/ancient, synchronic/diachronic, and practical/learned — is problematized by the fact that the ancient, learned languages both exhibit their character as such and are spoken by Panurge as if they were equivalent to the modern languages.[21] His Utopian speech becomes paradigmatic here: a language invented (for the reader) in imitation of a Renaissance high-culture written text, with connotations of perfection and venerable antiquity, is for the characters the spoken language of Pantagruel's own country, a "natural" language like French from the garden of France. The most earthy of cabbage planters in Pantagruel's kingdom would, if questioned, turn out to speak Utopian.

The problematization of what might at first appear a neat opposition is also, as I have suggested, a mediation or negotiation. Cultural strands or fragments deriving from different areas and types of experience are connected, and even fused, in a way that clarifies and modifies their relative position. One could no doubt build a larger and more complete model of the elements in play here, together with their coordinates in Rabelais's work and, crucially, beyond it. One could show that other texts, not belonging to the literary canon, display connections of a similar kind in a less complex way; this is already true of the language manuals and of Nicolay and Belon. But this trial model already makes the essential point in synecdochic form. *Pantagruel* 9/14 is a critical sample of French culture, datable very precisely to the early 1530s, and its historical value is a function of its literary uniqueness. Only there do we see so many strands interwoven, so many mediations; only there do we begin to see an unfamiliar code printed out in such graphic and immediately tangible forms.

At first sight, it would seem that a study of Rabelaisian journeys and voyages should give priority to the *Quart livre*, where the whole narrative deploys and depends on the motif, and references are made to actual voyages of discovery.[22] In the apodemic episodes of the first two books, traveling generates only fragmentary instances of narrative and appears as a theme rather than as an overall structure. However, the equation is balanced by the fact that, in the fourth book, travel is only intermittently a theme. The alien encounters of Rabelais's later work are certainly inserted into a fantastic cosmography, but the aliens are for the most part allegorized representations of ethical, religious, and political phenomena (Quaresmeprenant, Mardi Gras and the Andouilles, the Papimanes, Gaster); the celebrated storm scene is primarily a theological and ethical parable that, despite its technical shipboard language, gives little scope to the imagination of maritime space. The voyage of the *Quart livre* is thus an adapted version of the *pérégrination*.

And yet the mapping of strange and monstrous bodies in the *Quart livre* continues the process of the earlier books. It prolongs the dialectic between the strange and the familiar and demonstrates the impossibility of imagining, say, Cartier's voyage without reference to legendary accounts of exotic travel. Preexisting materials and structures create and define the space within which the unprecedented is understood.

What has changed is primarily the narrator's attitudes to the disturbing Other. The episodes we considered earlier seem designed to resolve or defuse the disturbance, and this is indeed broadly the pattern of the first two books. Already at the Abbey of Thélème, however, a system of inclusions and exclusions is in force, implying a marked defensiveness.[23] At the end of the prologue to the *Tiers livre*, as Thomas Greene cogently points out in his contribution to this volume, defense turns to open aggression as the narrator growls and curses at readers who refuse to take his work in good part. The book itself is identified in the same prologue with Ptolemy's grotesque offering to the Egyptians.[24] The confident mastery of Alcofribas Nasier in Pantagruel's mouth seems to have collapsed by 1546, and the disquiet about how the text will be read reappears in the prologue to the 1548 version of the *Quart livre*. Even more striking is the proliferation in the 1552 *Quart livre* of monstrous figures that cannot, in many cases, be suppressed or defeated and are best evaded or even appeased. This applies especially to the figure of Quaresmeprenant and to the Papimanes episode, but there are many other instances. Michel Jeanneret's formula "signs gone wild" in this collection makes the point admirably if it is read in this context: the signs point away from home, towards a wild and threatening Other that refuses domestication.

Far from following what might seem to be the logical movement towards greater familiarization with alien spaces and beings — the movement which is normally regarded as a distinctive feature of Braudel's "long sixteenth century" — Rabelais's representation of otherness is centrifugal. Instead of a reassuring cabbage planter, we encounter strange amalgams of words that defy comprehension; the nonsequiturs of Quaresmeprenant's anatomy are virtually a paradigm here. This shift may no doubt be explained as a highly personal response to historical events of the 1540s that have little to do with travel as such. But it is perhaps legitimate to posit, as one strand in this response, a sense of vertigo, of intellectual and psychological uncertainty, in the face of a bewilderingly rapid expansion of cosmographical space.

This large and complex group of examples helps to clarify some of the ways in which the high/low opposition may be misleading, if not simply false. There is a distinction, it is true, between learned publications such as the polyglot Bible and nonlearned ones such as polyglot word lists for travelers. There is a distinction between official ideology and the actual principles people apply in their daily lives. There are languages of power and others that are denied power. But there are many kinds of high or learned culture, which operate in different ways and have different degrees of authority, and there are many kinds of so-called low or popular culture: practical and artisanal skills such as cooking and learning modern languages, printed books claiming to teach these skills, nonlearned imaginative compositions such as the *Chronicques gargantuines* that are written down and printed, oral stories and verse, collective entertainments such as the carnival, and so on. The high and the low, the learned and the popular, are in any case not separate antithetical categories: many phenomena are mixed, or on the borderline between these poles, as for example sermons, *mystères* and other dramatic forms, while many texts and phenomena shift between different social and cultural contexts.

Rabelais's work is the paradigm of such a mixture. That is what makes it so historically interesting: there is no other sixteenth-century text where so many things are so strangely and so lucidly connected. Rabelais, who was by no means of noble birth, who seems to have acquired a late medieval education and then a humanist one, and who worked for noble and even royal patrons, must have experienced a broad segment of the culture of his day, and his decision to draw on every part of that experience makes his work unique and uniquely powerful.[25] If we make him into a single-minded evangelical humanist who used comic materials as a kind of smokescreen or red herring, we reduce the historical value and interest of his writing almost to zero (although of course the evangelical humanist elements are an essential part of the text as a historical document); if we make him into the voice of the people, uttering visionary truths from the lower bodily stratum, we reduce him no less (although age-old images and stories are reused in his writing as a source of great imaginative power).

The same applies, *mutatis mutandis*, to the new/old opposition. As the opening example showed, this is often unreflectively regarded as interchangeable with the high/low hierarchy, as if high culture were always the primary vehicle of novelty. Of course, we cannot help reading history diachronically and analeptically: we look for signs of change, of difference, and when we find them we value them. But the historical sense of a text like Rabelais's does not reside merely in what remains when everything that can be marked as old is subtracted, as in the traditional attitude towards a text and its "sources." It resides in the work as a whole, seen now as a complex network of mobile but connected traces. All the materials of all levels of culture are subject to historical process; all change and shift, but they do so at different speeds. Sometimes learned culture moves faster than the forms and practices conserved by a given society; sometimes the reverse occurs, and social practices change in such a way that official ideologies no longer seem appropriate or relevant. Some parts of both learned and nonlearned culture move faster than others. In addition, Rabelais's text has its own movement, reflecting rapid responses to some phenomena, such as his representation of changes in pedagogy, and slow responses to others, such as attitudes to money and to the Columbian voyage.[26] The point here is not to award good marks for being quick on the uptake; it is to be able to conceive of the whole of Rabelais's writing as having a dynamic relation to the historical. It will be particularly pertinent to note the way the text thematizes novelty or the archaic, as it frequently does: the sense of the past, of changing generations, changing styles, is central in Rabelais.[27] But even this will be one strand in the complex of relations between older and newer materials and perceptions.

Such a model, by setting aside unqualified antitheses, removes the pressure to find a single interpretative frame. It leaves one free to follow up historical questions raised by the text and to return from those excursions with a clearer sense of how certain threads are woven into connection with others, a clearer view of the cultural map that the work in question sketches for us. The key notion in this approach is *connection*: it is the encounter between different elements and levels of culture that only a text as complex as Rabelais's will give us. Elsewhere they usually appear separately, at least in the available evidence, although we know that they must indeed have been connected, in indefinite permutations, in the consciousness of those who lived in the sixteenth century.

Focusing on connection means focusing on cultural mediation, whether the mediation takes effect through form (narrative structure, dialogic exchange) or through materials from cultural borderlands (ancient Greek spoken with a modern Greek pronunciation). It also means exploring the way in which the new in Rabelais grows out of a changed use of earlier materials. Some of the best recent work on Rabelais, including Lestringant's article, has been in this area.

In the instance of Alcofribas's meeting with the cabbage planter, such an approach would insist that the mouth of the giant is not just the outworn relic of a crude and unsophisticated way of thinking, soon to be discarded. It is still a dynamic part of Rabelais's culture, and in his writing it acts as an enabling frame for precisely that which will eventually create a difference. For the giant is here benignly anthropomorphic; in the remainder of Rabelais's first book, he has been a friend and an ally, a heroic protector in the face of the alien threat of Loup-Garou.[28] Pantagruel is himself already a defused and familiarized alien; his gigantic size can thus become the medium through which the mapping of a global unknown, a whole new world, can begin to be viable. That Alcofribas can choose to walk into his mouth is crucial; he doesn't appear to think he will come to any harm.[29] In this way, the narrator's sang-froid mediates between the gigantic body of Pantagruel and the reassuringly human comportment of the cabbage planter. Similar remarks can be made about the constant oscillation between allusions to the mouth as a frame of reference and the evocation of a landscape of quasi-European proportions. The episode works by a dialectic, which is not a dialectic between polar antitheses of new and old, although something new is undoubtedly carried by materials from earlier periods. Even in Voltaire's *Contes*, where myths and legends are consistently marked as absurd, irrational, and outdated, those myths and legends remain a potent point of reference; which reminds one that the latter end of the early modern period is characterized, in its high culture, precisely by the belief in a rational progression beyond myth. Rabelais moves in and out of the mythical register with the ease and confidence of Alcofribas, profiting from the enormous latent power of these images of the body to imagine new departures and reversals.

This point may be further illustrated by a consideration of the episode which, as *Pantagruel* draws to a close, forms a sequel and sibling to the world in Pantagruel's mouth. The descent into Pantagruel's stomach in *Pantagruel* 33 to remove an intestinal blockage is not mentioned by Auerbach. One suspects that, for him, it was simply a continuation of those absurd and obscene jokes that block the development of the insight achieved in the cabbage planter episode. Lestringant makes only passing reference to it. Yet it too has its "novelty." The technology that enables brass spheres to be made, supplied with springs so they can be sealed for the descent and opened again on arrival; the precision of the interventive surgery; the confidence with which the operation is planned and executed and its successful outcome: all these have become part of our own imagination, the imagination of H. G. Wells and of the science fiction film in which miniaturized medics in a tiny submarine are injected into a human body (now appearing gigantic) to remove a threat to life. Rabelais's story is thus early modern in the sense that we retrospectively recognize in it adumbrations of what will be the very mark of the modern. Yet it is impossible to separate the early modern elements from the corporal narrative, from the ogre-like swallowing and vomiting and the descent into an infernal body.

The exceptional character of Rabelais's telling of such stories derives first from the number of strands he brings into play, the extraordinarily complex mixture he constructs, and second from the way the mixing process is controlled. One of the manifestations of that control is the notion of a cure, which runs through his writings from first to last and is too well known to require further illustration here. The successful removal of Pantagruel's intestinal blockage repeats in another mode the bold entry of the narrator into the giant's mouth, and the therapeutic properties claimed for the book *Pantagruel* in its prologue are echoed in many other local episodes of cure, literal and metaphorical. Rabelais's control of his materials is also realized through structural features such as the turn or return that occurs at crucial points in the micronarrative, a device that operates simultaneously, in the apodemic episodes, with the theme of a return from the alien Other or indeed of a cure. This *peripeteia* is the means by which the narrator exerts leverage on his materials or connects different levels; it would repay extended analysis not only as a literary form but also as a historical phenomenon, for it provides the precise angle of perception from which the many strands of the text are connected and mobilized. The perception may be idiosyncratic, but if so the idiosyncrasy is one which by definition belongs to a given moment in history.

The view of Rabelais's work as a structure of endlessly differentiated and endlessly mobile elements is not meant to preclude determinate interpretations of given points or elements in that structure. The local meanings that can be conveyed by connecting different strands and thus the discrete histories attached to each may be extremely precise and focused. The notion that Rabelais's text can mean anything one wants it to is untenable. But I believe that the opposite view — namely, that all the strands (or, failing that, those deemed worthy of serious attention) serve a unitary intended meaning — is equally untenable. Rather, there are an indefinite number of local meanings connected by an intricate, kaleidoscopic structure and an overall dynamic that may at any moment defamiliarize the familiar or naturalize the alien. There is a totality and a coherence in Rabelais's writing that any reader may identify, but it cannot be represented as a coherent interpretative product. The coherence is heuristic; the structure is a discovery structure, a network of experimental connections.

From a historical angle, this point can be restated simply by saying that the novelty of Rabelais's writing as a representation of his world does not lie primarily in the use of new materials that displace old ones and make them redundant, but rather in the restructuring of the whole gamut of culturally loaded textual materials that Rabelais had to hand.[30]

That restructuring shows us the way in which the various parts of the culture could cohabit. It shows us the frictions, the tensions, the asymmetries and inconsistencies that characterize the perceptions of a privileged observer at precisely that moment in history. It shows us the accommodations, the reconciliations, the momentary solutions that an accomplished player and storyteller could impose on the world he lived in by transposing it into fiction.

And so we return once more to the theme of an encounter with the alien. Pantagruel meeting Panurge, Alcofribas meeting the cabbage planter, may become the model for the reader who encounters the strange text of Rabelais and recovers from it something familiar, a pre-echo of our own thoughts. But that familiarity should not be a source of self-congratulation, and above all it should not lead to a move which seeks to strip from the alien every sign of its difference. Rather, it should perhaps lead us back to the sense that our own structures of thought are traversed by tensions and contradictions; that they are perilously fragile and time-bound; that we too, in the next millenium, will no doubt become someone else's aliens.

# Michel Jeanneret

# Signs Gone Wild:
# The Dismantling of Allegory

Not long after the beginning of the *Tiers livre*, Panurge starts wondering if he should get married. Four hundred pages and one hundred ten chapters later, at the end of the *Quart livre*, he still doesn't know. This is much ado with not much to show for it.

In each of the two cycles, the consultations of the *Tiers livre* and the sea voyage of the *Quart livre*, there is a succession of episodes that more or less follow the same pattern: the friends listen to an opinion or witness an event, whereupon there is a pause in which they take stock of what has just been said or happened, and, since no certainty can be reached, they go on and on and on.

It may have seemed at the outset that Panurge's query was to serve as a program for this lengthy quest. But the reader soon realizes that neither the character's future, nor the enigma of woman, nor the complexities of marriage are the only or the real problems. The two-part structure of most episodes consists of the phenomenon and its commentary, suggesting that the real issue is neither psychological nor moral, but about epistemology. To put it more precisely, signs crop up, messages that may be loaded with double meaning show themselves. How should they be handled? I suggest that the question of signs and their interpretation, already active in the first two books and central in the last two, is in fact a constant in Rabelais's work.

The giants and their friends look around, listen, and ponder the meaning of the data perceived. But even before they start interpreting, they are challenged by a first obstacle: How is one to distinguish between things that are signs and things that mean nothing more than themselves? How is one to identify from among the undifferentiated objects of experience those that request interpretation?

From one island to the next, the navigators of the *Quart livre* meet with unusual phenomena: strange populations of ill-shaped bodies, weird customs, atmospheric accidents, all this challenges the natural order. The travelers could ignore them as fortuitous and unintentional, but they are not sure. Don't the peculiar events point to a secret, a supernatural message lying under the surface? For Rabelais's contemporaries, this is the question raised by monsters. Are they only an error of nature with no other interest than the physical, or are they a meaningful accident invested with hidden values? An extended sequence in the *Quart livre* rehearses the different solutions.[1] The sea tempest (*QL* 18–28) turns out to be a "prodige," a "monstre" (2:120) that cries out for interpretation and is indeed deciphered as meaning something else. The whale (*QL* 33–34) is also called a "monstre" (2:137), but it has nothing to show apart from its enormous size. The first is then a sign, the second is not. The status of two other monsters in the same sequence, Quaresmeprenant [Fastilent] (*QL* 29–32) and the Andouilles [Chitterlings] (*QL* 35–42), is much less clear. Their weirdness might be an invitation to look for a higher meaning, unless they are just the crazy and meaningless products of an unbridled imagination.

The hesitation does not apply only to the status of things. It can also affect the status of words, following a scholastic distinction between *allegoria in factis* and *allegoria in verbis*. Does a given discourse hide an indirect message? Should it be deciphered as an allegory? The "Enigme en prophetie" at the end of *Gargantua* (ch. 58) receives two readings: under the "obscure parolles" [obscure words] of the poem, Frère Jean recognizes a mere "description du jeu de paulme" (1:209) [description of the game of tennis (130)], whereas Gargantua identifies it as a veiled allusion to the persecution of evangelical thinkers.[2] Throughout the *Tiers livre*, Panurge and his friends go on quarreling about problems of reading: Should a given statement be understood at a literal or a figurative level? For things as well as for words, the picking out of what needs interpretation is no clear-cut matter.

In fact, both message and bearer can be open to doubt. An object claims to be a sign, but how is one to establish its authenticity? Here the question moves from the content to the subject of enunciation and touches on the legitimacy of the messenger. Panurge and his friends ask for the Sibyl of Panzoust's predictions (*TL* 16–18), and they are submerged by enigmatic words and gestures. But can one take such a show at all seriously? Is the old woman an inspired pythia, a genuine mediator of the gods, or is she a vulgar sorceress, a disturbed mind, an imposter? Here again, we are faced with an uncertain boundary between mystery and mystification, between white and black magic. Some signs are forgeries; they smell of brimstone and would be better ignored.[3]

Supposing the selection is achieved, the interpreter still has to solve the main difficulty: If a secret lies under the words or the things, how is one to understand it? What is the appropriate code? Here again Rabelais, in his survey of semiological possibilities, acknowledges problems. The famous chapters (*G* 8–10) on the symbolism of colors, about the young Gargantua's dress, graphically illustrate conflicts between the available systems. According to the usual interpretation, white means faith and blue, steadfastness. But Rabelais considers these analogies to be arbitrary, attributes them to charlatans, and instead seems to adopt another code: white for happiness and blue for heavenly matters. So will he now stick to this symbolical system and tell us how to deal with these semiological intricacies? Some commentators believe that he has made his choice. Others, such as Rigolot (1976), say that, far from committing himself, he is having a good laugh at everybody's expense. So the question remains open. Here we have the narrator who stokes up the doubt, whereas in other episodes it may be the characters acting as interpreters and showing their perplexities or disagreements. No matter who is on stage, the path that leads from sign to sense is uncertain.

All these difficulties in the identification and reading of signs are symptoms of a crisis. In the rest of this article, I propose to clarify

Rabelais's position in the semiological and hermeneutical debate that takes place in his period. Let me apologize now for many simplifications; I will be reducing to its skeleton what in fact should be the matter of a book.

The fathers of the church and the scholastic philosophers established a theory of signs and interpretation that was remarkably coherent. Defended by the church, this theory was transmitted to Renaissance scholars as a massive legacy, which they would have to take into account. I will briefly outline this doctrine as it was perceived by the humanists.[4]

Medieval semiology is divided into two fields: the meaning of things and the meaning of words. The world is a book through which God talks to men. Natural phenomena on the one hand and historical events on the other are so many divine messages for humans to interpret. But the signs are so diverse and there are so many possible readings of them that the theologians had to build a rigourous symbolism, assigning to each thing one meaning only or a limited number of meanings. In this way, a set of strictly codified correspondences allowed the church to control the interpreter's activity.

Now to the words. The Bible and pagan texts both call for another hermeneutics. The central issue is familiar. How is one to square the teachings, apparently so different, of the Old and the New Testament? How is one to reconcile the classical legacy with Christian thought and morals? In both cases, the solution is in the treatment of words as signs. The Old Alliance is interpreted as a series of prophecies announcing the coming of Christ and the lessons of the Apostles. In the same way, an ancient poem is moralized and, through figurative reading, systematically transferred into the realm of Christian truths. The famous method of quadruple interpretation, whether it is used in the exegesis of the Bible or in the commentary of Ovid's *Metamorphoses*, allows for the non-Christian to be made to conform to the Christian; it controls the proliferation of the heterogeneous by submitting it to the unique truth of Revelation.

Medieval hermeneutics applies a very particular strategy. Its problem is not what it is about to discover, since this is known in advance, but how it is going to reach it. *Non nova, sed nove.* A pre-determined telos dictates the choice of method, and method in its turn aims at overcoming the discrepancies and ambiguities in order to minimize the threat of difference or the uncertainties of polysemy. Allegory, insofar as it rests on the general acknowledgment of a network of equivalences between signs and meanings, is perceived by the humanists as a typical expression of a theory that is both narrow and strictly determined.[5]

The evolution from the Middle Ages into the Renaissance coincides with a major crisis in the semiological and hermeneutical system. Without giving a complete picture, I will look briefly at the developments in two fields that are at the core of humanist philosophy.[6]

There is no need to recall the utmost importance of Neoplatonist thought in the sixteenth century, but it may be useful to establish that Neoplatonism plays an active part in breaking the univocal relationship between sign and meaning, thus accelerating the liquidation of scholasticism.[7] The Supreme Being—the ideal one—of Neoplatonists is conceived as an Absolute, too enigmatic for human language to grasp. Like the God of the mystics, it escapes all logical determination and challenges the signifying power of words. It can be grasped through intuition, but can be talked about only indirectly, through paradoxes and the mediation of figures or signs.

The signs of the divine, then, are no more than inadequate substitutes, which, as bearers of a diffuse revelation, are the better for being ambiguous and opaque. The best language to speak about what cannot be known is a self-defeating language that points to its own object as always beyond its reach. Two consequences can be drawn from this. Because they cannot come to a final stop, signs refer to each other in an endless drift. A given word alludes to another, one thing implies another, so that a statement or object never reaches the ultimate truth, but only fragments and shadows of this truth that have to be completed and that then lead to other fragments and so on. For the same reason, the signs, being absorbed in a network of multiple relations and testifying for a reality that is infinitely complex, are naturally polysemic. Their meanings are plural and escape totalization.[8] It is obvious that we are a long way from the rational hermeneutics and the neat set of equivalences of scholasticism.

The other witness is Erasmus, because he also takes part in the emancipation of signs, but for reasons connected with the lesson of the Gospels and the need to restore a religious life that should be experienced as a spiritual and intimate adventure. The Word of God, as revealed in the Bible, is infinitely richer and deeper than anything human beings can conceive. It is beyond all expectation. Any attempt to subordinate it to mechanical procedures like the quadruple interpretation is bound to weaken its effect. The genuine Christian should rid himself of all mediations and constraining methods and instead rely on God's grace and, with its help, read the Bible in spirit.[9] The signs of Revelation are saturated with hidden meanings, but only an intuitive quest or a personal meditation will grasp some of these riches, without ever being able to exhaust them.

So there is a convergence in sixteenth-century thought of two central trends that agree on some semiological principles. In Neoplatonism as well as in Erasmism, the semantic density of signs inhibits any attempt to systematize. Instead of the retrospective method of scholasticism, which confirms the already known, humanists assume the risk of a prospective interpretation; there is always something more to be found, not only one meaning or a few, but an indefinite number. Reading can no longer rely on stable procedures and formal methods. It is a very personal, intimate affair; it has turned into an open-ended process and, as a result, has become highly problematic.

Rabelais is closely implicated in this crisis and, through his own strategies, takes part in the liberation of signs. I suggest that the dismantling of allegory, the adoption of polysemy, and the inscription within the narrative of the uncertainties of reading are but one more aspect of his involvement in the debates of his period.[10]

For different reasons, the shaking of constraining codes is a major issue for Rabelais. His sympathy for Erasmian evangelism would be enough to pull him in this direction.[11] Against the external rites and superstitions of the church, the Christian humanists, as I have pointed out, plead for a religion that should be lived from within and inspired by faith and by love. In opposition to the scribes and phari-sees, to all the advocates of a formalist theology, yoked to a literal respect of the ancient law, they propose freedom of the spirit, ac-cording to the example of Christ, who transformed the meaning of signs and injected a new content into the rigid framework of Judaic ceremonies. The ideal of Pantagruelism seems to correspond pre-cisely to this state of mind; it interprets "toutes chose à bien" (1:495) [all things for the good (321)], rejects prejudices and dogmatic prin-ciples, and relies on the tenets of trust and generosity.

Rabelais as a writer and composer of fiction is no less concerned with this break. The trend in the Middle Ages was to impose a didactic or edifying meaning on legends, stories, and plays; narra-tives were meant to illustrate a moral message or the articles of faith. I refer the reader to the moralization of the novella, the writing of history as example, hagiography, and so on. The danger is that a text, when it is subservient to allegorical devices, may no longer be pro-ductive or inventive. Instead of holding the curiosity of the reader, it may actually inhibit it.[12] In a way, the *Tiers livre* is a parody of this situation. Pantagruel listens to a series of oracles and interprets them allegorically. We have the same repetitive pattern: a cryptic discourse is elucidated, an equivalence between sign and sense is given, and each time the same message unfolds — Panurge will be a cuckold. With no surprise, the new is modeled on the old. Truth and morality may profit from this, but the literary gain is nil. Once the predictions have been translated and commented upon, the narrative can stop. If Panurge with his self-deception and Frère Jean with his jokes did not push the text along, it would soon get exhausted and the reading of it would come to a standstill. Rather than solve the enigmas and ignore the difficulties, the plot stays alive through the reader's doubt.

To ensure that the mind is never saturated and that literature may act as a liberating and stimulating force, the reductive devices and the authoritative, exclusive methods must be condemned. Rabelais's narratives are interspersed with episodes that more or less directly thematize the problems of interpretation and unmask the excesses of overconfident readings.

The Papimanes in the *Quart livre* (ch. 48–54) become fanatical through their materialism and literalism. Unable to follow a religion that is not grounded on the evidence of the senses, they replace God with the Pope and the Bible with the Decretals. They worship a visible, tangible God, an idol, and refuse to go beyond the literal meaning of their Holy Book. Thus the supernatural is reduced to the natural in the same way as in the domain of language: signs can have only one meaning, and reading can never be figurative. The book of the Decretals is followed literally and invested with magical power; it imposes blind obedience, a whole ritual of gestures and formulae that, in the same way as the rabbinical legalism condemned by Erasmus, reduces faith to a series of superstitions. But there is another aspect to the story. The words that the Papimanes respect religiously are also imposed on others as an inescapable rule. Whoever does not bow to the letter of the law is considered a heretic and exposed to the worst punishment. So the words, when they are fixed into one exclusive meaning, become a tool for the repression of others. Restrictive interpretation of texts in this episode leads to intolerance and violence.

The result is similar with allegory, even though the mechanism is different. Insofar as allegory reduces the meaning of a discourse to its figurative value, the paralyzing effect is the same as before. Rabelais suggests that the automatic quest for a hidden meaning is no less dangerous than the cult of the literal meaning. Raminagrobis is a poet, and he is dying. For these reasons, he has access to divine truths and has been consulted by Panurge and his friends (*TL* 21–22). After he has written a poem, which evades the question, he tells his guests that he has just had to chase away "un tas de villaines, immondes et pestilentes bestes" (1:491) [a bunch of ugly, filthy, pestilential creatures (319)] that were preventing him from dying in peace. Whereupon we have, as usual, the interpretative pause; the identity of the mysterious animals is discussed and once more we have the opposition of the two canonical methods. For Epistemon, the poet "parle absolument et proprement des pusses, punaises, cirons" (1:494) [speaks literally and properly about fleas, bedbugs, gnats (my translation)]. But Panurge doesn't agree; his understand-

ing is based on allegory and he has no doubt in explaining that Raminagrobis was being rude about the "bons pères mendians Corde-
liers et Jacobins" (1:492) [good mendicant Franciscan and Jacobin
friars (319)]. This explanation is not unlikely but it freezes the poet's
words. It does not allow for any possible mistake and resembles
terrorism insofar as it imperiously attributes to somebody an intention that he may not have had.

Panurge's allegorical reading, along with the Papimanes' literalism, not only twists the words, it also threatens a man in his liberty
and his safety. As a result, the debate on interpretation that seemed
innocuous and purely theoretical turns out to be extremely serious, a
question of life and death. If Panurge's reading is correct, it follows
that the old poet, because he dares accuse monks, is considered by
the ecclesiastical authority to be a "heretic," a "blasphemer," and, as
such, deserves to be burnt. Once more, hermeneutical excess and the
fixation of words, captured by the church, are associated with sec-
tarianism, violence, and the methods of the Inquisition.

As a specialist in the occult sciences, Herr Trippa (TL 25) is an
expert in the art of manipulating signs in order to terrorize others.
He displays frightening magical tricks and, through his gesticulations and his jargon, attempts to fascinate the good folk. Here the
wizard is denounced as an impostor who exploits the mystery, the
misleading appeal of the hidden meaning, and thus blackmails ordinary people. This episode is no longer about physical violence, but
about intellectual terrorism.

Rabelais himself suffered the pressure of abusive interpretations.
His difficulties with censorship show that, when he vindicates polysemy and calls for a generous reading inspired by charity, he is in fact
talking about his own situation and safety. His books were condemned by the Paris Faculty of Theology, and the attacks from Geneva were no less violent. The fact that Rabelais spent part of his life
in hiding and managed to avoid prison or even the stake with the
help of enlightened and powerful protectors can be put down to
aggressive critics searching for and eventually finding scandalous
and condemnable passages in his works. As with Raminagrobis, he
was the victim of readings that were suspicious of him and that used

the interpretative device of allegory in order to label him a heretic. Those whom he called the "calumniators" claimed to be outraged by innocent wordplay, like *âne* for *âme* (*TL* 22–23), and attempted at all costs to see sacrilege in what was in fact, he says, "folastries joyeuses" (2:6) [joyous fooleries (423)]. Driven by hate, they see everything in a bad light, "comme qui pain interpretroit pierre; poisson, serpent; oeuf, scorpion" (2:7) [as if someone interpreted bread as stone, fish as snake, egg as scorpion (423)]. At a time when you could be killed for a few words too many, the choice of method becomes a question of life and death.

In the same text where Rabelais complains about the censor's accusations, he represents himself as the good doctor who, through his stories, heals the sick and comforts the afflicted. As soon as the threats and fears, which for most people were part of daily life, are taken seriously, the project no longer looks absurd. There is no doubt that one of the novelist's main objectives is to demystify impostures, reply to violence with laughter, and show up the complicity of dogmatic interpretative methods and repression. I would like to suggest two ways by which Rabelais achieves this end.

The first is familiar, but so important and so often overlooked by commentators who are all too serious that it deserves a brief mention. The comical acts as both a defense and a remedy. For instance, it allows the terrorists to be neutralized through ridicule. Herr Trippa wanted to convict Panurge of cuckoldry; Panurge returns the compliment. Through laughter, roles are reversed; the powerful man and his tricks are reduced to a farce.

But the liberating power of the comical is not only released through satire. To escape from sectarian intimidation and dissipate sadness or anxiety, the friends sometimes allow themselves a moment of relaxation and recreation; they meet together to attend to their own good pleasure. Instead of employing language as a weapon, they tell stories, reveal their dreams, and play with words. Frère Jean is very good at this; through his jokes, oaths, and tall stories, he exorcises tensions and worries. Rabelais put one of these moments of pleasure and rest at the center of the *Tiers livre* (*TL* 26–28), where Jean and Panurge tell jokes as if they were trying to escape melancholy and efface all the discourses of power they had heard. These episodes seem frivolous or bawdy and, because they are short on scholarly references, they are often neglected by critics. But this is wrong, insofar as they have an essential part to play in Rabelais's overall project as antidotes to fear.

The dismantling of allegory and the disabling of constraining herme-neutical codes also adopt another device. Rabelais builds up signs or pseudosigns that challenge traditional reading methods, escape any sort of control, and generate meanings that are unexpected, uncer-tain, and disturbing. He sketches out a kind of wild semiosis, which, by opening out onto obscure regions, sends interpretative systems into a spin. When it comes to giving a name to these irreducible images, he often uses the word *estrange*. I propose to take a trip into the territory of the strange and stop at episodes where the word effectively appears.

Towards the beginning of the *Tiers livre*, Panurge puts on a new set of clothes to show that he wants to return to civil life and get married (*TL* 7). "En tel estat se praesenta davant Pantagruel, lequel trouva le desguisement estrange" (1:430) [In such state he presented himself to Pantagruel, who found the disguise strange (277)]. The friends do not understand or at least are hesitant about the meaning of the message. What has happened? The new dress gives up the breeches and codpiece and replaces them with a robe and spectacles. In other words, Panurge eliminates the sign of masculinity — the codpiece — and instead adopts a disguise that makes him look like a monk — a robe and eyeglasses. His intention was to exhibit his sex-ual power, but his garment suggests the opposite. It seems as if, when he was encoding his message, he had improvised a private language so personal that it not only distorts the intention of the sender but also sends out information that is misleading and uncontrollable. Medieval semiotics was coherent enough to unite members of a given social group around a common code, and they understood each other. But Panurge is a modern man; he no longer has access to a stable hermeneutical system, he has to put together his own system with signs that are bound to be misunderstood and, worse, signs that generate disturbing representations beyond his control — a man in heat who hides his sex, a big mouth who speaks at cross purposes.

Panurge is not alone in being deceived by his own constructions. Rabelais from time to time also presents himself as a sorcerer's apprentice, so that he and his reader are faced with signs that are too much for them. The reader is often struck by strange images that are worrisome and generate a deep resonance somewhere within, without our being able to identify a content and find a key. The giant Bringuenarilles (*QL* 17), who normally feeds on windmills, has fallen ill from a surfeit of pots and pans and is finally finished off by a piece of butter (2:92 [476]). The Sibyl at Panzoust (*TL* 17) is surrounded by a strange decor. She performs a disturbing ritual and exhibits her obscene body (1:472 [306]). These objects are not innocent: they should normally convey a hidden meaning and, having performed their function, let themselves be forgotten. But they are opaque, they strike our imagination, they are like signifiers that attract all the attention and deny access to the signified. The fascination of the *unheimlich* disturbs the usual mechanisms of meaning.

Other signs spread messages that not only escape the dichotomy between the literal and the figurative but also seem to open a perspective onto what we nowadays would call the unconscious: erotic fantasies, sexual frenzies, visions of strange anatomies or perverse couplings. As in dreams, shocking or weird images crop up, bringing to light repressed anxieties or affects, all the more powerful for being normally censured.

The *Quart livre* has many of these disturbing representations. The people of Ennasin subvert the system of genders and of family relations and see no difference between human beings and objects (*QL* 9); the Chicanous [Shysteroos] earn their living by being beaten (*QL* 12–16); the inhabitants of Ruach eat wind and die of farting (*QL* 43). The reader is bombarded with symbolical suggestions, which, because they do not belong to any familiar code, cannot be rationalized and hence neutralized. The quick fire of disturbing images is even more intense in the parallel episodes of Quaresmeprenant (*QL* 29–32) and the Andouilles (*QL* 35–42): on the one hand, a sinister carcass, in the taste of Arcimboldo, which mingles the organic and the instrumental; on the other, female warriors in the shape of phallic sausages. These two monstrous figures seem to be the outcrops of a primitive and nightmarish world where the human and the animal, the living and the lifeless are confused, a world where the fancies and chimeras of a delirious imagination can come true. These preposterous effigies are the signs of something hidden, but instead of pointing to an abstract and graspable meaning, they pull us down into the sphere of instincts and release traces of the repressed.

One episode illustrates this displacement. Pantagruel has recommended to Panurge the use of Virgilian lots: you open the text of Virgil at random and you interpret the passage you have just come across as a sign of the future (*TL* 12). This is a tried and tested method that dates back to antiquity: mythological references are treated allegorically, they are moralized, so that not only do you draw a useful lesson from them but you also erase the weird and worrisome aspects of the primitive version. But what happens here? Instead of transferring the myth into the domain of the true and the good, the commentary lets insanities unfold and allows a monstrous procession of sexual aberrations to emerge. Virgil the wise man and prophet, when he is no longer domesticated through moralization, speaks of gods and goddesses transformed into animals, of Jupiter being fed by a goat or a sow; he pictures Minerva as a warlike and masculine woman; he draws on Vulcan and the Giants, emblems of brutal force with their deformed bodies; and finally he mentions two cases of incest, two stories of castration, and one episode of cannibalism. The signs of myth in this chapter release wild images and build up a representation of mankind overcome by bestiality and set free from all rules and prohibitions.

This is what *l'estrange* is about: images that cannot be incorporated into a preestablished system, wild signs emancipated from morals that bring to the fore phantasms normally repressed.[13] I have attempted in this article to show that the liberation of signs is not a modern invention, but corresponds to a historically documented aspect of sixteenth-century culture. The passage from the Middle Ages to the Renaissance, from the rigor of scholasticism to the intellectual uncertainties of humanism, is marked in part by a profound crisis in the way signs and their interpretation work. It seems to me that this crisis has not been considered seriously enough by specialists. When its impact is acknowledged, it will no longer be possible to argue that it is anachronistic to see Rabelais as problematizing interpretation and exploiting polysemy. On the contrary, some of his most powerful effects derive from his concern with the weird workings of signs.

# II    Marrows
## of Discontent

## Carla Freccero

# Feminism, Rabelais, and the Hill/Thomas Hearings: Return to a Scene of Reading

## Prefatory Remarks

Friday, November 1, 1992: When deciding how to proceed with this contribution, I was torn between several impulses. The first, represented only intermittently here, was an impulse to educate the readers patiently and responsibly on the matter of tokenism. The second was an impulse, strengthened in the wake of the United States Senate confirmation hearings for Clarence Thomas, to vent my anger and rage. Though apparent in the article, this impulse has been in part sublimated, as Freud would have it, in humor. The third impulse was the one that is bound to prevail even among those who aspire to the status of virago, if they have been schooled for as many years as I have in the academy, and that is the impulse to submit obediently to the scholarly task in the hopes of winning approval, if not praise.

When I was first invited to participate in this collective project in order to write about Rabelais and women, I thought I would do just that and entitled my talk "Rabelais and Women." When I noticed that I was the only woman presenting a paper at the symposium, I began to feel too much like Christine de Pisan joining the *querelle des femmes* as the only feminine voice defending her sex, so I changed the title to "Rabelais and Feminism." That way, instead of feeling as though the critical focus were on my body with its markers of sexual difference, I could rationalize the accommodation as having been made to an intellectual and political positionality, feminist criticism, the way one adds Marguerite de Navarre to one's canonical survey of early modern French prose to accommodate feminism's political impact on the academy.

Of course, since I am still here as the only woman feminist represented in these pages, body, mind, and politics converge to overdetermine both my position and my performance. Rather than being in drag and playfully passing as one of the men, I face the dilemma of the token virago, the virile woman whose visible sexual difference is the scandal she uses to interrogate the contents of the codpiece she wears. I am thus framed by a text that both inscribes my resistance and contains its force. A text or scene not unlike the one we have witnessed on the Senate floor. This scene is overdetermined: it constitutes a repetition of which the genealogy includes the Rabelaisian text, its masculinist readers, and ultimately liberal democracy itself.

I might have foregone the role of token virago by refusing to mention the obvious and refusing to perform the script I had been given. In that case as well, I would have been contained, for the critique that is required would have been silenced and another goal might have been met. I could not refuse because subsequently I might have been used to justify the absence of other women critics; after all, some might say, we did include a woman and a feminist too. It would therefore have been my fault had the absences of the collection gone undenounced. This is the dilemma facing female feminist and minority critics within the academy as a whole and particularly within those disciplines most invested in the foundational narratives of western civilization, such as the Renaissance. Like the *haute dame de Paris*, we can either accept the dubious honor of being courted by academies that distrust us and thus reveal ourselves to be hypocritical in our protestations, or we can refuse and continue to be effaced.

This paper is about Rabelais and critical filiation, about the masculinist genealogy of a repeated scene of reading moving from a moment in Rabelais to a moment on the U.S. Senate floor. A queer moment, one might say, though its queerness is quickly suppressed by a homosociality that exposes the relation between homophobia and misogyny. It is feminism, the denunciatory virago, the woman who does not laugh at the men's smutty joke, whose disruption in this scene both exposes and reconfirms the exhaustively performed exclusionary inclusion constitutive of liberal democracy in the United States. I dedicate this to Anita Hill and the rest of us.

## Return to a Scene of Reading

In 1985 and 1986, I responded to what is to date one of the most ethical attempts to engage the relationship between Rabelais and feminist criticism from a masculinist position, Wayne Booth's "Freedom of Interpretation: Bakhtin and the Challenge of Feminist Criticism."[1] Booth acknowledged that feminism diminished the humor of reading certain passages in Rabelais and thus the pleasure of the text itself. Booth's essay is the critical occasion in this genealogy, for he enacts an allegory of the relationship between Rabelais and woman, the masculinist critic and feminism, the polity and the challenge of democratic inclusion.

In this essay that tropes the question of the constitutional right to free speech, Booth first sketches a "sympathetic" (read "liberal") male reaction to the challenge of feminist criticism as it interferes with the pleasure of reading Rabelais and enjoying his humor (women see harassment where there is humor). He then impersonates a feminist critic who argues that "Rabelais's work is unjust to women . . . in its fundamental imaginative act" (66). While seeming to acknowledge the seriousness of the feminist claim (senators protesting that they acknowledged Anita's pain), he goes on to threaten the women with the "masters" (70), Rabelais and Bakhtin. Rabelais will "survive gloriously" while Bakhtin will "respond triumphantly" (70). Why? Because, he says, "what has been most obviously missing from my account is the sheer pleasure of *his* text, the exuberance, the subversive, vitalizing laughter that survives the worst that can be said about its sources" (70). Booth's Bakhtin, of course, praises the multiculturalism that feminism adds to interpretation; he calls it heteroglossia and welcomes the new voice into the academy.

In an allegory of liberal democracy, which the anti-PC contingent in its most benign form tells and retells about American democracy, Booth asks rhetorically, "Can we not say that if there is no freedom of interpretation, there is no significant freedom of any kind?" (76). In this way he simultaneously validates and undercuts the feminist challenge he has presented, since he often by his own admission parodies that challenge as a call to "repudiate almost the whole of Western literature" (74). Moreover, he returns to the question of freedom after, in his own words, making a "concession . . . to perspectivism" (76). The concession he makes to perspectivism (multiculturalism? diversity? inclusion?) is this: "Perhaps it remains true that the freedom to make new interpretations by exercising freedom from old methods and assumptions is more important in some epochs than in others" (76). The allegory of liberal democracy is complete: feminism has the constitutional right to add its voice to the many, to exercise its right to speak (to interpret), and this will (*perhaps*) be good for the rest of us (men). We (men) can make this concession to the feminist challenge, to hear it out. But the coda to this democratic process is a return to the same, couched in the form of a threat: "If you do not return to Rabelais for that fun . . . your freedom to add an *alien* voice to Rabelais's dialogue will have been dearly bought" (70, my emphasis). I would like to point out why and how this is not and has never been freedom for the rest of us, the alien voices.

Booth's essay focuses on and curiously repeats a moment in the Rabelaisian text. Why the repetition? Why does Booth choose the episode of Panurge and the Parisian noblewoman to address the question of feminist criticism, humor, and the pleasure of the text? Could it be because it constitutes a primal scene of sorts, a scene of masculine confrontation with alterity and its attempt to incorporate that alterity through seduction or erasure? Could it be because, as Jane Gallop has argued in "Why Does Freud Giggle When the Women Leave the Room?", it is precisely the woman who does not leave the room who interrupts the homosocial economy (academy?) of dirty jokes told among men?

The primal scene of sexual difference is, in this case, a primal scream of hilarity. Rabelais's episode of Panurge and the Parisian noblewoman sets up Freud's paradigm of the tendentious joke, in particular, of the passage from obscenity, which is regressive, infantile, lower class, and aimed at seducing a woman, to the dirty joke, which is sublimated, civilized, upper class, and aimed at entertaining another man (Freud, 100–101).

Freud's discussion of the dirty joke begins with an analysis of tendentious jokes, of which there are two kinds. Hostile jokes serve the purpose of aggressiveness, satire, or defense; obscene jokes serve the purpose of exposure (97). Although he initially calls the exposure joke a marginal type, Freud's characteristic rhetorical move is to focus on a pathology that then comes to stand in for the norm, so that the marginal kind of joke soon becomes a type for all jokes in which aggression is mobilized. "Obscenity," or "smut," as the English translation of Freud calls it,

> is like an exposure of the sexually different person to whom it is directed. By the utterance of the obscene words it compels the person who is assailed to imagine the part of the body or the procedure in question and shows her that the assailant is himself imagining it. . . . If the woman's readiness emerges quickly the obscene speech has a short life; it yields at once to a sexual action. It is otherwise if quick readiness on the woman's part is not to be counted on, and if in place of it defensive reactions appear. In that case the sexually exciting speech becomes an aim in itself in the shape of smut. Since the sexual aggressiveness is held up in its advance towards the act, it pauses at the evocation of the excitement and derives pleasure from the signs of it in the woman. In so doing, the aggressiveness is no doubt altering its character as well, just as any libidinal impulse will if it is met by an obstacle. It becomes positively hostile and cruel, and it thus summons to its help against the obstacle the sadistic components of the sexual instinct.
>
> The woman's inflexibility is therefore the first condition for the development of smut. (98–99)

So far so good. Here Freud might be describing Panurge's progress as he meets resistance in attempting to seduce the Parisian lady. When the initial aim of seduction is frustrated, he gets hostile. This scene, however, as Freud depicts it, is not yet funny; it is not a joke, it is an act of aggression. Humor, at least refined humor, requires a male third term:

> The ideal case of a resistance of this kind on the woman's part occurs if another man is present. . . . This third person soon acquires the greatest importance in the development of the smut; to begin with, however, the

presence of the woman is not to be overlooked. . . . The men [at higher social levels] save up this kind of entertainment, which originally presupposed the presence of a woman who was feeling ashamed, till they are "alone together." So that gradually, in place of the woman, the onlooker, now the listener, becomes the person to whom the smut is addressed, and owing to this transformation it is already near to assuming the character of a joke.

Generally speaking, a tendentious joke calls for three people: in addition to the one who makes the joke, there must be a second, who is taken as the object of the hostile or sexual aggressiveness, and a third in whom the joke's aim of producing pleasure is fulfilled. . . . Through the first person's smutty speech the woman is exposed before the third, who, as listener, has now been bribed by the effortless satisfaction of his own libido. . . .

And here at last we can understand what it is that jokes achieve in the service of their purpose. They make possible the satisfaction of an instinct (whether lustful or hostile) in the face of an obstacle that stands in its way. (99–101)

The humorous pleasure derived from Panurge's discomfiture of the Parisian lady depends upon a (masculine) third term. In the episode itself, that term is supplied by Pantagruel, whom Panurge calls over to watch as the six hundred dogs urinate on the woman. Pantagruel is also, as I have argued, a figure for the masculine reader whose pleasure the scene is orchestrated to produce. In his essay, Booth fulfills the role of that masculine reader/onlooker: "When I read, as a young man, the account of how Panurge got his revenge on the Lady of Paris, I was transported with delighted laughter; and when I later read Rabelais aloud to my young wife, as she did the ironing (!), she could easily tell that I expected her to be as fully transported as I was. Of course she did find a lot of it funny; a great deal of it *is* very funny" (Booth, 68).

Something about his wife's reaction disturbs Wayne Booth; his defensive "of course, she did find a lot of it funny; a great deal of it is very funny" suggests that she was not as fully transported as her husband. Perhaps she sensed the danger of her situation. Freud remarks that, "A person who laughs at smut that he hears is laughing as though he were the spectator of an act of sexual aggression" (Freud, 97), and one might wonder whether she or any woman could manage more than an uneasy chuckle. For Booth has warned us that we too may meet with the noblewoman's fate should we resist the humor ("If you do not return to Rabelais for that fun . . . your freedom to add an alien voice to Rabelais's dialogue will have been dearly bought" [Booth, 70]). As I remarked of this passage at the time: "The female reader, newly espoused [young wife!] as she must feel to the venerable society of critics, finds herself once again in a position of complicity against her sex, laughing along with the joke or becoming, herself, an object of revenge, like Panurge's Lady, paying dearly for her lack of humor and her willingness to resist" (Freccero 1985, 57–58).

The woman on the scene of reading in Booth's essay is a "young wife" who remains mute and whose graphically castrated presence does not wholly interrupt either Booth's transports of delighted laughter or his expectation that she shares the joke. Indeed, she subsequently disappears, and Booth is left alone with the masters/fathers, Bakhtin and Rabelais. At that point, of course, the humor reasserts itself: "What has been most obviously missing from my account is the sheer pleasure of his text, the exuberance, the subversive vitalizing laughter that survives the worst that can be said about its sources" (Booth, 70). It's one in the morning and the boys are left alone to revitalize themselves with exuberant accounts of their days at Yale Law School.[2]

In "How to Read Freud on Jokes: The Critic as Schadchen," Jeffrey Mehlman has pointed out that the triangular structure of Freud's joke scenario is oedipal; a difficult ménage à trois resolves itself into male bonding when, at last, the woman leaves the room. This is the homosocial contract of ruling-class men. As Jane Gallop has remarked of Mehlman reading Freud on jokes, "The woman is lost, but the man consoled. Rather than a woman he has a homology. The second person, the other sex, has been irretrievably lost. But no matter, it was worth it to gain a sameness, to find an identification. . . . The Oedipus is good: one loses the mother but gains entry into the world, into the exchange between men — Levi-Strauss's exchange of women, Freud's exchange of dirty jokes. The Oedipus is good, for the man. He escapes from his difference with the resistant, other sex into the world of homologies; man's economy" (Gallop, 34). However, in the joke scene also lurks what Freud would later call the negative Oedipus: "besides the familiar Oedipus, every boy also has the desire to murder his mother and marry his father" (Gallop, 37). Booth talks about the "sheer pleasure" of Rabelais's text. But to marry the father/master, to submit to the Law in Lacanian terms, is to become like a woman; Booth comments on the marginality he has experienced as a feminist critic. What is missing is IT, the capacity to laugh, the phallus. Booth says of his loss, "the effect is something like that of losing a brother, or a part of my past, or a part of myself" (Booth, 73). There is a problem here: feminist criticism is missing "it," the feminist critic does not have "it," becoming a feminist critic means losing "it" for Booth. Now he's not laughing either.

There is another woman in the room, a woman who refuses to leave so that Booth and Rabelais can enjoy their joking. She is a castrating bitch, a virago, a virile woman; she is not mute, she vexes the critic out of his laughter, and her presence has a scandalous effect:

> But now, . . . I draw back and start thinking rather than laughing, taking a different kind of pleasure with a *somewhat* diminished text. And neither Rabelais nor Bakhtin can be given the credit for vexing me out of laughter and into thought: it is feminist criticism that has done it.
> . . . here is a scandal indeed — I find that my pleasure in some parts of this text has now been somewhat diminished by my critical act. This is not a theoretical matter. If it were, I could perhaps reject it or change my theory to fit my reading. The fact is that reading now, try as I may to "suspend my disbelief," reading *now* I don't laugh at this book quite as hard or quite as often as I used to. (Booth, 68)

The phallic woman exposes the text as a fetish, a Rabelaisian codpiece; the critic is now uncertain as to whether the text has "it" or not. The critical confrontation and contamination with the object (now subject) of the humor diminishes it; an identification with the resistance that is feminism makes him (laugh) less hard and less often than he was (used to). Feminist criticism's intrusion into this voyeuristic scene of pleasure "is not a theoretical matter"; it is the intrusion of the denunciatory virago into the pleasurable scene of reading between a man and his book, his master, his father. And three, in this case, is a crowd.[3]

Gallop offers a clue to the threat experienced by the (straight) male critic as he imagines himself becoming, like the woman, the butt of the joke ("The essential artistic drive of Rabelais will thus criticize both himself *and* me, no doubt with raucous laughter" [Booth, 70]): "Whereas the homosocial is the realm identified with the father, the realm of power, the homosexual is associated [by Freud, by Booth] not with power but with humiliation. Identification with the father equals patriarchal power; desire for the father equals castration, humiliation" (Gallop, 38). The confrontation with feminist criticism thus unveils the desire behind the male critic's homosocial bonding for an originary identification with the mother. This desire must be denied lest it expose the domination of women upon which the homosocial contract is founded, by exposing as well the submission to the master/father that such desire must, in the critic's economy, entail. Here Gayle Rubin's (1975) and Eve Kosofsky Sedgwick's (1985) observations are confirmed that, in the present social order, patriarchy and homophobia are intimately related.[4]

Booth's essay does not conclude with desire for the masters/fathers, but identification with them (he even impersonates their voices), identification with what he takes to be their values, multiculturalism or heteroglossia, and democratic inclusionism. He is not humiliated but vindicated. How does he do this? Could there be a connection here between the denied desire that is rescripted as identification with the fathers and the oppression of women that is rewritten as liberal democracy? Might such equality in fact mean submission?

There is a feminist motto that goes, "She who laughs, lasts." Not an easy thing for a woman to do these days. But in Rabelais's text, it is indeed the woman, or rather her trace as woman, who has the last laugh. For when Pantagruel deciphers at last the message from his abandoned lady, it is a message that establishes an identification. The fact that it is a message, signifiers, and not a body, an object, is also significant, for it accedes to subjectivity, to the "ownership of desire," in Marjorie Garber's terms, rather than remaining the effaced object of masculine desire (Garber, 118–27). As I have previously shown, the text repeats the words of the crucified Son to the Father: *lamah hazabtani* (Why have you abandoned me?), words that articulate Pantagruel's desire for his recently deceased dad. In the symmetry of their abandonment, the lady is to Pantagruel as Pantagruel is to his father. And this father crucifies and castrates his son, whose obedience is redefined as a submission, albeit transfigured.

I think by now you will have seen how the circuit of desire is completed and repeated in this scene of reading and how and why this is not freedom, either for me or for anyone. The tokenistic inclusion of the virago's voice in Rabelais studies, in the academy, in the Senate, continues to repeat a scene of revelation, an exposure that is simultaneously a covering up and veiling over of the phallus and its paternalistic law. What then, to distort a famous question, does a feminist want? Not to have her voice added to the Senate or the text, perhaps, but to reconfigure them completely. And in this Rabelais will not, as Booth would have it, survive gloriously. He, the fetishized master, may not survive at all. And the pleasure of this text may well depend on it.

*François Rigolot*

# The Three Temptations of Panurge: Women's Vilification and Christian Humanist Discourse

> *Là vous verrez ... petites joyeusettez toutes*
> *veritables; ce sont beaux textes d'évangilles en*
> *françoys.*

— Rabelais, *Pantagruel*

For several decades now, the interpretation of Rabelais's works has been greatly influenced by scholarship on Christian humanism and the revival of evangelical thinking in the early sixteenth century. For the last thirty years, serious critical work has been done to establish a horizon of expectation that removes our author from anachronistic libertine or rationalist suspicions and places him squarely, though not exclusively, within the Erasmian brand of humanist culture (Defaux, Duval, Screech, Weinberg). Few Rabelais scholars today, even those who question the validity of reconstructing authorial intentionality, disagree with the need for sound historical recontextualization.[1]

Yet problems do arise when we turn to the interpretative reading of specific passages and characters, especially in Rabelais's first book, *Pantagruel*. For there is always the danger of "reducing the text either to a single ideological reading, or to a reading that posits an author having at all times recoverable intentions and meanings to convey" (Schwartz, J. 1992, 2). For example, what are we to make of the innumerable antisocial, immoral, disruptive elements that seem to interfere with the positive valuation of a humanist new order? Although Mikhail Bakhtin's approach may often sound grossly overstated today, the significance of folk and popular culture must still be retained to a large extent for the proper understanding of Rabelais's early fiction.[2] As modern social historians have amply shown, upper-class participation in popular culture was an important fact of sixteenth-century European life.[3] Even Richard Berrong, who has undertaken a systematic refutation of Bakhtin's carnivalesque interpretation, agrees that folk culture is given a prominent role in *Pantagruel*, although not to the exclusion of learned humanist culture (Berrong, 121).

In the context of the times, the systematic vilification of women was the prevailing attitude, practiced routinely by monks to blunt their natural desires; the Franciscans and later the Capuchins were particularly noted for it. This was paradoxically reinforced by the newly revived Platonism, which identified woman as the changeable, fickle, and treacherous *luna* as opposed to the constant, proud, and dependable masculine sun.[4] As a former Franciscan himself, Rabelais must have been well acquainted with the particular brand of misogynous clichés that loomed large in many of the types of works he must have known: Jean de Meung's *Romance of the Rose*, the fabliaux, and various antifeminist satires written from the thirteenth to the fifteenth centuries (Bloch, 37–58).

The question I would like to raise here is, how can unbridled male sexual aggression, as exemplified in many episodes of *Pantagruel*, together with humiliation and degradation of the female, coexist with the evangelical doctrine of *caritas*, so dear to Rabelais's friends, which says "Love thy neighbor like thyself"? In other words, what happens to the exemplarity of Christian humanist discourse when it is expressed with the simultaneous presence of profoundly disturbing elements in moral behavior? More specifically, if we take the characteristic patterns that emerge from Rabelais's first book, to what extent can the recurrence of trickery, obscenity, and violence against women still qualify, in the Rabelaisian narrator's words, as "beaux textes d'évangilles en françoys" [fine Gospel texts in French]?[5]

In the following pages, I propose to concentrate on the single episode of *Pantagruel* devoted to Panurge's and Pantagruel's twin amatory adventures with a lady of Paris.[6] Although the episode has been the object of some probing critical scrutiny (Freccero), I do not think enough attention has been paid to the evangelical intertext that must have been easily recognized by the Christian humanist entourage of Rabelais. First, I will try to reconstruct the horizon of expectation for the episode on the basis of direct biblical allusions and contemporary evangelical commentaries. I will then offer a set of possible interpretations that may problematize the modern evangelical readings of the episode and question the exemplary status of Rabelais's and, more generally, Renaissance fiction.

Few modern readers may fail to interpret the attitude of Panurge toward the Parisian lady as a classic case of sexual harassment. Here, the usually ambivalent figure of the rogue appears at its basest and most vile; he becomes the repugnant "figure of phallologocentrism par excellence" (Freccero 1986b, 47). Although his offensive attempt to seduce a woman may be seen as a replay of Genesis as well as an attack on the conventional language of love in civilized society, the implications of the episode go much further. Recent critics have presented radically opposite views, which can be summarized as follows: Is Panurge subverting the foundations of social order by "dissolving all respect for hierarchy, feminine honour and marriage" (Schwartz, J. 1990, 39)? Or, in a more positive way, is he humbling a rich, haughty, pharisaical character, who sinned against *caritas*, thus serving the larger "redemptive design" of Rabelais's "Christian epic" (Duval 1991, 75, 119, 140)?

Before addressing these questions, let us turn to chapter 21, "Comment Panurge feut amoureux d'une haulte dame de Paris" (1:326) [How Panurge was smitten by a great lady of Paris]. The narrative of Panurge's sexual advances is divided into three neatly distinct parts, corresponding to three consecutive seduction scenes: the initial declaration (1:327–28) is repeated twice the next day, at church (1:329) and after dinner (1:330–31). Most sixteenth-century learned readers would have recognized a scenario familiar to them, namely the three temptations of Christ in the Gospels. Although the narrative is available from two of the four evangelists, Matthew and Luke, with only slight variations, I will concentrate on Matthew's version for reasons that will become clear. As we shall see, a parallel reading of Matthew 4:1–11 and *Pantagruel* 21 is revealing.

In the first temptation, Satan the tempter says to Jesus: "If thou be the Son of God, command that these stones be made bread." But Jesus, quoting Deuteronomy 8:3, replies, "It is written Man shall not live by bread alone, but by every word that proceedeth out of the mouth of God" (Matt. 4:1–4). In *Pantagruel*, from his very first appearance in chapter 9, Panurge is portrayed as a famished rogue who "lives by bread alone." He manages to seduce Pantagruel by begging for bread in several languages. His obsessive urge to feed on bread alone is reflected in his own name, *Pan/urge* (in need of bread), as he himself playfully indicates to his newly found master: "Seigneur . . . *mon vray et propre nom de baptesme est Panurge* . . . car pour ceste heure j'ay necessité bien *urgente* du repaistre" (1:269–70, my emphasis) [My Lord . . . *my true proper baptismal name is Needbread* . . . for right now I have very *urgent* need to feed].[7]

During his first attempt to seduce the Parisian lady, Panurge the tempter uses food metaphors, especially manna, as he mixes obscene language with hyperbolic clichés of Petrarchan love to taunt his victim: "Ce n'est que miel, ce n'est que sucre, ce n'est que *manne celeste*, de tout ce qu'est en vous. . . . Doncques pour gaigner temps, bouttepoussenjambions" (1:328, my emphasis) [All that is in you is nothing but honey, nothing but sugar, nothing but *celestial manna*. . . . So, to save time, let's push-thrust-straddle (204)].

In Christ's first temptation, the complete Old Testament verse from which Jesus quotes to Satan also talks about celestial manna: "And He [the Lord] humbled thee, and suffered thee to hunger, and *fed thee with manna*, which thou knewest not, neither did thy fathers know; that He might make that man doth not live by bread only, but by every word that proceedeth out of the mouth of the Lord doth man live" (Deut 8:3, my emphasis).

The lesson is clear. If man does not only live by bread alone, he certainly should not live either by the kind of *manne celeste* (i.e., sex) that Panurge has in mind. Biblical language has been twisted by the lecher to serve his own purpose, but the reader who knows the Gospel narrative will know the difference.[8]

Panurge's second seduction attempt happens the following day at church: "Au lendemain il [Panurge] se trouva à l'eglise à l'heure qu'elle [la dame] alloit à la messe" (1:329) [The next day he was in the church at the time when she was going to mass].

Interestingly enough, in Matthew's version, the second temptation of Christ also happens in a holy place. The devil takes Jesus to Jerusalem and places him "on a pinnacle of the Temple" (Matt. 4:5). Here again Satan plays the game of biblical quotations, using a truncated verse of Psalm 91 to justify his claims: "And [Satan] saith to Him, If thou be the Son of God, *cast thyself down*: for it is written, He shall give his angels charge concerning Thee: and in their hands they shall bear Thee up, lest at any time Thou dash Thy foot against a stone (Matt. 4:6, my emphasis).

Likewise Panurge literally urges his lady to "cast herself down" by yielding to his sexual desire. She should not worry because he will protect her as a guardian angel; he makes a deep bow and kneels close beside her. He tells her that his "cousteau" (i.e., his penis) is entirely at her service: "il est bien à vostre commendement, corps et biens, tripes et boyaulx" (1:329) [it is at your command, body and gods (sic), tripes and bowels (205)]. And lest she hurt herself with the precious stones of her rosary ("ses patenostres"), he cuts them off and sends them to the pawn shop ["les couppa très bien, et les emporta à la fryperie" (1:329)]. One could hardly find a more devious and self-serving transposition of Psalm 91. Panurge has obviously learned much from Satan about the art of textual manipulation. But the Parisian lady rejects the second temptation by retorting to Panurge, "Allez (dist elle), allez . . . laissez moy icy prier Dieu" (1:329) [Go away, go away . . . leave me alone here to pray to God]. This is a direct echo of Christ's response to Satan as he rejects the second temptation. Undaunted by his enemy's textual mastery, Jesus quotes Deuteronomy 6:16 and says: "It is written again, Thou shalt not tempt the Lord thy God" (Matt. 4:7).[9]

Panurge's third and final attempt to seduce the Parisian lady probably offers the clearest parallel with the narrative of Christ's encounter with the devil. In Matthew's version (Matt. 4:8–11), the devil takes Jesus to a high mountain and shows him "all the kingdoms of the world and the glory of them." Then he says to him, "All these things will I give thee, if thou wilt fall down and worship me." In Rabelais's transposition, Panurge shows his lady a great purse which she believes is full of money: "Après disner, Panurge l'alla veoir, portant en sa manche une grande bourse pleine d'escuz du Palais et de gettons" (1:330) [After dinner Panurge went to see her, carrying in his sleeve a big purse full of law-court counters and tokens (205)].

The trickster uses these valueless tokens to lure her, promising to buy her much richer rosary beads than the ones he has stolen from her. By displaying a cornucopia of precious stones in front of her eyes, he hopes to arouse her desires. The tempter's verbal virtuosity is just as dazzling as the gorgeous turquoises, sapphires, and diamonds he promises her:

> "En aymerez vous mieulx d'or bien esmaillé, en forme de grosses spheres ou de beaulx lacz d'amours, ou bien toutes massifves comme gros lingotz? ou si en voulez de ebene, ou de gros hyacinthes, de gros grenatz taillez, avecques les marches de fines turquoyses, ou de beaulx topazes marchez, de fins saphiz, ou de beaulx balays [rubis] à tout grosses marches de dyamans à vingt et huyt quarres?
>
> Non, non, c'est trop peu. J'en sçay un beau chapellet de fines esmerauldes, marchées de ambre gris coscoté et à la boucle un union Persicque gros comme une pomme d'orange! elles ne coustent que vingt et cinq mille ducatz. Je vous en veulx faire un present, car j'en ay du content." (1:330–31)

[Will you like some better in nicely enameled gold in the shape of great spheres or nice love-knots, or else all massive like gold ingots? Or do you want them of ebony, or big hyacinths, great cut garnets, with markers of fine turquoise or of lovely marked topazes, fine sapphires, or beautiful rubies with great markers of twenty-four carat diamonds? No, no, that's too little. I know of a beautiful chaplet of fine emeralds, with markers of dappled ambergris, at the clasp a giant Persian pearl as big as an orange! It costs only twenty-five thousand ducats, and I want to make you a present of it, for I have enough ready cash for it. (205–6)]

The temptation is great indeed and, we are told, makes the lady's mouth water: "Par la vertus desquelles parolles il luy faisoit venir l'eau à la bouche" (1:331). Nevertheless, she does not give way. Her moral strength is clearly demonstrated when, politely but categorically, she refuses the offer: "Non, je vous remercie; je ne veulx rien de vous" (1:331).

In the Gospel narrative, Christ's last reply to the tempter is just as categorical. It is the famous *Vade [retro] Satana* [Get thee hence, Satan].[10] We can see an echo of this imperative command in the lady's earlier plea to her tormenter: "Je vous ay, (dist elle), jà dict tant de foys que vous ne me tenissiez plus telles parolles . . . *Partez d'icy*" (1:330, my emphasis) [I've already told you ever so many times, said she, not to talk to me that way any more . . . *Get out of here* (205)].

To Satan, Jesus then quotes from Deuteronomy 6:13: "for it is written, Thou shalt worship the Lord thy God, and him only shalt thou serve." It would be out of character for the Parisian lady to quote the Scriptures. In her response to Panurge, she nevertheless refers to God's commandment of *caritas*: "Quant est de moy, je ne vous hays poinct, car, comme Dieu le commande, je ayme tout le monde" (1:330) [As far as I am concerned, I don't hate you, for, as God commands, I love everyone (205)].

And just as Matthew's narrative of the Three Temptations ends with the vanquished Satan leaving the scene, Rabelais's chapter 21 ends with the defeated Panurge running away for fear of a beating.[11]

At this juncture, one more textual detail should be pointed out that adds considerable credibility to the biblical intertext. At the beginning of chapter 21, Rabelais's narrator contrasts Panurge with "ces dolens contemplatifz amoureux de *Karesme*, lesquelz poinct à la chair ne touchent" (1:327, my emphasis) [those doleful and contemplative *Lent* lovers who never tamper with the flesh]. This allusion to the season of Lent must have functioned as an interpretative signal to sixteenth-century readers. *Quaresme*, also spelled *Karesme* (modern French *Carême*), comes from Latin *Quadraqesima*, the ordinal form of the word for forty. It denotes the fortieth Sunday (*Dominica Quadragesima*), the day on which Lent, the forty-day period of fasting before Easter, was to begin (Kinser, 277–78). Therefore, properly speaking, *Quaresme* designates the first Sunday in Lent. Interestingly enough, Matthew's narrative of Christ's Three

Temptations was the major liturgical reading of the mass for *Quadragesima* Sunday. There was a logical reason for it, since Jesus had fasted for forty days and forty nights before being submitted to temptation.

Moreover, in the edition he provided of the *Evangile* for the "Premier Dimenche de Quaresme," Jacques Lefèvre d'Etaples had written a rich commentary on Matthew's version of the Three Temptations (121–24). Lefèvre's text was, of course, compulsory reading in Christian humanist circles. Between 1525 and 1533, his elaborate commentary enjoyed considerable success, at at time when Rabelais was busy writing his *Pantagruel*. It is not surprising to find echoes not only of Matthew's text but of Lefèvre's own "Exhortation" in the three temptations of Panurge. Take, for instance, Lefèvre's uses of the double metaphor of the sword and the stick as powerful weapons to resist the sin of despair in adversity: "Pour nous monstrer où c'est que nous debvons en temps d'adversité cercher consolation, il (le Christ) a prins ung bon appuy, *ung bon glaive et baston* contre luy (Satan), c'est assavoir la parolle de Dieu" (122, my emphasis) [In order to show us where we should look for solace in time of adversity, Christ took a good aid, *a good sword and a good stick* against Satan, that is the Word of God].

In Rabelais's first seduction scene, the Parisian lady tries to deflect Panurge's advances by threatening him twice, first with "ung bon glaive" of her own invention: "Meschant fol, vous appartient il me tenir telz propos? A qui pensez vous parler? Allez, ne vous trouvez jamais devant moi; car, si n'estoit pour un petit, *je vous feroys coupper bras et jambes*" (1:327, my emphasis) [You crazy wretch, have you any right to talk to me that way? Whom do you think you are talking to? Go away, never come near me again; for but for one little thing, *I'd have your arms and legs cut off* (203)].

Then, as Panurge remains undeterred by these threatening words and keeps harassing her, she threatens him with a good "baston": "Allez, meschant, allez. Si vous me dictes encores un mot, je appelleray le monde, et vous feroy icy *assommer de coups*" (1:327, my emphasis) [Go away, you wretch, go away. If you say one more word to me, I'll call for help and have you *beaten* on the spot].

In a typical stylistic twist, Rabelais has literalized Lefèvre's double metaphor. In his hands, the spiritual meaning of the "bon glaive et baston" has been displaced to retrieve its original, physical sense. Is Rabelais telling us that stark, unmediated violence must sometimes be used against the dark powers of Satan? Is he drawing a clear parallel between Panurge and the devil, based on recognizable allusions to the Gospel narrative and the liturgical reading of the First Sunday in Lent? Or is he lightly musing about Lefèvre's evangelical commentary, much in the spirit of his book, offering his readers "petites joyeusettez" [little jollities], which his narrator wishes to pass off as "beaux textes d'évangilles en françoys" (Saulnier, 177) [fine Gospel texts in French]? Before proposing an interpretation, let us continue our reading of the evangelical intertext in the same episode.

The portrayal of Panurge, *mutatis mutandis*, after Satan's model, as a devilish tempter with no redeeming value in his harassment of the Parisian lady, should not come as a surprise. Much information has already been given about the rogue's "meurs et condictions" (1:300) and his obsessive interest in "mille petites diableries" (1:304). The question can be raised, however, whether Panurge becomes totally diabolical in Rabelais's fiction. To be sure, the narrator never conceals his contempt for the vain "glorieux" (1:326) whose masterfully hidden deception is betrayed by his "faulx visaige" (1:331). Yet, at the same time, Panurge is presented as a wonderful storyteller, a dazzling word player, and a great punster whose verbal resourcefulness seems to have no limits. Can Panurge be condemned as satanic by Rabelais, the embodiment of linguistic virtuosity?[12]

Here the evangelical commentary on the Second Temptation of Christ may be helpful again. In Matthew's narrative, Lefèvre remarks, Satan misquotes the Bible and uses Psalm 91 out of context to serve his purpose: "En la maniere d'ung trompeur, d'ung faulx prophete et seducteur, il [Satan] *sincopoit* et laissoit aucuns motz du texte. . . . Et ce voyant, nostre seigneur l'a derechief confondu par l'escripture *non sincopée* ou changée, mais purement et veritablement alleguée" (122–23, my emphasis) [In the manner of a cheater, a false prophet and a seducer, he (Satan) would *syncopate* (cut off) some words and leave others in the text. . . . And seeing this, our Lord confounded him again, *not* through *syncopated* or adulterated Scriptures but through pure, truthful quotations].

Like Satan, Panurge is a great "sincopeur" of texts. In an earlier chapter, we recall, he had tried to justify his petty larcenies by playing with another passage from Matthew: *Centuplum accipies* (1:309) ["You shall receive a hundredfold" (Matt. 19:29)]. In the second temptation, he embarrasses the respectable lady with shocking double entendre, playing on "A Beaumont le Vicomte" and the obscene meaning of his "cousteau" (1:329).[13] But the narrator himself shares his taste for equivocation: "Panurge commença estre en reputation en la ville de Paris . . . si bien qu'il entreprint *venir au dessus* d'une des grandes dames de la ville" (1:326, my emphasis) [Panurge began to get a reputation around the city of Paris . . . so much that he decided to *come on top of* one of the great ladies of the city].

The erotic meaning of "venir au dessus" is obvious.[14] But the narrator's point of view is interesting here. If, in the light of evangelical *caritas*, Rabelais wants to condemn Panurge as Satan, how can he afford to have Alcofribas share Satan's deceitful language? One possibility would be to consider the sentence "il entreprint venir au dessus" as a form of free indirect discourse ("discours indirect libre"), that is, a discourse in which the narrator adopts his character's voice. In terms of historical stylistics, such a usage might be viewed as anachronistic (Genette, 194). It may be simpler and safer to allow for the narrator's own playful space and recognize the participative role of Rabelais's persona in Panurge's delight for "satanic verses."

Such an interpretation is confirmed by Pantagruel's attitude in the episode. Far from distancing himself from Panurge's dirty tricks, he shows unequivocal approval of what he considers to be his friend's creative genius. When Panurge urges him gleefully to watch how he took revenge of the Parisian lady, he gladly accepts the invitation and acknowledges his enjoyment of the show: " 'Maistre, je vous prye, venez veoir tous les chiens du pays qui sont assemblés à l'entour d'une dame, la plus belle de ceste ville, et la veullent jocqueter.' A quoy voluntiers consentit Pantagruel, et veit le *mystere*, qu'il trouva fort beau et nouveau" (1:334, my emphasis) ['Master, I beg you, come and see all the dogs in the land gathered around a lady, the fairest in this town, and they want to ride her.' To which Pantagruel readily agreed, and saw the *show*, which he found very fine and novel (208)].

If the Christian law of *caritas* ("Love thy neighbor like thyself") is the central issue of Rabelais's epic, then the eponymous hero has obviously forgotten his mission. As a Good Samaritan, he should have rushed to the lady's rescue. Instead, by siding with the devil and forsaking an innocent victim, Pantagruel has become a problematic hero, fascinated by and acquiescent to the antisocial instincts of his friend in an offensive way.

Panurge is not, however, the triumphant Satan of Genesis who was able to lure Eve and make her eat the forbidden fruit; he is cast, rather, as the Satan of the Gospel, thrice defeated by the Word of God. If this is true, then his victim, the Parisian lady, should be seen as a Christlike figure. Such an interpretation runs counter to the traditional view, which holds that the "haughty dame" somehow deserves the degradation Panurge inflicts upon her (Duval 1991, 140–41). As we shall soon see, however, further evidence can be found to reconstruct the lady's character as an unexpected example of *imitatio Christi*.

Rabelais's portrayal of the lady as a Christlike figure is particularly striking in the second part of chapter 22, "Comment Panurge feist un tour à la dame Parisianne qui ne fut poinct à son advantage" (1:332) [How Panurge played a trick on the Parisian lady that was not to her advantage (207)]. In a most humiliating scene, Panurge, who had promised to avenge himself, has all the dogs of Paris run up to the lady, mount her, and piss all over her: "Tous les chiens qui estoient en l'eglise accoururent à ceste dame, pour l'odeur des drogues que il avoit espandu sur elle. Petitz et grands, gros et menuz, tous y venoyent, tirans le membre, et la sentens et pissans partout sur elle. C'estoyt la plus grande villanie du monde" (1:333, my emphasis) [All the dogs that were in the church ran up to this lady, for the smell of the drug he had sprinkled over her. Great and small, stout and tiny, they all came, freeing up their members, and sniffing her and pissing all over her. *It was the dirtiest mess in the world* (208)].

This time, the narrator shows unequivocal disapproval. Indeed we are asked to witness the most dreadful thing in the world, a spectacle that paradoxically may also have reminded sixteenth-century readers of an equally dreadful passage in the Gospel narrative.

In the text of Christ's Passion, the paradigmatic scene of degradation is known in the Vulgate as the "Flagellatio et Coronatio" scene. It takes the form of a mock homage staged by Roman soldiers before the Crucifixion. A comparison between *Pantagruel* 22 and Matthew's version is revealing. Following Pilate's orders, a band of soldiers, like Panurge's dogs, gather around Jesus to humiliate him ("Tunc milites . . . congregaverunt ad eum universam cohortem"). They smite him, mock him, and spit on him (Matt. 27:27–31; Mark 15:16–20; John 19:1–3). Allowing for Rabelais's proper style, could the transposition of soldiers into dogs be conceivable? "Ces villains chiens compissoyent tous ses habillemens, tant que un grand levrier luy pissa sur la teste, les aultres aux manches, les aultres à la croppe" (1:333) [Those nasty dogs pissed all over her clothes, to the point where a big greyhound pissed on her head, the others in her sleeves, the others on her crupper (208)].

In Matthew's text, the soldiers wrap Jesus in a scarlet robe ("chlamydem coccineam") and place a crown of thorns on his head. We may note that, in Rabelais's version, the Parisienne is also dressed in red: "ladicte dame s'estoit vestue d'une très belle robbe de satin *cramoysi*" (1:332, my emphasis) [the said lady had put on a very beautiful gown of crimson satin (207)]. Although she wears no headgear, her "cotte de veloux blanc bien precieux" may be seen as a semantic inversion of the crown of thorns; the rich white velvet serves as a foil to the dark prickly twist placed on Christ's head. But the crucial clue is given by Rabelais's narrator in the first line of the chapter. In the *editio princeps* we read, "Or notez que le lendemain estoit la grande feste du Corps-Dieu" (Saulnier, 122) [Now note that the next day was the great holiday of Corpus Christi (207)].

Rabelais may have felt that the allusion to the feast of Corpus Christi did not fit with the liturgical calendar he had in mind. At any rate, he later amended this line, presumably changing the wording slightly to give a clearer sense of his intentions. In the definitive edition, we read, "Or notez que le lendemain estoit la grande feste du *sacre*" (1:332, my emphasis) [Now note that the next day was the great feast of the *Coronation*].

In sixteenth-century usage *sacre*, as a substantive noun, could refer both to the Holy Sacrament and the crowning of the king.[15] This fully attested ambivalence may highlight Rabelais's correction as it now allows for an allusion to the mock-coronation ceremony of both Jesus and the "Dame de Paris."

In Rabelais's rewriting of the *Ecce homo* scene (John 19:5), the Parisian lady has thus taken the place of the humiliated Christ; she has become the Woman of Sorrows. Perhaps this is the most unexpected example of *imitatio Christi* one could find in the literature of the period. As we shall see later, Rabelais was also keen on hinting at the lady's ambiguous attitude toward her sexual harasser; his deliberate portrayal of her coyness and of the masculine view of woman as "saying no but meaning yes" cannot be ignored. Yet, at the same time, the lady-as-Christ figure fully conforms with the normal expectations of Rabelais's humanist readers. In his commentaries on the Epistles, Lefèvre d'Etaples had done much to establish the notion of *Christiformité* (Rom. 8:26, Rom. 13:14, Gal. 4:19, and Col. 3:1): "cette finalité de la vie chrétienne qui nous conduit à revêtir le Christ, à l'imiter, à nous assimiler à lui" (xxxii). Similarly, in his letters to Marguerite d'Angoulème, Guillaume Briçonnet, the leader of the evangelical "groupe de Meaux," had exhorted the queen to patient resignation in the face of suffering. To imitate Christ was above all to suffer with him and in him the pains of his Passion. The goal of a religious woman like Marguerite was thus to realize the opportunity to merge her own painful flesh with that flesh whose agony was salvation, in Briçonnet's words, "puisque toute la vie du chrestien doibt tendre à mort et plus en approche, plus est *christiforme*" (1:72, my emphasis). A case might even be made for Rabelais's recognition of Christ's feminine side. The motif, which could be traced back to the Fathers of the Church, was closely linked with the theme of the *indignitas hominis*.[16]

Although it would be exaggerated to see Marguerite as a model for the Parisian lady, some aspects of Rabelais's fictional character may have reminded the readers of the queen's religious fervor. To be sure, the Parisian lady offers a lesson of *caritas* to Pantagruel. Her words to Panurge in chapter 21 are suffused with *Christiformitas*: "Je ne vous hays poinct, car, comme Dieu le commande, je ayme tout le monde" (1:330) [As far as I'm concerned, I don't hate you, for, as God commands, I love everyone (205)].

Like Christ mocked by the soldiers, she was abjectly humiliated: "*She* looked for some to have pity on *her*, but there was no man, neither found *she* any to comfort *her*" [Psalm 68(69):20]. Not even Pantagruel, whose identity as a type of Messiah is promoted through the mock-epic fiction, showed the slightest pity on her. He simply abandoned her to the dogs in heat. To Pantagruel, the lady's degradation is simply a good show, a fine and original "mystere" (1:334). The word *mystere* may serve here as a reminder of the biblical text. Although it generally translates as *show* (spectacle), its religious meaning ("mystery") may be more relevant to the present situation. The three great mysteries of Christianity are Christ's Incarnation, Passion, and Resurrection. Here, Rabelais may play on the ambiguity of the word to refer to the second *mysterium fidei* as well as to the most famous of all mystery plays, the "mystère de la Passion." But Pantagruel is totally blind to the implications of his religious vocabulary.

Finally, the narrator's detached comment on Pantagruel's attitude may be read as another sign pointing to the ambivalent flavor of the whole dramatic episode. Just as blind as his hero, Master Alcofribas gleefully stresses the comic aspect of the climactic dog scene with total disregard for the lady's tragic distress: "*Mais le bon feut à la procession*: en laquelle feurent veuz plus de six cens mille et quatorze chiens à l'entour d'elle, lesquelz luy faisoyent mille hayres: et partout où elle passoit, les chiens frays venuz la suyvoyent à la trasse, pissans par le chemin où ses robbes avoyent touché" (1:334, my emphasis)

[*But the good part was the procession,* in which were to be seen over six hundred thousand and fourteen dogs around her, giving her a thousand annoyances, and everywhere she passed, newcomer dogs followed in her tracks, pissing along the roadway where her clothes had touched (268)].

Yet, as we shall see, Pantagruel will soon receive a message from another Parisian lady, making him understand that he has forsaken her and sinned against Christ's New Commandment of *caritas*.

The thematics of the Passion narrative can be traced even further in the second part of the episode, the one dealing with Pantagruel's own love story (ch. 23 and 24). As he is about to set sail for Utopia, the giant hero receives a diamond ring from "une dame de Paris" of whom we hear very little except that he has courted her for some time ("laquelle il avoit entretenue bonne espace de temps" [1:337]). After examining the ring carefully, the companions find Hebrew words engraved inside: "LAMAH HAZABTHANI (1:339)," which means "Why hast thou forsaken me?" As an expert in reading rebuslike devices, Panurge is able to decipher the lady's message: "J'entens le cas. Voyez vous ce dyament? C'est un dyamant faulx. Telle est doncques l'exposition de ce que veult dire la dame: 'Dy, amant faulx, pourquoy me as tu laissée?' " (1:339) [I understand the case. Do you see this diamond? It's a fake diamond. So this is the explanation of what the lady means: "Say, false lover, why hast thou forsaken me?" (212)].

Pantagruel then remembers that, on leaving from Paris, he did not bid his lady farewell: "et luy souvint comment, à son departir, n'avoit dict à Dieu à la dame" (1:339–40) [and he remembered how, on leaving, he had not said farewell to the lady (212)]. For a while he is so depressed that he considers returning to Paris to ask for her forgiveness: "et s'en contristoit, et voluntiers fust retourné à Paris pour faire sa paix avecques elle" (1:340) [and it saddened him, and he would have been inclined to return to Paris to make his peace with her (212)]. But he is reminded of Aeneas's conduct toward Dido and decides to press forward, sacrificing his individual preference to higher ideals. He must set off to defend his fatherland and fulfill his epic destiny (1:340).

Although much critical attention has been given to the ring episode, including interesting comments on an Italian parallel story (Freccero 1986, 48 ff), no one seems to have noticed the profound meaning of this message in the context of Rabelais's transposition of the Passion narrative. Most sixteenth-century humanist readers knew that the Hebrew words engraved on the ring came from the first line of Psalm 21(22), "My God, my God, why hast thou forsaken me?" From the Gospel narrative, they knew that Christ had uttered these words in their Aramaic form ("Eli, Eli, lamma sabacthani") before expiring on the Cross (Matt. 27:46; Mark 15:34).

They also knew that, according to ancient practice, by quoting the *incipit* one meant to refer to the entire psalm. Last but not least, they knew that Psalm 21(22) talked about mockery by ugly creatures named *dogs*:

> Omnes videntes me, deriserunt me.
> [All they that see me laugh me to scorn]
>
> Quoniam circumdederunt me canes multi
> Concilium malignantium osedit me
> [For many dogs gathered around me
> An assembly of wicked creatures closed in on me]
>
> Erue a framea, Deus, animam meam:
> Et de manu canis unicam meam.
> [Deliver my soul from the sword:
> And my darling from the power of the dog.][17]

When Pantagruel finds the Hebrew inscription on the ring, he immediately establishes a textual connection between the line he reads and his own situation.[18] This was common practice in applied allegorical readings of the Bible. As in the case of Augustine's "Tolle, lege," a scriptural fragment could open the reader's eyes and make a powerfully revealing statement about his own destiny. Unlike Pantagruel, Panurge is totally blind to the implications of the message he has deciphered. Ironically, he is the one who discovered the literal meaning of the rebus, proudly claiming his victory ("J'entens le cas" [1:339]) [I understand the case]. Yet he misses the tropological sense that the biblical quotation obviously has for himself. In the horrible dog scene he has just engineered, he behaves as the worst possible false lover ("amant faulx"). He humiliates the person he was supposed to love. He fails to realize that Pantagruel's "dame de Paris" is speaking to him in unambiguous terms when she quotes Psalm 21(22). No matter how great a decipherer of texts he may be, he never recognizes himself as the one who "laughed her to scorn" when "the dogs gathered around her" and submitted "his darling to their wicked power." As a typical sexual harasser, he remains unable to realize that the psalm bears a special meaning to him, namely that he has sinned against the law of *caritas*.

At this point, several questions of interpretation should be raised that problematize the evangelical reading I have offered. As we have seen, reconstructing a Christian humanist horizon of expectations is an essential step in the hermeneutical process. Just as modern readers must be acquainted with philology to understand the meaning of Rabelais's words, they must also be able to recognize biblical intertexts in order to grasp the meaning of Rabelais's staging of Panurge's misogyny. Yet the interpretative reading of a Renaissance work does not stop here. Contextual fluency is only a prerequisite for a fuller textual understanding of humanist fiction.

In Rabelais's hands, the evangelical scenario is submitted to stylistic manipulations that destabilize the normal relationship between text and ideology. This may involve extratextual satire, intertextual parody, and intratextual irony (Hutcheon, 142–43). By stuffing his narrative with half-recognizable biblical motifs, Rabelais goes beyond the norm of allegorical motivation. His book welcomes all forms of excess, including the overabundant use of evangelical references. This is where Bakhtin's notion of dialogism may be useful in a Christian humanist perspective (Bakhtin 1986). We can see it at work in the case of Panurge. In many ways his character is patterned after Satan's, but Rabelais's playful style lends its redeeming power to the rogue's "diableries" (1:304). Otherwise, how could Pantagruel, the good Christian hero, keep Satan in his company? We soon learn that, no matter how lecherous and roguish Panurge may be, he remains 'au demourant le meilleur filz du monde" (1:301) [for the rest the best fellow in the world]. This is a radical departure indeed from strict moral exemplarity.

As several critics have pointed out, Panurge is "a sign of ambivalence" that cannot be reduced to a single dimension (Schwartz, J. 1990, 210, n. 63). To be sure, the sexual harassment scene is the most gratuitous and loathsome of his pranks. It offends our modern sensitivity to a greater extent than his cheating the priests or whipping the kids. The Parisian lady seems to be cast as an allegory of the suffering Christ. Yet her character also carries certain marks of ambivalence. In the first temptation, she tricks Panurge by making believe that she will call for help: "Et [Panurge] la vouloit embrasser, mais elle *fist semblant* de se mettre à la fenestre pour appeler les voisins à la force" (1:328, my emphasis) [And (Panurge) tried to embrace her, but she *made as if* to go to the window to call the neighbors for help (204)].[19]

"Faire semblant" [make as if] is an expression often used in the sixteenth-century to characterize female duplicitous attitudes toward sexual advances.[20] Similarly, in the third temptation, as Panurge tries to kiss the lady, she is not at all determined to call for help and makes sure to keep her voice down: "elle commença à s'escrier, toutesfoys *non trop hault*" (1:331) [she started screaming, however not too loud]. Her attitude thus involves some degree of complicity, which adds to the realism of the story but contradicts her portrayal as an innocent victim and Christlike figure (Schwartz, J. 1990, 39).

The utopian plenitude of a lofty ideal, like evangelism, cannot be neatly separated from the cornucopian movement of a proliferating fictional text (Cave). Many disruptive elements do interfere with the essentially positive valuation of a Christian humanist new order. To be sure, in Rabelais's creative language, abundance and excess are not easily distinguishable (Jeanneret 1991, 107). The French words *très* [much] and *trop* [too much] are amazingly close cognates, and the most seriously committed evangelical message is not exempt from excessive free play, because it must also be part of the book's regenerative process. One thing is sure: Pantagruel will love Panurge for ever. Paradoxically, a thoroughly undisciplined pattern of life must coexist, even though it be based on humiliation and degradation, with the luminous evangelical doctrine of *caritas*.

In more general terms, this complex episode could be read as a striking illustration of what modern critics have come to recognize as the Renaissance crisis of exemplarity. In the sixteenth century, the rhetoric of example went through a major epistemological change (Hampton; Lyons). Humanist education opened up a more mobile space into a rather sclerotic concept and, despite much early reluctance, marked a clear move away from older didactic certainties. Medieval imitation essentially posited fictional texts as extensions of a unique source of undifferentiated truth and an infinitely expandable master text, the Holy Scripture. By contrast, Renaissance imitative theory became essentially metaphoric (Greene). It posited the relationship to paradigmatic figures as strictly one of analogy. Rabelais's early fiction seems to partake of this new brand of epistemology. His characters can no longer bridge the human time and historical difference that separate them from their models. Panurge may be similar to Satan in some ways, but he is essentially worthy of Pantagruel's love. The same can be said in reverse of the Parisian lady who, although patterned after a Christlike figure, exhibits a radical departure from her holy model. Many humanist readers were undoubtedly familiar with the long literary tradition which, through Origen's influential commentary on *The Song of Songs*, had stressed woman's identity as the bride of Christ. The archetypal tale was that of the beautiful lady who refuses blandishments and threats and accepts physical degradation in the name of chastity and wifely fidelity. It was recast many times in medieval literature. The most famous and probably oldest exemplary text in the vernacular is *The Sequence of Saint Eulalia* (ca. 880). But there were numerous similar stories, like Wace's *Life of Saint Margaret* (ca. 1145?) and the Old Provençal *La Chanson de sainte Foi*. Obviously, Rabelais's Parisian lady both reminds us of the medieval women saints' *Lives* and vigorously contrasts with that traditional source of exemplarity.

In his classic article strikingly entitled "L'Histoire comme exemple, l'exemple comme histoire" [in English: "History as Example, Example as (Hi)story], Karlheinz Stierle draws our attention to the problematic moral character of Boccaccio's *novelle*: "Le caractère exemplaire ne disparaît pas totalement," he writes, "il devient susceptible du réflexion" (Stierle, 187). Much like Boccaccio, Rabelais is still in many ways a profoundly medieval author.[21] Yet his works also usher a new process that may subtly make his readers reflect on and perhaps question the validity of exemplarity in Renaissance fiction.

Strangely enough, because our modern critical sensitivity is more finely attuned to problems of misogyny in our daily lives, we can better understand some of the semantic conflicts Rabelais so brilliantly built in his *Pantagruel*. At any rate, it is no longer possible to read Panurge's harassment scene as Wayne Booth and his young wife once did when, at an earlier stage, they were "transported with delighted laughter." Like the older Booths, we are forced to "draw back and start thinking rather than laughing" (Booth, 68).[22] In so doing, we may paradoxically become closer to Rabelais's own humanist readers who interpreted his early fiction for what he claimed it to be: a puzzling mixture of "beaulx textes d'évangilles en françoys" [fine Gospel texts in French] and "mille aultres petites joyeusetez toutes veritables" (1:385) [myriad other little jollities, all true (244)].

III     "Médullaires"

*Thomas Greene*

# Rabelais and the Language of Malediction

R abelaisian comedy is subject to pressures from two ostensibly unlike directions. It is on the one hand offered to
the reader explicitly and repeatedly as a source of moral
health. The writer or the narrator figuratively hands his
volume to us with the invitation that closes the "propos des bien
Yvres": "Avallez, ce sont herbes!" (1:29) [Swallow it, it's restorative
(*my translation*)]. Not only the "Fanfreluches" of the first book but
the whole work is presented as medicinal, "antidotées" (1:14). But
the comedy and the comic language are also placed at the service of
the writer's powerful if intermittent aggressivity, not only in those
episodes loosely and perhaps misleadingly described as satirical but
also in briefer explosions of searing verbal abuse. This abuse may
take the form of a literal curse or, more frequently, of invective,
which is not phrased as formal anathema but whose destructive
force is no less fearsome. The relation between the announced therapeutic intent and the terrible instances of execration pose problems
for an understanding of the work's internal economy. Thus an analysis of Rabelaisian malediction needs to begin with a glance at his
work's aspirations as well as physical restoration. We have to do
with a text explicitly produced by a doctor of medicine who also
happens to be a master of vituperation.

Rabelais writer: Rabelais physician. The interplay of the two roles
and the metaphoric substitutions they invite constitute a common
motif in his text. This interplay recurs with particular frequency in
the prologues, in the precious liminary reflections where Rabelais
discourses most freely on his own literary enterprise. The motif of

writing as therapy appears in all the prologues that are certainly authentic, and it is perhaps worth noting that the author of the prologue of the *Cinquième livre*, whoever he was, refers to his book as an "opiatte cordialle" (2:284) [an opiate for the heart (613)], thus sustaining the thematic continuity. It is in fact unbroken through all the preceding prologues, although it allows a broad shift of emphasis.

The accent in the prologue to the first-published volume is ostensibly farcical. The *Grandes Chronicques* have served to mitigate the suffering caused by many infirmities, from toothache to syphilis, just as the life of Saint Margaret aids women in labor. Other books may have appeared possessing analogous "proprietés occultes" (1:218), but they cannot be compared to the truly miraculous *Chronicques*. Only the book one is about to read, the *Pantagruel*, belongs to the same category. The prologue to the *Gargantua* is notable for the alteration in the contents of the boxes to which he likens his writing. Unlike the boxes in Plato and Erasmus to which he alludes briefly, boxes with a representation of Silenus outside and the statuette of a god inside, those boxes on which Rabelais dwells are sold by contemporaneous apothecaries; they are adorned outside with images of fantastic animals, but contain within them precious drugs and balms. So it is with this book: "la drogue dedans contenue est bien d'aultre valeur que ne promettoit la boite" (1:7) [The drug contained inside is of quite other value than the box promised (4)]. Thus the "sustantificque mouelle" [substantific marrow] is to be understood as essentially therapeutic. In the prologue to the *Tiers livre*, the medicinal drug becomes the inexhaustible wine offered by the writer as steward to the Pantagruelist armies of the world, the writer as "architriclin" restoring his readers with the marvelous liquor that confers "bon espoir" (1:400, 402). The medical motif emerges more explicitly than ever in the two prologues to the *Quart livre* and in the dedicatory epistle to cardinal Odet de Coligny. These three texts develop the metaphor very suggestively and will receive closer scrutiny. From their perspective, one can see that the entire work is ostensibly offered to its readers out of a concern for physical and moral health, offered with growing seriousness and growing emphasis as a life-enhancing restorative for us who need it. And our need is repeatedly assumed.

But these same texts raise implicitly a question that is perceived as problematic: What is the role of abuse, insults, execrations, and curses in a book guided by those announced goals? We cannot ignore the insistence of those reiterated claims of therapeutic intent, but neither can we ignore the aggressivity of the work, the writing of a man deeply wounded who also knew how to wound. Rabelais, when he chooses this instrument, takes his place in a line of masters of execration in western literature, a line that may be said to begin with Archilochus, a historical figure of the seventh century B.C. whose murderous power became legendary. Rabelais may not have known the fulgurous fragments of Archilocus that we possess, but he would have known the Ovidian or pseudo-Ovidian *Ibis*, a long versified curse against an unnamed enemy, and he would have known, among more recent vernacular texts, the sulphurous "Ballade des langues envieuses" of Villon. He would also have known, of course, the power of the Old Testament curse in prophecy, narrative, and psalm. It is notable that the Song of Deborah in the Book of Judges, the oldest surviving passage in Hebrew literature, contains a curse [Judges 5:23]. In the New Testament, Jesus's preaching of charity did not preclude the kind of ritual invective against whited sepulchres we find in Matthew 23, that terrible jeremiad with its maledictory refrain, "Woe unto you, scribes and Pharisees, hypocrites!" Rabelais had before him these most prestigous models and many others less prestigious as well.

The language of malediction still retained in Rabelais's age much of the destructive force attributed to it through much of human history. Did he in fact believe that he could literally injure others by the magical force of the imprecations which flowed so often from his pen? No answer can be conclusive, since there are degrees and levels of belief. It is possible to accept an assumption intuitively, viscerally, but not cerebrally — all the more possible if the assumption remains current as a vestige of immemorial credence. A belief in the efficacity of curses underlay the belief in sorcery, a belief that Rabelais apparently held. Pantagruel's remarks on the sybil of Panzoust dismiss the possibility that she is a witch, but not the existence of witchcraft itself. The intensity of Rabelais's reaction to the attacks upon him by the Sorbonne, by Calvin, and by Puy-Herbault attest to the power he attributed to the written word. Thus his own counterblasts have to be read as to some degree apotropaic, defensive shields against assaults that were not merely metaphoric. The belief in maledictory power can of course be traced back to the dimmest reaches of prehistory, and few peoples anywhere have been unaware of it. Any notion that this belief had disappeared among the literate elite of the Renaissance is refuted by the routine use of book curses against theft, commonly inserted by scribes in their manuscripts and by owners in valuable printed books. I cite one example from a Book of Hours of the early sixteenth century:

> Descire soit de truyes et porceaulx
> Et puys son corps trayne en leaue du Rin
> Le cueur fendu decoupe par morcealx
> Qui ces heures prendra par larcin.[1]

The question I would like to raise and to begin to answer asks how compatible are the apotropaic abuse, the anger toward and fear of the target of abuse, the aggressivity, and the vestigial magic of malediction with that therapeutic intentionality claimed for a health-enhancing text. I want to suggest three responses to this question that, in my view, are not necessarily mutually exclusive.

A first response would simply claim that there is no serious problem, that therapy and abuse are completely compatible and that, if anything, the therapy requires the abuse. A healthy text like a healthy subject needs a safety valve. Thus the occasional bursts of billingsgate are essentially sanitizing; without them, the Pantagruelistic good humor might strike us as too facile and too bland. Rabelais's text refuses to repress its hostilities, and the very refusal of repression guarantees the authenticity of the "joyeuseté." This argument could be extended by recalling the well-documented ethnographic links between fertility and abuse. The links between playful raillery and fertility were particularly apparent in the age-old fescennine abuse common at weddings, the verbal equivalent of those blows used by the seigneur de Basché to maul the Chiquanous.

Praise and blame are the two functions assigned to poets by many preliterate and traditional societies, in ways that pair the functions as mirror opposites.[2] Aristotle traced the origins of comedy to abusive phallic songs, which appear to have been common in fertility rituals throughout much of Europe and Asia Minor. These "still survive," he wrote, "as institutions in many of our cities" (Aristotle 1984, 1449b). Insults can be ludic; among men in particular, one finds insult games in many societies. The *tenzone* between Dante and his friend Forese Donati, a series of scurrilous insults packed into alternating sonnets, is doubtless best understood as a kind of zestful macho exercise. The long execration that concludes John Donne's elegy "The Bracelet" has to be read as an example of lyrical anathema, piling up catastrophes upon the unknown thief of his mistress's bracelet with a witty invention not to be taken seriously.[3] Comedy involves release, including the release of hostility, and the intuition that links this release to fertility may bear something like profundity within its irrational logic. At any rate, the connection seems to animate the pages of Rabelais. Part of Frère Jean's charm lies in the copia of his oaths, his "couleurs de rethorique Ciceroniane" (1:150) [colors of Ciceronian rhetoric (92)]. One hears a kind of robust good fellowship in the threats of Alcofribas against readers tempted to disbelive his veracity: "Pareillement le feu sainct Antoine vous arde, mau de terre vous vire, le lancy, le maulubec vous trousse, la caquesangue vous viengne . . . et comme Sodome et Gomorre puissiez tomber en soulphre, en feu et en abysme, en cas que vous ne croyez fermement tout ce que je vous racompteray en ceste presente *Chronicque*" (1:219) [May Saint Anthony's Fire burn you, the falling sickness spin you, squinancy and the wolf in your stomach truss you. . . . And, like Sodom and Gomorrah, may you fall into sulfur, fire, and the abyss, in case you do not firmly believe all I will relate to you in this present Chronicle (135)].[4]

I might remark here parenthetically that curses against a reader's incredulity appear to have been traditional and were normally not playful. But here we have a mock curse that invokes mock infirmities and mock disasters, that renders them impossible as it promises the copia to come. The therapy lies in making the dangerous impossible.

That would be one response to the question posed about the compatibility of therapy and malediction, but I think it needs to be complemented with a second response that takes the maledictory impulse more seriously. Leo Spitzer, in his memorable essay of over forty years ago, "Linguistics and Literary History," was right to be frightened by what he called the horror of Rabelais's execrative power.[5] Not all the invectives are mock invectives; some correspond to a genuine wish to destroy through the inherent force of charged language that transcends the playful and the aesthetic. The magic of anathema was preserved in the practice of the Roman church itself; the Council of Trent would routinely anathematize whoever refused to accept each article of doctrine promulgated.[6] But an analogous power of anathema could be wielded by individuals, most effectively by those gifted with the strength of linguistic invention. That invention, the power to make phonemes destructive, is what we find in Rabelaisian malediction.

We find it, for example, in the great inscription over the gate of Thélème, an inscription that does more than exclude; it exorcises and ultimately destroys its enemies in torrential annihilation.

> Cy n'entrez pas, hypocrites, bigotz,
> Vieulx matagotz, marmiteux, borsouflez,
> Torcoulx, badaux, plus que n'estoient les Gotz,
> Ny Ostrogotz, precurseurs des magotz
> Haires, cagotz, caffars empantouflez,
> Gueux mitouflez, frapars escorniflez,
> Befflez, enflez, fagoteurs de tabus;
> Tirez ailleurs pour vendre vos abus. (1:194)

> [Hypocrites, bigots, do not enter here,
> Blanched sepulchers, who ape the good and true,
> Idiot wrynecks, worse than Goths to fear,
> Or Ostrogoths, who brought the monkeys near;
> Imbecile sneaks, slippered impostors too,
> Furred bellybumpers, all, away with you!
> Flouted and bloated, skilled in raising hell:
> Go elsewhere your abusive wares to sell. (120)]

It would be wrong to ignore the wealth of semantic suggestiveness in this catalogue; each noun and each adjective contributes something to the misshapen and hideous distortions of humanity that swell and twist in the grotesque litany. The abuse of the human body committed by the *torcoulx*, the *boursouflez*, the *frapars* — this offense to the body is always in Rabelais a symptom of the radical evil that denies joy and denies life. There is rich and dense meaning in this single stanza that would support more analysis than it has received. But the language, so much more insidious than the word games of the *rhétoriqueurs* that inspired it, draws the reader away from the purely semantic toward an incantation of phonetic nightmare — Spitzer's "chaotic word-world situated somewhere in the chill of cosmic space" (Spitzer 1988, 20). As in most incantatory malediction, there is a drift away from the semantic toward sounds reified as missiles, sounds that acquire the density and substantiality of dangerous objects. Verbal reification emerges as a means to moral power. As language calls attention to itself as sound at the expense of meaning, as it hardens into a set of reified instruments, it acquires the uncanny momentum of withering efficacity. As "hoc est corpus meum" becomes hocus pocus, it becomes meaninglessly dangerous. A passage like the bans in the Thélème inscription does indeed make the danger felt, both the danger from the *bigotz* and the danger to them. The English word *ban* is indeed the right word, passing as it does from exclusion to curse. Hence the therapy of the word lies precisely in its power to exorcise the diseased from the protected enclosure of the verbal architecture.

It is worth pausing here to glance at Rabelais's brilliant use of the catalogue of monsters, the kind of catalogue we find in the Thélème inscription and will meet repeatedly in this paper. Rabelais liked to enumerate his supposed enemies one after another, stringing out the epithets of his contempt in marvelously inventive series, multiplying his crazily apt, whimsically malicious names for people who themselves begin to multiply in these savage typologies. The enemies doubtless were all more or less the same, but the *copia* of names tends to make them more various and abundant. They begin to swarm upon the page in their barbaric disfigurement; we hear them growling through the accumulating consonants; their teeming deformity becomes dangerous. A zoo of the misbegotten takes a menacing shape around us as the pitiless list calls out each ungodly species in turn. The plural nouns that compose each catalogue imply categories of evil, battalions of the loathsome, ready to assault the reader as they have the writer, so that it seems only the corresponding power of the deadly rollcall can keep at a distance this misshapen spawn of Antiphysie.

There lies in this phantasmagoria of abuse something of that Cratylism that François Rigolot has analyzed in an essential essay.[7] But there is also a drift toward an autonomy of sonorous elements that acquire a kind of independent febrile dynamism. Rabelais himself, in the Ancien Prologue of 1548, refers directly to the revolting force of the sound of his names, "caphards, cagotz, matagotz, botineurs, papelards, burgotz, patespelues, porteurs de rogatons, chattemittes; ce sont noms horrificques seulement oyant leur son" (2:574) [hypocrites, dissemblers, impostors, gumshoes, phonies, drones, hairypaws, indulgence-peddlers, catamites. These are horrific names, just to hear the sound of them (418)]. The reader senses that this horrific character of verbal sound preoccupied a writer sensitive to the opacity of words sprung from their semantic moorings. This preoccupation does not in itself violate the anti-Cratylan belief in the conventionality of language expressed by Pantagruel in the nineteenth chapter of the *Tiers livre*. If the link between sound and thing is arbitrary, the free-floating chain of sounds has more freedom to attain its own formidable independence. Thus the fiercely ebullient exorcism that closes the third prologue reaches a wordless snarl which is absent from all dictionaries: "Arrière, cagotz! Aux ouailles, mastins! Hors d'icy, caphars, de par le Diable hay! Estez vous encores là? Je renonce ma part de Papimanie, si je vous happe. Gzz. gzzz. gzzzz" (1:403) [Out of here, you phonies! In the name of the devil, out! Are you still there? I give up my share of Papimania, if I can just catch you. Grr. Grrr. Grrrr! (260)].

In passages like this one, Rabelais seems to be seeking a language strong enough to expel the unnatural and the antinatural from his book and perhaps even from the world outside his book. The resort to the alexical "Gzzz," half-humorous as it is, bespeaks the bestiality of those children of Antiphysie who are "mastins cerbericques" [Cerberian curs] both diabolical and subhuman.

Did Rabelais have a theory of language that would have allowed him to formulate the workings of the maledictory language? Can we reconstruct that theory today? Against the theory of conventionality I've already cited ("les voix . . . ne signifient naturellement, mais à plaisir" (1:480) [words . . . signify not by nature but by our pleasure (311)]), one can recall Pantagruel's comment on the "paroles gelées": "Me souvient . . . que Aristoteles maintient les parolles de Homere estre voltigeantes, volantes, moventes, et par consequent animées" (2:205) [I . . . remember that Aristotle says that Homer's words are prancing, flying, moving, and consequently animate (557)]. That theory of inherent linguistic animation seems truer to Rabelais's own practice, not least in his passages of verbal disinfection. Only a living language breathing with Pantagruelist health can deal with the poisonous power of the "caphars." We owe to the learning of Glyn Norton and especially Gérard Defaux a reminder of the passage in which Erasmus evokes a linguistic "occulta quadam energia" in his paraphrase of the gospel of Saint John, that occult energy of *oratio* that renders it, writes Erasmus, the most efficacious means of affecting the impulses of the soul. Erasmus would seem here to be echoing a passage in one of Saint Jerome's letters that affirms this mysterious energy: "habet nescio quid latentis energeias viva vox" (The living word has I know not what hidden force).[8] Pantagruel's conception of words as "animées" can be read in the Christian tradition of the "viva vox" as well as the Aristotelian encomium of Homer in his *Rhetoric* (1412a) for the life-giving character of Homeric tropes.

The occult vivacity of the word that produces "joyeuseté," which serves as a therapeutic drug, is also the means of fumigating the "cagotz," the cannibals, the agelasts, and other monsters of Rabelais's unholy zoo. The occult power is a power of health and of upright nature, a power drawn on to dispel the unholy monsters on the edge of the text, who are threatening to intrude and corrupt it. One feels that awesome power in play in the verbal *sparagmos* of the oppressors at the Sorbonne: "Sophistes, Sorbillans, Sorbonagres,

Sorbonigenes, Sorbonicoles, Sorboniformes, Sorbonisecques, Niborcisans, Borsonisans, Saniborsans" (1:318, n. 2). The plastic character of language, its "voltigeant" volatility, the animate energy of a changeable substance — these are the elements of the word permitting the destruction of the inhuman. In a page added to the close of the *Pantagruel*, Rabelais had already discovered the artistic possibilities of the half-rhyming, chiming catalogue of monsters, all the more monstrous for their grotesque disguises: "un grand tas de sarrabovittes, cagotz, escargotz, hypocrites, caffars, frappars, botineurs, et aultres telles sectes de gens, qui se sont desguizez comme masques pour tromper le monde" (1:386) [a big bunch of Sarabaites, bigots, snails, hypocrites, fakers, bellybumpers, monks in buskins, and other such sects of people, who have disguised themselves like masters to deceive people (244)]. The Cratylan faith that Defaux finds throughout the century surfaces here only to empower the word to undo the disguise of its referent, to expose its masqued deformity.[9]

This exposure, the occult power of undoing, would constitute a second means of reconciling therapy and malediction. Yet one is obliged to notice the persistence of the monstrous and even its growing presence in the succession of Rabelais's volumes. No exorcism seems definitive, and the prologues that invoke health with progressive emphasis also betray the lengthening shadows of the unnatural accusers. The sense of monstrosity is reflected in the brilliant evocation of the accusers' writhing gesticulations added to the second volume. They are portrayed "articulant, monorticulant, torticulant, culletant, couilletant et diabliculant, c'est à dire callumniant" (1:386) [articulating, monorticulating, torticulating, buttock-wagging, ballock-shaking, and diaboliculating that is to say calumniating (245)]. As Rabelais grew older, and notably as he wrote certain passages of the *Quart livre*, his sensitivity to what he calls calumny seems to have grown more acute, so that one can distinguish a third, more troubled response to the problematic relationship between therapy and execration.

The prologue of 1548 reveals in fact a level of overpowering resentment unprecedented in the first three volumes, and this resentment could only have been deepened by the attacks of Calvin in

1549 and 1550 and Gabriel de Puy-Herbault in 1549. It is important to note that among the activities imputed to Rabelais by this latter critic was the sin of slander; he is said to "lancer la calomnie et l'injure . . . attaquer les honnêtes gens, les pieuses études." Rabelais strikes back with one of his now familiar catalogues in Chapter 32 of the *Quart livre*, purporting to list the offspring of the unnatural goddess Antiphysie and naming for the first time his two most recent accusers: "Depuys elle engendra les Matagotz, Cagotz et Papelars; les Maniacles Pistoletz, les Demoniacles Calvins, imposteurs de Geneve; les enraigez Putherbes, Briffaulx, Caphars, Chattemites, Canibales, et aultres monstres difformes et contrefaicts en despit de Nature" (2:137) [Since then she engendered the Matagotz, Cagotz, and Papelars, the maniacal Pistols, the demoniacal Calvins, impostors of Geneva, the rabid Putherbeuses, the Gut-Guzzlers, Hypocrites, Toadies, Cannibals, and other monsters deformed and misshapen in despite of Nature (507)].

Part of the destructive effect of this passage lies in the continuous use of the plural, suggesting that "les Calvins, les Putherbes" belong to a misbegotten species like the dog-faced "canibales." Here the writer seems quite as much in control of his invective as in the preceding volumes, but other passages in the same *Quart livre* call that control into question.

The sections most relevant to our purposes are the three prefatory texts of 1548 and 1552, that is, the '48 prologue, the dedicatory epistle of '52 to Cardinal Odet de Coligny (which draws on the earlier prologue), and finally the new prologue of '52. Nowhere previously had Rabelais dwelt as fully as in the first two of these texts upon his role as physician-writer, and nowhere previously had this role appeared so problematic. Each of the three texts has a distinctive place in Rabelais's canon, but I want now to read them with each other and against each other.

One can say that the texts reaffirm explicitly two principles already implied: first, the intimate rapport between bodily health and moral or psychic health; second, the radically medical purpose of Rabelais's writing in succoring both kinds of infirmity. Thus the epistle to Odet begins by asserting its healing function: "plusieurs gens languoureux, malades, ou autrement faschez et desolez, avoient, à la lecture d'icelles, trompé leurs ennuictz . . . et repceu alaigresse et consolation nouvelle" (2:3) [many languishing, ill, or otherwise vexed and heart-sick people had, in the reading [of the first three volumes] beguiled their troubles . . . and received new blitheness and consolation (421)].

To lighten the burden of the afflicted had in fact been the writer's only goal: "seulement avois esguard et intention par escript donner ce peu de soulaigement que povois es affligez et malades absens" (2:3). The implication is clear that writing, which is itself healthy, can in fact heal the infirm. The idea is present as early as the prefatory verse of the *Gargantua*: "Aultre argument ne peut mon cueur elire, / Voyant le dueil qui vous mine et consomme" (1:3) [No other subject can my heart hold dear, / Seeing the grief that robs you of your rest" (2)]. In these prefatory texts of the *Quart livre*, however, we find for the first time a doubt concerning the writer's capacity to play this role, a doubt directly linked to the verbal attacks directed against him. The epistle to Odet states, whether truthfully we cannot say, that the calumnies directed against the writer had decided him to write no more and that only the approval of the king of France had persuaded him to continue. This hints at least at a danger of artistic sterility. It is difficult not to apply to the writer the proverb quoted in the '52 prologue, "medicin, o, gueriz toymesmes" (2:12) [Physician, heal thyself (425)]. It is difficult not to conclude that the writer-physician invests this proverb with the "horrible sarcasme et sanglante derision" (2:12) [horrible sarcasm and biting derision (425)] which he alone seems to find in it. Although he protests that his own health is good, he will associate himself with those readers who need to pray to God so that the legal maxim may be confirmed in their lives: "le mort saisit le vif" (2:13) [the dead man seizes the quick (426)]. "J'ay cestuy espoir en Dieu," he writes, "qu'il oyra *nos* prieres" (2:14, my emphasis) [I have this hope in God, that He will hear *our* prayer (427)]. The same question arises in all three of these late prefatory texts: Is the writer-physician healthy enough to heal the afflicted for whom his book is allegedly composed? Is he rather too wounded by the maledictions intended to silence him? Or is it possible that he himself is afflicted by his own counter-hostility and counter-malediction?

This last question has to be posed in the light of the astonishing conclusion to the '48 prologue, later to be suppressed. That text closes with a fearful fantasy of the "mesdisans et calumniateurs" (2:577) [backbiters and calumniators (419)] running amok like lunatics, pillaging and grimacing in a frenzied orgy of destruction and suicide. The writer makes to such as these the offer once made by Timon of Athens, "Timon le Misanthrope" (2:577), to his ungrateful countrymen: they are free for a given time to hang themselves from a tree he will provide; after the new moon, they will have to fend for themselves (2:577–78) [(420)]. The '48 prologue ends on this note remarkable for its anti-Pantagruelism. The intent rather is quite deliberately murderous; in the language of the text, it is misanthropic. As the prologue to a work of healing gaiety, it fails and it allows the reader to wonder if the writer's powers of abuse have not poisoned his own spirit. The risk of self-contamination on the part of the curser is in fact an article of faith in many traditional societies. Rabelais could have found its reflection in the remarkable Psalm 109. That psalm, spoken by a victim of malediction, turns the effect of the curse which has injured him upon its author:

> Curses he loved: may the curse fall on him! . . .
> He clothed himself in cursing like a garment:
> may it seep into his body like water and into his bones like oil!
> May it wrap him round like the clothes he puts on.

In that wish of the psalmist lies a plausible psychic truth, and after reading the embittered prologue of 1548, it is reasonable to wonder whether the truth is not exemplified by François Rabelais. The writer's vituperation, borrowed from Plutarch's Timon, seems so to have wrapped him round as to have degraded him from Pantagruelist to misanthrope.

The epistle to Odet four years later turns this word back upon the usual enemies, "certains Canibales, misantropes, agelastes" (2:6) [certain cannibals, misanthropes, *agelastes* (423)]. But the reader may now wonder to what degree the writer is distinguished from the other misanthropes. What is clear in this epistle is the effort required of the physician-writer in that combat or drama played by three actors: the patient, the doctor, the illness. The role is no longer played spontaneously, and it requires, we are told, a disguise: "le medicin, ainsi desguisé en face et habitz . . . [pourroit] respondre à ceux qui trouveroient la prosopopée estrange: 'Ainsi me suis je acoustré . . . pour le gré du malade lequel je visite, auquel seul je veulx entierement complaire, en rien ne l'offenser ne fascher' " (2:4–5) [the doctor, thus disguised in face and clothes . . . could reply to those who might find the costume strange: 'Thus have I clad myself . . . for the taste of the patient I am visiting, whom alone I want to please entirely, not offend or vex him in any way' (422)].

The word "prosopopée" is glossed in the *Briefve Declaration* as "disguisement, fiction de personne" (2:249). The disguise or mask, formerly attributed to the "cagotz" and "caffars," is now worn by the healer as a necessary medical measure, because the healer's mood is transferred to the patient and determines the success of the therapy. It is "trescertain" that Hippocrates was correct in perceiving this transference; the only open question is whether the physician's cheer or gloom has a corresponding effect because the patient reads his own destiny in the physician's facial expression or whether, as Plato and Averroes would have it, the physician emanates spirits that, depending on his mood, have a positive or negative effect. If, as we have been told, the writer-physician Rabelais must disguise himself before visiting his reader-patients and have recourse to a "fiction de personne," the disguise would suggest he cannot spontaneously present a cheerful face, cannot transfer spontaneously health-giving emanations. One is led to suppose that his true demeanor, undisguised, would be that of the "medicin chagrin, tetrique, reubarbatif, catonian, mal plaisant, mal content, severe, rechigné" (2:5) [doctor's mien that is gloomy, cross, harsh, Catonian, unpleasant, unhappy (422)].

A threat emerges from this passage to the efficacious role of the writer-physician: Will the disguise prove sufficient? Isn't there a risk that the malign spirits will affect the afflicted reader? At the end of his life, Rabelais seems to fear the emanations of his own corrosive and debilitating anger, which had earlier empowered his righteous maledictions. Can the embattled author win his combat against moral disease? The evidence is not clear, and the text suggests in fact the danger of creative sterility stemming from the cannibals; their calumny was so outrageous that it overcame the writer's resolution and he decided to write no more ("plus n'estois deliberé en escrire un iota") (2:6) [I was determined not to write one more jot of this (423)]. Only the approval of the king had encouraged him to continue. But as he writes, he still feels the need of a protector who will be an "Alexicacos," that is, according to the *Briefve Declaration*, a "defenseur, aydant en adversité, destournant le mal" (2:250) [defender, helping in adversity, warding off evil (593)]. This apotropaic protector is to be Odet. The language of malediction will not in itself suffice.

In the *Tiers livre*, Frère Jean remarks of the mendicant friars that "ilz mesdisent de tout le monde; si tout le monde mesdit d'eulx, je n'y pretends aulcun interest" (1:493) [They speak ill of everyone; if everyone speaks ill of them it's no skin off my nose (320)]. But by the end of his career, it would appear that Frère Jean's creator could not achieve the same detachment. He had come to see calumny as diabolic: "En grec," he wrote, "calumnie est dicte diabole" [For in Greek, calumny is called *diabole*"] and his own calumniators are "appariteurs et ministres" ["attendants and ministers"] of the devils in hell (2:574–75) [(418)]. The *Quart livre* is haunted by the fear of the demonic in the language of the enemy, and, as I read it, by the less visible fear of the demonic in the writer's own text. The volume can be regarded as a struggle on the part of the writer-physician to heal himself so he can heal his reader-patients, but it is never clear that the struggle is definitively won.

This paper offers three perspectives on the relationship between therapy and malediction in Rabelais. The first of these, a ludic theory of malediction as safety valve, is the simplest and most reassuring. The second, a magical theory attributing real destructive power to charged language, draws out the primitive and even atavistic assumptions apparently latent in Rabelais's book. The third theory, which is the darkest, suggests that the malediction turned back corrosively upon the writer to nullify his therapy and threaten his Pantagruelistic health. Having sketched this triad, I repeat that these three perspectives do not seem to me mutually exclusive. Perhaps the entire work reflects the gradual discovery of the diabolic poison and cleansing power in malediction. We watch Rabelais acquiring the wisdom of Vladimir Mayakovsky on what he calls the "wrought-iron lines of long-buried poems": "handle them with the care that respects ancient but terrible weapons."

*Edwin M. Duval*

# History, Epic, and the Design of Rabelais's *Tiers livre*

The *Tiers livre* appears to be a book without a design. From a strictly formal and generic point of view, it is unprecedented, even absurd. It begins neither *in medias res* as classical epics do, nor *ab ovo* as historical narratives do, but *in finem*, with a climactic epic telos transposed almost verbatim from the end of the preceding epic. It ends not with a climax or even a conclusion, but with an epic beginning, as the Pantagruelians prepare to embark on a new Odyssey or Argonautica. And between its opening conclusion and its concluding overture, the book contains an open-ended quest whose point is never entirely clear and whose telos is indefinitely deferred. If there is a design to this peculiar book, it must be an anomalous one indeed.

I do not propose to investigate here the design of the *Tiers livre*, though it does have a coherent and rational design, first appearances notwithstanding. Instead, I would like to consider two highly self-conscious, emblematic representations of the *Tiers livre* contained within the book itself, both of which suggest that the apparent incoherence and directionlessness of the *Tiers livre* are themselves an effect of a deliberate design.

The first of the book's self-representations is contained in the author's prologue, where Rabelais compares his book to the futile tub-rolling of the cynic philosopher Diogenes. As Floyd Gray pointed out almost thirty years ago, the analogy of the prologue draws attention to the uniqueness of a literary structure that, as Gray rightly observed, was "quite unlike anything the world had ever seen," being informed by "no narrative progression" and "revolv[ing] constantly and furiously about its own axis . . . as a kind of transfigured Diogenic tub" (Gray 1963, 61–62).[1] Ever since Gray's article it has been a critical commonplace that Diogenes's frantic tub-rolling in the prologue functions as an emblem of the *Tiers livre* as a whole, and of Panurge's futile and unending quest in particular. The quest and the book, like Diogenes's pantomime, appear perfectly Sisyphean in their repetitiveness, endlessness, and infinite futility.

But the prologue's suggestion of non-design in the *Tiers livre* is even more focused and ironic than this, for the anecdote about Diogenes, and indeed the articulation of the whole prologue, are borrowed directly from a work that was very well known to literate readers of the 1530s and 40s, a book by Lucian of Samosata entitled significantly: *How to Write History*.[2] Rabelais intended for his readers to recognize this book as the direct source of his prologue, as will become evident in a moment.

In the prologue of *How to Write History*, Lucian, like Rabelais in the prologue to the *Tiers livre*, tells the story of Philip of Macedon's attack on Corinth, of the Corinthians' panic, and of Diogenes's mimetic mock-frenzy (Lucian 1538, 3[4]).[3] Like Rabelais, he compares his own situation to that of Diogenes, proposes to imitate the cynic, and finally offers the following book as the equivalent of Diogenes's parodically censorious tub-rolling (Lucian 1538, 4[6]). But there is a crucial difference between the two prologues. For Lucian, the crisis that corresponds to frantic preparations for war at Corinth is not pandemic war fever, as it is for Rabelais in a bellicose France, but rather a comical epidemic of history writing triggered in an excessively literary Greece by the events of current wars. "There is no one," Lucian laments, "who is not writing a history. What is more, they all claim to be our Thucydideses, Herodotuses, and Xenophons. The old proverb is true, it seems: 'war is the father of all things,' since it has engendered so many writers all at one blow" (Lucian 1538, 2[4]).

Lucian, not wishing to remain the only "mute" (ἄφωνος) in such a loquacious (πολυφώνῳ) [6] time, decides to play Diogenes to the

Corinthian madness of mass historiography, not by writing yet another history — such an undertaking is beyond his means, and the perils of doing so are all too evident from the flood of artless histories now being published — but rather, by offering some lessons in writing history from a safe distance and out of harm's way, like Diogenes (Lucian 1538, 4[6]). The original, Lucianic equivalent to Diogenes's censorious tub-rolling is *How to Write History* — that is, Lucian's humorous textbook designed to ridicule the failings of modern historians and teach them to write good narrative history according to the rules of the genre (Lucian 1538, 4[6] and 63[72]).

By appropriating the prologue to this book of rules as the prologue to his own unruly book, Rabelais assimilates his own tub-rolling not only to Diogenes's but to Lucian's as well, deliberately inviting his readers, who in 1546 knew Lucian's book well, to consider the *Tiers Livre des faictz et dictz Heroïques du noble Pantagruel* alongside *How to Write History* and in the light of the norms of historical narrative as they are codified in Lucian's book. For Rabelais's intended audience, the prologue thus contained a subtle but unmistakable signal that this sequel to the history of Pantagruel acknowledges, but deliberately ignores, the rules of writing good history. It breaks the rules of narrative history not out of negligence, but by conscious, deliberate design.

These implications of Rabelais's appropriation appear even more obvious when we recall that Lucian goes on in his prologue to evoke the futility of his own tub-rolling in the following terms:

> Yet most [of these mad historians] do not even think they need instruction in their work, any more than they need some special skill to walk, look around, and eat. They think that nothing is simpler or easier than writing history and that anyone can do it simply by putting into words whatever comes into his head. . . . I know that I shall not convert many of these and that I shall even seem a nuisance to some, especially to those whose histories are already completed and published. . . . Nevertheless, it will not hurt to speak even to these, so that if another war should ever occur — say between the Celts and the Getes, or the Indians and the Bactrians (for surely no one will ever make war on us, since we have subdued everyone by now) — they will be able to construct better histories by using this rule . . . if the rule seems straight to them,

that is. If not, they can continue to measure their work by their own cubits, as they do now (Lucian 1538, 5[6]).

As a latter-day Diogenes in a nation devoted to war, Rabelais is one of those writers who, as Lucian foresaw, would someday find themselves witness to another war and thus have a second chance to write a proper history.

Yet in the *Tiers livre*, Rabelais apparently remains one of those impenitent, raving historiographers for whom Lucian played his Diogenes in vain. Uncured by the tub-rolling of *How to Write History*, he rolls his own tub by putting down whatever comes to mind with no respect for the art of composition, that essential art by which, Lucian promises, the writer may never "stray from the staight path that leads directly onward" and that consists in knowing precisely "what kind of beginning to begin with, what kind of order to impose on the parts, what proportion to give each part, what to leave out, what to dwell on, what to mention only in passing, and how to express and arrange everything harmoniously" (Lucian 1538, 6[8]).

This art of composition, as Lucian defines it in his prologue and goes on to teach it throughout the rest of his treatise, is precisely what appears to be wanting in Rabelais's bizarre sequel to the *Pantagruel*. By appropriating Lucian's famous prologue as his own, adapting it to his own purposes and allowing the model to resonate within the imitation, Rabelais uses and compounds Lucian's ironies, announcing from the very beginning of the *Tiers livre* that he knows Lucian's *How to Write History* very well but still does not know "how to write history." Or rather, that he has deliberately chosen to write his history otherwise. In this way, the prologue not only represents, emblematically, the anomalousness of the historical narrative that follows but also alludes, intertextually, to the fact that he acknowledges the accepted norms of narrative history but deliberately chooses to disregard them.

I would like to leave the prologue now to consider the second passage in which the *Tiers livre* represents itself emblematically. This passage is less often recognized for what it is, though it is even more specific and ironic in its self-representation. It is a textbook case of what we now commonly call a *mise en abyme*. The passage occurs near the center of the work, in chapter 24. By this point, it has already become painfully clear that Panurge's search for a resolution to his doubts concerning marriage is leading nowhere and that the sequence of consultations could conceivably go on forever. But here the quester, much to the reader's dismay, renews his original vow to "porter lunettes au bonnet, ne porter braguette en chausses" until he has had a "resolution aperte" to his "perplexité d'esprit" (1:501–2) [(325–26); compare with 1:430–33 (277–79)]. At this, Panurge's companion Epistemon loses patience. Speaking for all of us, it would seem, Epistemon angrily derides Panurge for his foolish obstinacy, comparing his vow to one made by a Spanish knight, Michel d'Oris, to wear on his leg a painful "trançon de greve," that is, a mutilated fragment from a torn shin guard, until some English knight accepted his challenge to do single combat with him. As Epistemon goes on to state, this example of a foolish vow is recorded in a modern historical narrative, Enguerrand de Monstrelet's fifteenth-century chronicle of the Hundred Years' War.[4]

Book I of Monstrelet's work, from which Epistemon draws his anecdote, chronicles the first twenty-two years of the fifteenth century, the bleakest period of the entire Hundred Years' War (and indeed one of the bleakest in all French history), beginning with revolts and civil war and culminating in the disaster at Agincourt (1415), the legal demise of the Kingdom of France sealed by the Treaty of Troyes (1420), and the death of the insane king Charles VI, known derisively as the "king of Bourges" (1422). But in Monstrelet's narration, the very first event of the fifteenth century and of this entire tragic period is the utterly frivolous, trivial, and inconsequential episode alluded to by Epistemon. Immediately following a background chapter on Charles VI's insanity and its devastating consequences for the political stability of France, Monstrelet devotes an interminable chapter — eight double-columned folio pages in the early sixteenth-century editions — to transcriptions of eight long letters by Michel d'Oris of Aragon and Jehan de Prendegrest, a knight in the service of the count of Somerset.

This epistolary exchange is actually a masterpiece of situation comedy, in which an amusing caricature of hispanic braggadocio gives rise to a long series of contretemps and comic errors — letters sent to the wrong address, unforwarded mail, mistaken identities, deliberately misinterpreted intentions, missed rendez-vous. These lead to quibbles about protocol, such as the question of which party is responsible for defraying travel expenses to the site of the duel. The correspondence finally degenerates into petty squabbles about the history of the correspondence itself — who said what to whom at what date and in answer to which letter. The last letters are devoted almost entirely to recapitulating the history of the whole exchange, introducing new errors and misunderstandings in the process. The final result of all this writing and wrangling about writing is . . . absolutely nothing. The chapter concludes, "Lesquelles lectres ainsi envoiees d'une partie et d'aultre, finablement quant au fait ne vint pas à nul effect."[5]

Now this comically impertinent, incongruous, and inconsequential opening to the chronicles of Enguerrand de Monstrelet is explicitly represented to us through Epistemon's little speech near the center as emblematic of the *Tiers livre* itself. Immediately after comparing Panurge's vow to the one made by Michel d'Oris, Epistemon digresses at some length to condemn Monstrelet for his poor historiography. As he does so, he suggests a clear analogy between Monstrelet and Rabelais himself:

> Et ne sçay lequel des deux seroit plus digne et meritant porter chapperon verd et jausne à aureilles de lievre, ou icelluy glorieux champion, ou Enguerrant, qui en faict le tant long, curieux et fascheux compte, oubliant l'art et maniere d'escrire histoires baillée par le philosophe samosatoys. Car, lisant icelluy long narré, l'on pense que doibve estre commencement et occasion de quelque forte guerre ou insigne mutation des royaulmes; mais, en fin de compte, on se mocque, et du benoist champion et de l'Angloys qui le deffia, et de Enguerrant leur tabellion, plus baveux qu'un pot à moustarde. (1:502)

> [And I don't know which of the two would be more worthy and deserving to wear the fool's motley and hare's ears, this glorious champion or Enguerrand de Monstrelet, who tells such a long, detailed,

and boring story about it, forgetting the art and manner of writing history, handed down by the philosopher of Samosata. For, as you read his long account, you think it must be the beginning and occasion of some mighty war or notable mutation of kingdoms; but when all is said and done, you laugh at the silly champion and the Englishman who defied him and at Enguerrand, their scrivener, who drivels worse than a mustard pot. (325)]

If Panurge's vow is comparable to that of the foolish Spaniard, then by analogy the narration of Panurge's quest — that is, the *Tiers livre* itself — is clearly no less comparable to the "long narré" of the Spaniard's quest. And indeed this sequel to the *Pantagruel* has begun to look very much like Monstrelet's sequel to Froissard. The epic that began with an "insigne mutation des royaulmes" [notable mutation of kingdoms] as Pantagruel established an ideal utopian colony in Dipsodie [1:405–9 (261–64)] has now degenerated completely into a "long, curieux et fascheux compte" [long, detailed and boring story] apparently written by some "baveux" [driveling] lunatic who is as mad as Panurge. In this *mise en abyme* lodged near the center of the *Tiers livre*, Rabelais deliberately represents his book as a history without a design, and himself as a historian as foolish and unskilled as the notoriously witless, verbose Enguerrand de Monstrelet.

At the same time, Epistemon's pointed allusion to the "philosophe samosatoys" in this passage links this ironic representation of the *Tiers livre* directly to the one in the prologue, for "the philosopher of Samosata" is of course Lucian and the book in which Lucian set forth the "art et maniere d'escrire histoires" is the same book whose prologue Rabelais had already borrowed and put to such ingenious, ironic use in his own. Here again, but more explicitly this time, Rabelais alludes to Lucian's *How to Write History* as the rule by which narrative histories, including his own, must be judged. By doing so, he points ostentatiously to the fact that the Diogenic narrator of the *Tiers livre*, as a "tabellion, plus baveux qu'un pot à moustarde" (1:502) [scrivener, who drivels worse than a mustard pot (325)] like Enguerrand de Monstrelet, has indeed forgotten "l'art et maniere d'escrire histoires."

As Epistémon continues to deride Monstrelet's history in this otherwise unmotivated digression on the rules of narrative, he simultaneously brings into even sharper focus the anomalies of the *Tiers livre*: "La mocquerie est telle que de la montaigne d'Horace, laquelle crioyt et lamentoyt enormement, comme femme en travail d'enfant. A son cris et lamentation accourut tout le voisinaige, en expectation de veoir quelque admirable et monstrueux enfantement, mais enfin ne nasquit d'elle qu'une petite souriz" (1:502–3) [The mockery is like that for Horace's mountain, which kept loudly crying out and complaining, like a woman in the labor of childbirth. At her cries and lamentations all the neighborhood came running up in the expectation of seeing some wonderful and monstrous delivery; but finally all that was born of her was a little mouse (325–26)].

Behind these remarks about the mockery of laboring mountains lies a well-known proverb, "ὤδινεν ὄρος," or "parturiunt montes." Epistémon's words are borrowed directly from Erasmus's commentary on this proverb in the *Adagia* (1.9.14).[6] According to Erasmus, this proverb was used in antiquity against "braggarts and show-offs [*homines gloriosos et ostentatores*] who, with their magnificent promises and their pompous mien and attire, raise expectations of marvelous things but in the end deliver nothing but trifles [*ubi ad rem ventum est, meras nugas adferunt*]."[6] Understood in this way, the proverb of course applies perfectly to that "glorieux" and "benoist champion," Michel d'Oris, and by extension, to Panurge.

But as Erasmus also notes, the same proverb had become a commonplace of literary criticism, thanks to Horace and Lucian of Samosata, both of whom Epistemon mentions by name in his speech to Panurge.[7] In *How to Write History*, the "philosophe samosatoys" singles out for special derision those ill-composed histories whose prooemia are "brilliant, dramatic, and excessively long," promising Herodotean "marvelous things" only to be belied by a narrative "so meager and base" that the work as a whole resembles a small child wearing the mask of Hercules or a Titan. The audience of such a history will immediately hoot: "ὤδινεν ὄρος" (Lucian 1968, 23 [32–34]).

In the *Ars poetica*, Horace used the same proverb to make precisely the same point, not about history but about epic. If an epic poet were to begin his poem with a tumescent line like, " 'Of the fortunes of Priam I sing and great and famous war' " ["Fortunam Priami cantabo et nobile bellum"] (Horace, 137 [Loeb 462]), what could he possibly deliver that would live up to such a promise? Horace's ironic answer to this rhetorical question is the proverb, "parturient montes, nascetur ridiculus mus" [mountains will labor, to birth will come a laughter-arousing mouse] (Horace, 139 [462]).

Understood in this way, as a critical commonplace having to do with overblown prooemia and epic incipits that promise wonders only to be belied by the work that follows, the proverb applies perfectly to that "baveux" chronicler of the Hundred Years' War, Enguerrand de Monstrelet, and by extension to Rabelais, the "tabellion" of Panurge's foolish and utterly inconsequential quest. In this completely ironic *mise en abyme* placed near the center, as in the Diogenic emblem placed at the beginning, Rabelais points ostentatiously to the fact that the *Tiers livre* is indeed a highly irregular and that he, the author of that successful epic, the *Pantagruel*, has forgotten — or rather — deliberately chosen to ignore not only the "art et maniere d'escrire histoires" but, as Epistemon's explicit allusion to Horace suggests, the rules of writing classical epic as well.[8]

The norms of writing with which both Lucian and Horace are concerned in the passages to which Epistemon alludes have to do specifically with proportion and congruence among parts and more generally with the arrangement and function of parts within an organic whole. Lucian, immediately after mocking inflated prooemia and quoting the proverb of the laboring mountain, continues, "It should not be so, I think; rather all parts must be similar in nature and tone and the rest of the body must be proportionate to the head, so that the helmet will not be made of gold while the breastplate is a ridiculous thing made of rags and rotten hides sewn together willy-nilly, the shield made of wicker, and the shin guards of pigskin" (Lucian 1538, 23 [34]). Similarly, Horace, after quoting the same proverb and praising the first two lines of the *Odyssey* as a model epic incipit, goes on to say, "Nor does [Homer] begin his poem about the Trojan War with the twins hatched from an egg [*ab ovo*], but always hastens toward the end [*semper ad eventum festinat*], plunging his listeners into the middle of things [*in medias res*] as if the circumstances were already known to them, leaving out whatever he thinks he cannot make interesting in the telling, and contriving through a mixture of truth and falsehood to make the middle harmonize with the beginning, and the end with the middle" (Horace, 147–52[462]).[9]

These questions of composition and design, linked to the image of the laboring mountain, are in fact major preoccupations throughout Lucian's *How to Write History* and Horace's *Ars poetica* and are announced as such from the beginning of each work. Lucian, as already mentioned, defines his subject in the prologue as the art of knowing how not to "stray from the straight path, and from the thing toward which it leads," and knowing "what kind of beginning to begin with, what kind of order to impose on the parts, what proportions to give to each part, what to leave out, what to dwell on, what to mention only in passing, and how to express and arrange everything harmoniously" (Lucian 1538, 6[8]).[10] Horace suggest the same thing negatively in the opening lines of the *Ars poetica* with his well-known image of the ill-composed work: "If a painter should join a horse's neck to a human head, add feathers to various limbs assembled from a variety of different animals so that what began as a beautiful woman ends as an ugly black fish, who would not burst out laughing at the sight? Believe me, Pisos, exactly like such a painting would be the book whose fictions are as incoherent as a sick man's dreams, so that neither its foot nor its head belongs to a single, coherent form" (Horace, 1–9[450]).[11]

From all of this we may identify two fundamental rules of historical and epic narrative, or perhaps one fundamental rule stated in two different ways, once statically and once dynamically: (1) the various parts must be congruent and proportional and must cohere as an integrated, organic work with a beginning, a middle, and an end; and (2) the work must be endowed from the beginning with a clear direction and finality and must progress quickly and ineluctably toward its end.

These fundamental rules are the ones Rabelais's epic history most conspicuously and systematically violates. Contrary to the first, static rule, the beginning, middle, and end are so incongruous as to seem to belong to three entirely different works. Contrary to the second, dynamic rule, far from beginning with a crisis (*in medias res*) and hurrying toward its end (*semper ad eventum festinat* (Horace 148 [462]), the book finds its direction only belatedly, progresses through the quest in the most desultory, circuitous manner, and never even approaches the telos toward which it should be moving swiftly and inexorably. To restate both points in terms of Horace's famous comparison, the *Tiers livre* resembles one of those composite, heterogeneous figures that start as a beautiful woman, degenerate into a chimera made of unrelated, plume-bedecked parts, only to end "turpiter atrum in piscem" or, as the French say, "en queue de poisson."

While the sequel to the *Pantagruel* is a unique and unprecedented book then, it is not quite true to say that it conforms to no known literary model. Rabelais's ironic, strategically placed representations of his work are designed to reveal that the *Tiers livre* conforms exactly to Lucian's and Horace's famous descriptions of what a history and an epic *should not be*.

The fact that Rabelais points so deliberately to the apparent ineptness of his book does more than simply confirm our initial impression of its anomalousness. It reveals that Rabelais knows perfectly well what he is doing. Despite all appearances, he is a self-conscious, self-ironic narrator who is in complete control of this highly irregular and apparently aimless narrative.

This being the case, we are not really at liberty to dismiss the formal anomalousness of the *Tiers livre* as something accidental and indifferent to the meaning of the book. It will simply not do to call this a Menippean satire and go on studying the individual scenes and episodes in isolation from one another, as if their position relative to each other and their place within the larger whole were of no consequence. On the contrary, we have to ask: Why does the *Tiers livre* so deliberately subvert the norms and forms of narrative history and of epic? Why are the beginning, middle, and end made to look as though they do not belong together, or that they appear in reverse order: end-middle-beginning? Why does the quest not end? Why is it so repetitive and its telos indefinitely deferred? In short, why is this epic sequel a perfect antiepic?

Only when we start asking questions like these will the real coherence and design of this strange book become evident and its meaning begin to be intelligible.[12]

# Richard Regosin

# Opening Discourse

After a long tradition of reading the prologue to the *Tiers livre* as the complex and veiled presentation of Rabelais's attitudes towards contemporary political, religious, and military events, we have developed in recent decades a better sense of its properly literary preoccupations. Thanks in large measure to Floyd Gray's insistence in his 1963 study, "Structure and Meaning in the Prologue to the *Tiers livre*," that the prologue be read as an artistic creation that both defines and demonstrates the norms and mechanisms of its own verbal production, we now speak routinely of the ways in which the text thematizes and illustrates the circularity of writing, the question of literary inspiration, the dangers of empty rhetoric, and the writer's anxiety about his readership. In this light, the prologue to the *Tiers livre* takes its place alongside the prefaces to *Gargantua* and to *Pantagruel* as another instance of Rabelais's self-reflexive writing, another expression of both the program of his writing and the problems it generates for the writer as well as for the reader.[1]

Read in this way, Rabelais's prologue appears to fulfill the traditional role of the liminary text by creating a horizon of expectation about writing and reading. The narrative persona invites the reader into a farcical text, into the space of spontaneous writing, of verbal proliferation and play, of circular movement, and of his own anxiety about the novelty of his form, thereby pointing the way to questions of genre, language, composition, authorial authority, and interpretation that are continuing obsessions of Rabelais's writing. But while the *Tiers livre* is certainly about writing, it is not exclusively and, some might say not even primarily about writing. It is also about things political, religious, economic, philosophical, legal, and sexual, about debts, marriage, paternity, and power, about knowledge and self-knowledge. But the prologue has little or nothing to say about this. In form and theme, there are no references to character, plot, or structure or to their meaning, not a word of anticipation about Panurge and his quest, nothing to shape the reader's expectations about Pantagruel or Pantagruelion. Much of what lies beyond on the horizon is not anticipated by the prologue and, conversely, some of what is in the prologue does not appear on the horizon. The narrator's concern with the reception of his innovative form and his desire to exclude hostile readers point outside the text and do not surface explictly as such at the discursive level of the *Tiers livre*. Other elements, like the narrator's digressive style and his final descent into madness, appear excessive or supplementary to the text that follows and to the anticipatory function of the prologue.

Rabelais's prologue thus enacts the uneasy and paradoxical opening to the *Tiers livre*, like all prologues neither wholly a self-effacing opening to the succeeding text nor wholly closed off and autonomous. It plays its conventional role by looking beyond itself and to the text it introduces to set readerly expectations, but not entirely or exclusively. It also looks outside of itself to history to confront its own enemies, and it looks as well into itself, into the working of its own discursive "inside." In fact, we might say that wherever the prologue looks, it is always also looking at itself, for its concerns are always self-reflexive, its preoccupations are always the mirror of its own composition and its reception. In this sense, the prologue reflects the writer, it is in the most profound way the image of writerly expectations and self-conscious writing, the image of the generation of writing itself. Perhaps all prologues to a greater or lesser extent serve writers as much as readers. Perhaps they have as much to do with writing as with reading, with setting writing in motion, with finding or determining authorial or narrative voice, mastering discourse, or establishing authority as they have to do with creating horizons for the reader. I want to argue that the prologue to the *Tiers livre* is most significantly a writer's prologue, which performs what might be called opening discourse not only as an instance of that generic form of prefatory writing we described earlier but more centrally as an instance of the opening itself of discourse, the pre-ambulary movement of writing that makes writing itself possible.[2]

Let me reiterate here, by way of opening, what we already know well: that a prologue opens the order of reading rather than of writing, that its placement at the opening is a rhetorical move that reverses and misrepresents the order of the writing. To fulfill its time-honored role of anticipating the text and the reading to come, the prologue must await their conclusion. Only in retrospect, with full knowledge of the ground already covered, can that ground be defined and its future crossings conditioned. These commonplaces bear repeating only because I want to propose that the prologue to the *Tiers livre* acts as if it anticipates the writing as well as the reading; it acts as if it were the necessary prelude to the generation of the text itself, a way of starting up without which writing itself could not occur. Rabelais's metaphor for textual production, as the prologue to the *Tiers livre* reminds us, figures writing as wine in a barrel, and his words seem at times to suggest that writing flows spontaneously from the verbal spigot, mature and full-bodied, onto the page. But the prologue to the *Tiers livre* also demonstrates that the opening of writing is a process that stutters and drifts as its seeks its way, a process that, like language itself, is unstable and unmasterable, and that constantly defies and escapes the full control of the writer.

In a sense, each of Rabelais's books raises the issue of opening discourse both by the sequence of textual material through which the reader passes from the opening of the book and by the questions of authorship, textuality, reading, and interpretation opened by the prologues. In their physical form and disposition, the books set before us the question of where the text opens. Where, for example, in the sequence of title pages, prefatory *dizains* and dedicatory letters, the *privilège du roi*, the prologues, the first chapters of the fiction, does the reading begin? The staggered appearance of the *Quart livre* as eleven chapters in 1548 and the completed sixty-seven in 1552 dramatizes the problem of openings by creating a different prologue for each of the publications. In *Gargantua* and *Pantagruel*, the prologues reveal their explicit thematic concern with the problematical origins and authorization of narrative discourse and with the ways in which it can be or should be read, and they enact as well the complex discourse that inaugurates the coming into prominence of the printed word. These few remarks suggest that we might have opened the discussion of opening discourse in a number of ways. I have chosen to concentrate on the *Tiers livre*, but I submit that there is both historical and textual support for proposing that here opening discourse functions dramatically and specifically to enact the opening of writing itself.

Twelve years separate the *Tiers livre* from the publication of *Gargantua* and, while it is difficult to know precisely what significance to attach to this hiatus between books, we might sense that the passage of time alone would complicate the process of starting to write again. More significantly, readers are almost unanimous in their belief that the *Tiers livre* represents a thematic and formal break with Rabelais's prior writing, a shift in critical preoccupation that some, like Floyd Gray, take to be almost complete: "Rabelais commence le *Tiers livre* à partir de zéro, sans l'appui d'une forme extérieure et sans connaître sa destination. Il lui reste des personnages qui ont déjà épuisé toutes les possibilités de la trame des *Grandes Chroniques* et à qui il faut suppléer une nouvelle nécessité romanesque. Il y a donc une coupure ici dans l'élaboration de l'écriture rabelaisienne" (Gray 1974, 125).

From the outset, the *Tiers livre* does stand apart in a number of striking ways. It is the first book in which Rabelais inscribes his own name and where he speaks in his own voice in the prologue, eschewing the narrative mask provided by Alcofribas. Its subject matter does depart radically from the parodic lives of the giant-heroes of the first two books to situate Panurge at its center and inaugurate the quest motif that will structure the last three books. Panurge may in fact be the appropriate figure for the *Tiers livre* for he too seems to start from zero, an orphan of unknown origin, a man without a genealogy, a character who appears full-blown from nowhere.

Even as we emphasize difference and privilege openings, we want to remind ourselves that no writing starts from zero. In the most profound sense all writing has antecedents, as Rabelais's texts so forcefully demonstrate. All writing rewrites prior writing, even and especially when it sets off in a new direction and when it does not know its destination. To use our own terms, we can say that no opening discourse opens absolutely, that the opening irresistibly and in spite of itself has always already opened. This is the lesson we drew from outlining the sequence of texts that open Rabelais's books. It is the case also of the *Tiers livre*, whatever its efforts to turn away from the past and to open anew. The author who signs his name for the first time had already inscribed it in anagrammatic form, scrambled, hidden but still present in the earlier books. The prologue he composes had already been written in part as the story of Diogenes that Lucian recounts in *Quomodo historia scribenda est* [*How to Write History*], which Rabelais rewrites to justify his writing.[3] This is, as the title informs us, the third book in a series, a book that entitles itself *Tiers livre* to mark its filiation, to insert itself in a genealogy, to claim a past as a way of identifying itself and entitling itself to open on its own and swerve from the story of the heroic deeds of the noble Pantagruel. Not surprisingly, in this book Rabelais claims ownership of *Gargantua* and *Pantagruel* in his own name and even promises a fourth in the future. In terms of its characters and of the thematic tension between them, the *Tiers livre* already had its opening in the first two books, in the dutiful, socialized sons of the giant-kings and in the maverick orphan Panurge, whom Pantagruel loved all his life. In structural terms, the narrative reaches back to its intertext in the *Grandes Chronicques*, where Gargantua served at King Arthur's court, to reopen the generic quest of medieval romance, as Carla Freccero has recently argued (Freccero 1991, 146–75). It may not be entirely coincidental that the quest shapes this particular book, for the quest, with its multiple departures and deferred endings, with its structures of repetition and its concern with origin, appears an appropriate form for the complex and problematical workings of openings, that inaugurate and perpetuate, that open to the future and link to the past.

Keeping the inaugural and reiterative openings in mind, let us return now to the opening discourses of the *Tiers livre* and most significantly to the prologue. What in fact is the opening discourse of the *Tiers livre*? Is it the title page that speaks of the author and for the author in his own name in an unusual address to the reader: "L'auteur susdict supplie les Lecteurs benevoles, soy reserver à rire au soixante et dixhuytiesme livre" (1:389) [The aforesaid author implores his kindly readers to refrain from laughing until the seventy-eighth book (247)]? Is it the *dizain* dedicated to Marguerite de Navarre, invoking her patronage to add stature and legitimacy to the writing? The "privilège du roi," establishing the political and legal authority to write? The prologue? Or is it the opening chapter that apparently inaugurates the fictional narrative and mirrors that opening by thematizing political beginnings, the establishing and maintaining of authority in the newly conquered land of Dipsodie? Is it chapter 2, which speaks of Panurge for the first time? Chapter 6, which introduces the central marriage theme? Chapter 7, in which Panurge himself begins to speak of marriage, or chapter 9, in which he poses the specific question of whether he should marry and opens the quest that structures the narrative? This proliferation of openings suggests that our initial question is a moot one, that in fact there is no opening discourse per se. We find ourselves confronted with multiple openings, with openings that have already opened, as we said, and that delay and defer the opening. The opening of Rabelais's *Tiers livre* demonstrates that what is proper to opening is that there is no opening proper and no proper opening.

The texts that comprise the opening of Rabelais's *Tiers livre* have as their effect to draw our attention to the complex process of opening the text and to how we are to open our reading. I want now to shift my perspective from issues of reading to the problem of writing the opening, although this too is for us an issue of reading. Perhaps the perseverated openings of Rabelais's books testify to what we readers also know as writers, that writing the opening is as difficult to master as reading it. How does the writer open the discourse entitled "prologue," as the discourse that precedes and opens the way, and what does that opening tell us?

Most readings of the prologue imply that it opens with the story of Diogenes and that the story of Diogenes is what the prologue is

about.[4] But the writing itself does not open there. The narrator
Rabelais may want to tell that story, but he does not or cannot begin
by recounting it in any simple way. He begins instead with a conventional address to familiar readers, with a formula that links his
writing to tradition and past practice and that facilitates his first
incursion onto the blank page. Whatever interpretive problems this
particular address to "Bonnes gens, Beuveurs tresillustres, et vous
Goutteux tresprecieux" (1:393) [Good folk, most illustrious topers,
and you, most precious poxies (253)] may have for us as readers, it
serves the writing by calling up a readership within the text to whose
call the writing can respond, it invents the audience without which
no literary invention can come into being.

Rabelais thus begins to write. He can write the name Diogenes as
he asks his reader, "Veistez vous oncques Diogenes, le philosophe
cynic?" (1:393) [Did you ever see Diogenes, the cynic philosopher?
(253)], but he cannot yet tell the story of Diogenes. In writing that is
already rewriting, that resonates with echoes of other texts and previous reading of the Gospels, Lucian, Erasmus and Budé, in writing
that teems with commonplace allusions and lowbrow puns, that
jumbles the sacred and the profane and mixes elements of written
and popular oral culture, the narrator produces an errant discourse.
He plays with words, commits verbal lapses, forgets about grammatical antecedents, asserts the obvious in the name of truth and
logic. Then he wanders off after surmising that the reader has at least
heard about Diogenes to evoke by association the genealogy of the
French and the large ears they inherited from the Phrygians, Midas's
donkey ears, Persian spies, and an unknown legend of "Belles aureilles." Just as the ears of the narrator's digression are deferred in
synecdochic substitution by the Phrygians, Midas, the "Otacustes,"
and "je ne sçay quoi" until they emerge as the "Belles aureilles" at the
end of the passage, Diogenes himself is displaced into a pronoun
after the initial mention of his name in the second line of the prologue ("Si l'avez veu," "Si veu ne l'avez," "avez vous ouy de luy
parler," "Si n'en avez ouy parler" (1:393–94) ["If you have seen
him," "If seen him you have not," "you have heard speak of him,"
"If you haven't heard of him" (253)], and his return is deferred until

he reappears as Diogenes Sinopien when Rabelais finally comes to tell his story.

Rabelais's opening thus enacts a vagabond, decentered discourse that displays a strong centrifugal tendency, an inclination to wander or to fly off on its own. It appears to have a subject in mind, a course it seeks to follow, and a story it wants to tell, but it cannot follow that course in any simple linear way. Nor can it simply tell its story. The discourse proceeds by moving tangentially, by diverging, and by a process of superficial association, substitution, and displacement that appears inevitably to defer the expression of its object. This is a contingent rather than a necessary movement and one that always risks losing itself in its own unfolding. Some readers might object that Rabelais the narrator is simply speaking to his audience and that this movement follows the spontaneous flow of oral discourse. Claiming that it reveals something about writing would thus be making too much out of it. But we must keep in mind that Rabelais is writing the prologue and that his preoccupation here is with the generation, composition, and reception of the written word, the book. Even if the writing looks or sounds like oral discourse, even if it seems to resemble speech, this resemblance is a consequence of the writing. It is a stylistic effect generated by the text, a deft illusion of oral discourse produced by the writer and not orality itself. The problems of writing the oral, like the problems of any other writing style, are the problems of writing itself.

As it seeks its way through its discourse, the writing of the prologue enacts a movement that is in every sense excessive. Rabelais's opening discourse apparently cannot occur without producing more than it intends or, we might say, more than it needs to say what it has to say. When the writer writes or when the reader reads, regardless of the meaning imputed to the discourse, there is always something that cannot be accounted for in strictly logical or linear terms, something that appears to be surplus and that clamors to be heard. From the narrow perspective of the logical and the linear, the narrow perspective of a narrative line, for example, excess may appear to be an empty discursive by-product, something to be evacuated and eliminated. Some readers have treated the prologue to the *Tiers livre* in this way, ignoring the rambling of Rabelais's opening discourse and doing what the writing itself cannot do, that is, proceeding straight through it to the story of Diogenes. But such excess can never be entirely set aside by the reader or wholly expelled from his discourse by the writer, because it is already in discourse, it is already what discourse is. Rabelais's prologue indicates that there is no discourse without excess, it shows that discourse needs the excess in order to be itself and to move toward whatever it intends to express. There is always the possibility that, knowing no bounds, discourse in its congenital excess will run on in vacuous proliferation. But it is also true that the fullness and complexity of writing and textuality are products of discursive excess and that it has its role to play in the constitution of meaning, even or especially in the meaning of emptiness.

There is then what we might take as an opening ritual, where the writer moves obliquely and haltingly toward his subject, a preambulary gesture whose movement is determined by the nature of discourse itself. This preamble to the story of Diogenes also enacts a certain clearing of the ground, an opening of the space which the narrative can then occupy. Rabelais begins with two questions addressed to his readers: Have they seen Diogenes? Have they heard speak of him? The assumption of a negative reply ("Si veu ne l'avez," "Si n'en avez ouy parler") creates the void that forces him to continue speaking. Only when he affirms or assumes that the readers do not know of Diogenes can he say, "De luy vous veulx presentement une histoire narrer" (1:394) [I want to tell you now a story (253)]. Only then can he will to speak and impose his will, announce the narrative and embark on its telling.

While I have chosen to emphasize the deferral of the story of Diogenes, both in Rabelais's words and in the general movement of the opening, it is essential to note the paradoxical truth that the narrative has already begun. In preparing to speak of Diogenes, Rabelais has already been speaking of him or, perhaps more precisely, he has been speaking of speaking of him. The opening to discourse is also the opening of discourse, as our remarks on the so-called prefatory texts of the *Tiers livre* have already suggested. Preambulary writing, whether we are referring to title pages, dedicatory poems, or prologues or whether we intend the opening within writing itself, preambulary writing is already writing just as all writing is in some sense always preambulary. We asked earlier, where does discourse open? Rabelais's opening discourse would seem to suggest Derrida's often misquoted remark about Lautréamont by way of a response, "Il n'y a que du texte, il n'y a que du hors-texte, au total une 'préface incessante'" (Derrida 1972, 50).

The story of Diogenes serves the writer to define his own activity, for it is only through the appropriation of previous discourse and the mediation of his own experience that the writer establishes or discovers what he wants to be and what he is doing. Rabelais presents the narrative as an allegory of his own activity; like all allegories, it requires interpretation. There is to begin with the problem of the meaning of Diogenes's symbolic actions, actions that are not meant to be taken literally and that need to be read. The story is first of all the writer's reading, a reading inscribed in the writing itself, in the elements of its composition (the cynical philosopher, the preparations for war, the rolling of the cask) and in its formal characteristics (its excess description, its juxtaposition of substantive and verbal weight, its image of Sisyphus). It is also Diogenes's reading, since, as he performs for others in a play of pure spectacle, he also reads his own actions explicitly, interpreting and explaining what he is doing for a friend who apparently cannot read: "Ce voyant quelq'un de ses amis, luy demanda quelle cause le mouvoit à son corps, son esprit, son tonneau ainsi tormenter. Auquel respondit le philosophe . . ." (1:397) [Seeing this, one of his friends asked him what cause impelled him thus to torment his body, his spirit, and his barrel. To which the philosopher replied . . . (256)]. And Rabelais reads as narrator. "Je pareillement" (1:397) [I, likewise (256)], he says, openly allegorizing as he appropriates the elements of Diogenes's story to recount his own, telling yet another narrative intended to situate him and to impart meaning to his action.

In this repetition of narratives, Rabelais is writing and writing about writing, performing his efforts to find his way and making the performance itself the way to that finding. In the most profound way, Rabelais is still moving toward the opening of discourse, he is still groping towards what he wants to say, even as he is already saying it. Rolling his cask, like Diogenes, he will be active and perhaps useful, and like Lucian and Budé before him he will write. But from that linear perspective we just referred to, this circularity, this endless repetition, appears the very sign of excess and of emptiness. So the writer turns back upon himself and his writing, describing another circle, to question reflectively where he is going and how he should proceed. Addressing himself to his reader, he asks, "a ce triballement de tonneau, que feray-je en vostre advis?" (1:398) [by this dingledangling of my barrel, what do you think I will accomplish?" (257)]. Rabelais answers his own question: "Par la vierge qui se rebrasse, je ne sçay encores" (1:398) [By the virgin tucking up her skirts, I don't know yet (257)]. The writing admits or declares its uncertain status, it reveals that it doesn't know yet what it is or what it is doing, it still doesn't know where it is going as it turns round and round. Perhaps it only knows that it is doing and going. "I don't know yet," the writer says, or "I still don't know," but the *encores* seem to suggest that the writing is searching to define itself in process, as if only in the writing, only from the writing in all its circular excess, can form and intention emerge to take it beyond the mere performance of its opening. Circularity and excess are not "nothing"; rather, as we suggested, they are the necessary and unavoidable accompaniments of any discursive move, even or especially of the move ahead.

At this point, there is a thematic pause. There is no pause in the writing, even though we might have anticipated that it would surrender to its ignorance and uncertainty and abandon its pursuit: "Attendez un peu que je hume quelque traict de ceste bouteille: c'est mon vray et seul Helicon, c'est ma fontaine caballine, c'est mon unicque enthusiasme" (1:398) [Wait a minute while I sniff down a snifter from this bottle; it's my one real Helicon. It's my Caballine spring, my one and only enthusiasm" (257)]. Having nourished itself on classical and contemporaneous subtexts, such as Lucian, Erasmus, and Budé, to sustain the Diogenic allegory, the writing now imbibes in the long tradition that seeks inspiration in wine, that conflates the philosophic and the bacchic, and thus it keeps itself going.[5] It inserts itself in the lineage of Ennius, Aeschylus, Plutarch, Homer, and Cato to give itself a genealogy that makes wine the origin of writing and writing the generator of drinking. Once its source and origin are established, the writing can proceed and announce a "sort" and a "destinée": "Puys doncques que telle est ou ma sort ou ma destinée" (1:399) [So since it is my lot or destiny (257)]. It can proceed to say what it is doing and where it is going.

The writer intends his writing to serve. He intends to build like the gods who built the walls of Troy, like Amphion whose music caused the stones to move and form the walls of Thebes. It turns out, of course, that Rabelais does not build this grandiose public building, he does not become the chronicler of the epic deeds of France's warriors. He has erred in the prologue to the *Tiers livre*. But that is the point, for in this error and the errant discourse in which it occurs, in this wandering and digressive writing that is also a mistake, Rabelais finds his calling as writer, a degraded Amphion perhaps, but an Amphion nonetheless. He can now situate this writing and what is to come in relation to his previous two books and thus confirm its lineage. He can now speak of his writing as draughts drawn from his barrel, this the gallant third and a jovial fourth draught of "Sentences Pantagruelicques" to come. The writing encourages our playful use of the English "draught," the confusion of written drafts and draughts of wine, the transfer from Bacchus, which lends to discourse not only its inspiration but its intoxicated frenzy and unbridled motion as well. When the writing in Rabelais's opening discourse locates its inspiration, it also discloses its tenuous control. In its errant movement, it recovers what it intends and discovers the parody of its intention, and in its puns, lapses, and "contrepetries" and in its mistaken identity, it demonstrates a certain mastery over language and reveals that language invariably eludes the master's grasp to generate its own signification.

The problem of the writer's mastery over his own discourse is mirrored in his lack of control over the reader's reception and use of that discourse. When discourse opens, how can the writer be certain that his intention will be appreciated, his meaning understood? How can he be assured that he will not deceive the expectations of his readers? The story of the Bactrian camel and the bicolored slave that mediates Rabelais's anxiety makes clear that the writing is a gift, offered to please his readers and elicit their love. But like all gifts and like language itself, it eludes the authority of the donor and author. The prologue's opening address to the "Bonnes gens, Beuveurs tresillustres, et . . . Goutteux tresprecieux" called up readers favorably inclined, familiar and receptive readers with whom the writer could play and joke and share his errant discourse as he would share a draught of wine. But there are other readers out there as well, perhaps even those whom he would seek to entertain and the warriors whose praises he would sing. And not only out there. These readers inhabit the writing, unnamed, anonymous, present only as the object pronouns that identify them, faceless readers capable of turning the writer's treasure to coal. To them, Rabelais ascribes the quality of Pantagruelism. He seeks to assure his success by imputing to them the unwillingness to take in bad part anything that they know to spring from a good, honest, and loyal heart. The story of the camel and the slave who, for lack of appreciation, exchanged life for death and that of Eudio's cock, which had its throat cut for its pains, are countered by another fiction in the hope of neutralizing them, that of the writer rescued by the generous and benevolent reader.

But there is more to the story. Even as the writer has said all that needs to be said to assure himself of his readership, even as he invites his friends and readers to drink[6] or not to drink, if they so desire, as if this writing is now completed, even, finally, as he plays the "Architriclin" and imposes his authority as the organizer of the festival ("Tel est mon decret" (1:401), he says), the writing is invaded by unwanted and uninvited readers, menacing and maddening. The writer can express his will and evoke his authority, but he cannot finally control who reads and how they misread. Over and above problems of meaning and interpretation inherent in any writing, problems generated by the way signs escape authorial intention and lend themselves to diverse and multiple understanding, there are real and dangerous enemies, powerful forces and institutions, disguised and hypocritical adversaries who stifle and suppress discourse. In the diabolical final scene which plays out the repressive politics of reading itself, these hounds of hell set upon the modern Diogenes, the dog, reducing him to a snarling mastiff fighting to sink his teeth into the curs who attack him. This reduction is also the reduction and muzzling of discourse.

The prologue to the *Tiers livre* thus performs what we might call the mimesis of its production, the uncertain and tentative opening of discourse, its insecure, digressive, and excessive movement toward the discovery of intent. It enacts the anxiety of its reception, its apprehension of being mistaken and misread. What is at stake is not the mediation of a truth that effaces the production, such as the truth of nature, which is outside of itself, but the truth of production itself, the action, rhythm, and practice of writing. The opening discourse also discloses, perhaps in spite of itself, its own precarious existence and that of all discourse, that is, the possibility that instead of continually opening up, it will close down, instead of going or flowing on, it will dry up and stop or be stopped up. Rabelais's narrator assures his readers, the "compaings," the "enfans," the "Beuveur [and] Gotteux de bien," that his cask is inexhaustible, its source endless. He suggests that, even if, at times, it may seem to be empty to the lees, it will not be dry. But Terence Cave has shown us how the celebration of fullness, of copia, reveals an inverse movement toward emptiness or absence and how, in this context, the examples of copiousness represented by the Danaides, Tantalus, and Pandora's box function to undermine the cornucopian ideal.[7] The seemingly self-generating impulse of Rabelais's writing, its production of excessive discourse, its centrifugal and digressive tendencies, all seem to express the unfailing perpetuation of his text, but are also signs of the potential for vain and impotent textuality. Even more is at stake here than textual plenitude, for the images of the empty barrel suggest not only the possibility of empty discourse but the possibility of the end of discourse. Don't be afraid that the wine will run out, as it did in Cana, Rabelais says, but "don't be afraid" means here that there is indeed reason to fear, that the barrel that seems only to be empty to the lees can indeed dry up. There is no assurance that discourse can open, there is no guarantee that it can proceed, and there is no certainty that it will not shut down or be shut off. But the stunning paradox of the prologue to the *Tiers livre*, a paradox that implicates all literature, is that it is precisely this uncertainty and fear, this anxiety and insecurity, that produce Rabelais's discourse, that are in fact his inspiration, and that fill the barrel from which he draws his text. The fear of not producing or of producing nothing has in fact given rise to some thing that is the opening of discourse.

# Jean-Claude Margolin

# Rabelais, Erasmus's Intellectual Heir?

My topic is not a new one. Many historians of literature, specializing in Renaissance time and civilization, have written books or articles on the intellectual and, so to speak, spiritual relations between two giants of European humanism.[1] Moreover, today, the influence of Erasmus on Rabelais is well acknowledged, if not well known. Some critics have underlined the convergence of many linguistic or semiotic reflections and sociopolitical, sociocultural, and socioreligious themes on the problems of education, marriage, war, peace, and so on. Michael Screech has shown in his book *Rabelais* the great number and the importance of the borrowings of the French novelist from Erasmus's *Annotations to the New Testament*, one of the most significant texts of the Dutch Christian humanist for our knowledge of his religious viewpoint about most of theological, social, and ethical problems of his time and our own.[2]

We can recollect the first lines of Rabelais's famous letter to Erasmus: "I have called you 'father,' I would also call you 'mother,' if by your indulgence that were permitted me" (Frame, 746). Rabelais then tries to justify his enthusiastic judgment and devotion, developing the parallel with women carrying children in their wombs, feeding and protecting them from the unpleasant and dangerous miasma in the air around them.

Erasmus was for Rabelais the prime master of culture, a famous editor or translator of many Greek and Latin texts from the classical authors to the most celebrated church fathers. Rabelais worked on Hippocrates and Galen; Erasmus had translated at least three of

Galen's short and philosophical tracts into Latin.[3] They held the same views on freedom and will and on the relationship between nature and reason, in spite of some differences of accent. Human reason, for both of them, must be in harmony with nature, both with a person's individual nature and with nature in general, that great world or universal nature created by God and human reason, which Paracelsus called "macrocosmos."[4]

Most of Rabelais's thoughts on education agree with those of Erasmus.[5] Their enemies are the same — medieval grammarians and scholastic theologians, lost in the clouds of a purely formal dialectic and imprisoned in the obscure arcanes of empty dogmatism. They attack the same methods and the same philosophical background, as we can see in the *De pueris* and the *Dialogus de recta pronuntiatione* (Erasmus ASD I-4 1973, 1–103) and in Gargantua's letter to Pantagruel (Frame, 158–62). Both make fun of the old and obsolete textbooks and ways of teaching and schooling; both are deeply shocked at the various marks of mental and physical cruelty against young schoolboys, deriving from genuine sadism. Both are determined propagandists of a highly liberal education, a true preparation for life, for a professional, civic, and religious life.

My first point will lay great stress on Erasmus and Rabelais as praisers of folly. As Walter Kaiser shows in *Praisers of Folly*, they are different and close at the same time. I think that most of their ideas have derived from their approaches to man and folly, folly in man and outside. My second point will deal with the authors' religious conception, Christian folly being a link between the first and the second points. And because Erasmus and Rabelais are great prose writers, Erasmus in Latin and Rabelais in French, my third point will consist of a short comparative analysis of two different styles, two ways of having a dialogue with readers, both of their time and of the future.[6]

It would be foolish to look at *The Praise of Folly* as a microcosm of Erasmus's works and thoughts.[7] We know that Erasmus later retracted some of his work, regretting having caused some trouble in the minds of respectful people or having offended the representatives of social or religious institutions. But in his defense against his detractors, Erasmus tells us that he had no other purpose in writing his *Praise of Folly* than in his fully Christian *Enchiridion militis christiani* (CWE 1988, 66:1–127).[8] Professor Halkin agrees, as he proved in Tours in his paper "A Religious Pamphlet of the Sixteenth Century: *The Praise of Folly*." I will try to show that the "jocoseria declamatio" is the best expression of Erasmus's deepest thoughts, his affective and intellectual ego.[9]

The sermon of the goddess Folly is full of knowledge, quotations, and references; it looks like a magnificent piece of classical and Renaissance rhetoric; it uncovers most of the social, political, or religious problems of the time; it is a door open on the world as it is and as it ought to be. Since Folly, who is both a woman and a goddess, speaks in the first person, Erasmus is more of an observer, so that author and reader experience to the utmost degree what I call ironic self-consciousness.

In Erasmian folly, we find at the same time the figure of the medieval fool and the ironic profile of the humanist of the Renaissance. So will it be with Rabelais. Dame Folly and the gigantic, ludicrous, but so human beings of Gargantua and Pantagruel act as reflective and distorting mirrors for their literary fathers and for the reader's self-consciousness.

The fool may reflect what I am, what I want to be, or what I appear to be; at other times, the fool may be my opposite, showing what I do not want to be or to appear. The fool is an ambivalent figure, hence his function, as deciphered by Robert Klein (1963) as an instrument of self-comprehension.

This ambivalent figure generates not only a series of paradoxes, as well as pleas for and against marriage, war, and folly, but also a paradoxical text corresponding to the ambiguous conscience of humanity.[10] As a writer who keeps his distance from his spokeswoman instead of speaking for himself and for us, Erasmus built a figure divided into two and even three parts: a bad and insane folly, a good and creative folly, a divine and superhuman folly. Rabelais also created good and bad fools, Picrochole and Panurge, Pantagruel and Epistemon.

The essence of humanistic folly is precisely its ambivalence, that is to say its ability to be converted into its opposite, namely into wisdom. Of course, the personality of Erasmus and Rabelais and the special features of their works imply a sense of humor and a taste for fun that cannot be separated from the sermon of Folly or the narrative discourse of Gargantua and Pantagruel. We are not dealing here with philosophical tracts or a procession of concepts. As readers, we seem to be spectators involved in a drama while Moria and her companions on one side and the Rabelaisian giants on the other side, with their gaily colored escort, play their parts before us. But we are not unconcerned spectators, for the play is our own play, humanity's tragicomedy of life. We become at the same time actors and spectators. Folly is ironic self-consciousness and the most effective tool for the discovery of our self by ourselves.

Sometimes, the fool's figure makes people laugh, because it shows us the state and harmless pattern of an exorcised and unidimensional antihumanity. Sometimes, as the iconographic topos of a skeleton, the appearance of the fool, from the Middle Ages until the Baroque Age, invites us to a kind of Socratic meditation.[11] We should not forget that life is a meditation on death and dying. We have to remember that Socrates was regarded as a fool by most of the people of his time and perhaps by some today as well. By the medium of the double mirrored figure, as we have seen, we are able to cast our eyes towards our true nature, our true ego, stripped of every false or wrong look. No wonder the figure of Socrates is central both in Erasmus's works in general and in Rabelais's novel.[12] We once again meet with the celebrated Sileni Alcibiadis, that is with the adage of Erasmus and with the prologue of *Gargantua* (5–9) [3–5].[13]

In *Gargantua*, especially the prologue, the intellectual and religious influence of Erasmus is obvious. Everybody knows Gérard Defaux's book on *Pantagruel et les sophistes* and Raymond La Charité's pages (1986) on that topic. The seminal text of the prologue, in which the author invites his readers to go deeper and deeper into the matter of the novel is the adage of Erasmus. The "substantifique mouelle" that any right reader must discover and absorb in order to assimilate it and also to be assimilated or mixed together is the inner true self of those ludicrous and grotesque figures known as Sileni, with which Alcibiades compared Socrates in the *Banquet.*

The concrete, colored representation of the philosophical dialectic of appearance and reality had been already used before Erasmus and Rabelais. But in the history of ideas in Western civilization, it had never been expressed more vividly or more convincingly. Erasmus carries his analysis to a very high point, which Rabelais does not try to reach. The most important figure of the Erasmian Silenus is Christ himself, while Rabelais does not go beyond human boundaries. Dorothy Coleman (1971) has also noted that, in spite of the derivation of the prologue from Erasmus's adage, Rabelais makes some very meaningful changes. First, the Sileni of Erasmus and Plato, which were ornamental statuettes, have been changed into apothecaries' boxes filed with drugs, spices, and preserves. Despite some spicy remarks, Erasmus gave us a purely functional description because he intended to use this concrete figure swiftly for a philosophical and ethical purpose, that is, to demonstrate the dialectical and abstract relationship between appearance and reality. By contrast, Rabelais lingers over a picturesque description, with familiar and popular allusions, many rhetorical devices and effects, and medical words. For instance:

> (Erasmus) Open the reversed Silenus, and you find a tyrant, sometimes the enemy of his people, a hater of public peace, a sower of discord, an oppressor of the good, a curse to the judicial system, an overturner of cities, a plunderer of the Church, given to robbery, sacrilege, incest, gambling — in short, as the Greek proverb has it, an Iliad of evils. There are those who in name and appearance impose themselves as magistrates and guardians of the common weal, when in reality they are wolves and prey upon the state. There are those whom you would venerate as priests if you only looked at their tonsure, but if you look into the Silenus, you will find them more than laymen. . . . There are those . . . who, judging by their flowing beards, pale faces, hoods, bowed heads, girdles, and proud truculent expressions, might be taken for Serapio and St. Paul; but open them up, and you find mere buffoons, gluttons, vagabonds, libertines, nay, robbers and oppressors, but in another way, I dare say

more poisonous because it is more concealed — in fact, as they say, *the treasure turns out to be a lump of coal* (Mann Phillips 1964, 276–77).

(Rabelais) boites . . . pinctes au dessus de figures joyeuses et frivoles, comme de harpies, satyres, oysons bridez, lievres cornuz, canes bastées, boucqs volans, cerfz limonniers [which contain] les fines drogues comme baulme, ambre gris, amomon, musc, zivette, pierreries et aultres choses precieuses (1:5) [boxes . . . painted on the outside with merry frivolous pictures, such as harpies, satyrs, bridled goslings, saddled ducks, flying goats, harnessed stags . . . but inside they preserved fine drugs such as balm, ambergris, amomum, musk, civet, precious stones, and other valuables (3)].

We will find again these differences of style and purpose when we speak about Erasmus and Rabelais as prose writers.

The central place occupied by the Church and its representatives in Erasmus's adage as in *The Praise of Folly* leads us to another comparison between the two authors in the status of Christian folly, according to Paul's Epistle to Romans and several others texts taken from the apostle. Through a great number of chapters, Rabelais is concerned with madness of all sorts, not merely with the joyful folly of Carnaval time, as Bakhtin has written (1972). As people know, according to the Scriptures, the number of fools is infinite (Eccles. 1:15). In *The Praise of Folly*, we can contemplate the variety of fools: some are merely insane; some are self-lovers (the *philautia*, [Erasmus 1979, 17, 34–35] whom we find already in St. Bernard's works); some are gluttons and ambitious while others are naive or unconscious. Sometimes, old men fall in love with pretty girls while old women are burning with desire for intercourse with young men; some are dying for a marriage which Erasmus calls a marriage that is an un-marriage (ASD I-3 1972, 591–600). Rabelais shows us some cases of diabolical possession, while Erasmus, through Lady Moria, denounces many cases of irreligious foolishness and stupid and endless quarrels about theology and philosophy. The point is that, for Erasmus, who is following St. Paul, a complete inversion of values springs up. There is a good Christian form of madness, a divinely ordered Christian folly that is opposed to worldly wisdom. Christian folly is perfectly compatible with true wisdom, which is a gift of the spirit. We again find the ambiguity of folly, the self-division of man's consciousness.

This Christian folly of Erasmus leads us to the problem of Rabelais's religious ideas and religion. This topic was not new when Lucien Febvre raised it in *Le problème de l'incroyance au XVIe siècle* or when Abel Lefranc compiled his critical edition of Rabelais's works (Rabelais 1912–55). Nor do we claim that all Rabelaisians agree on the religious status of François Rabelais, at least based on his works. Certainly, nobody looks on Rabelais today as did the Catholic censors who condemned him as an atheistic, obscene writer. However, the problem is still open.

We are indebted to some Rabelais scholars for their deep insight into this important field, especially Michael Screech, editor of Rabelais and the author of a seminal book on Rabelais (Screech 1979b) and another on Erasmus (1980). Although Roland Crahay (1977) has shown that the word "evangelism" is ambiguous, too general, and inadequate in discussing Erasmus, it is frequently used, since Lucien Febvre, about Marot and Rabelais: Screech has published two essays, *Marot évangélique* and *L'évangélisme de Rabelais*. So long as we specify what we mean by "evangelism," it is a useful approach to Erasmus and Rabelais.

Erasmus is indeed a biblical author, an exegete, a deep connoisseur of the four Gospels and of the commentaries of the Church Fathers on these gospels.[14] He is also a commentator on the New Testament in his *Annotations* and *Paraphrases* and a commentator on old biblical commentaries.[15] For these reasons, we can call him an evangelical writer. The Bible and the church fathers are always literally and spiritually present in his writings, in those that do not concern religion or theology, as in his pedagogical tracts or in his pacifist works.[16] Moreover, some of the latter are built as commentaries on Psalms, such as his *Consultatio de bello Turcis inferendo* (ASD V–3 1986, 1–82), a commentary on Psalm 28, which exalts the virtues of peace.

The problem of Rabelais's evangelism is a little more complex. He cannot be considered a commentator on the Bible, and in his novel it is not always easy to disentangle him from his characters who are attributed many features, a great number of which are not properly evangelistic. Almost every picture of positive Christian life and creeds stands not on its own, but in contrast to satiric descriptions or ironic representations of ridiculous, crude, even cruel portrayals of representatives of the Roman Catholic institution, such as Frère Jean des Entommeurs. By contrast, in addition to Erasmus's satiric patterns of what a Christian ought not to be, there are many instances, especially in his last works, in which the fair and sublime aspects of the true religion of Christ are generously displayed.[17]

Underlined or not, the biblical references spring out everywhere in Rabelais, but they are overwhelmed by waves of comedy and are therefore not identified, especially by a modern reader.[18] Of the extraordinary birth of Gargantua, Screech writes, "In the sixteenth century, every reader of Rabelais who was more or less educated or uneducated in the Bible was able to associate Gargantua's birth and the reflections which stem from it with the miraculous conception of Sara and that of the Holy Virgin. Rabelais does not allude to either; both are under his eyes" (Screech 1979a, 2; my translation).

Our reading of Rabelais has evolved, and we are now much more impressed by the comic descriptions and the narrative discourse of Rabelais's characters than by the biblical or classical allusions aimed at other scholars of his time. For us, Rabelais is writing, in many passages, a parody of the Bible, even though Screech says, "Rabelais ne parodie point la Bible" (Screech 1979a, 12). I agree with him when he says we do not have to seek an interpretation of Rabelais in cynicism or atheism. But a parody does not necessarily mean a cynical mockery, corrosive or destructive of faith. Rabelais is winking at his learned reader, but his parody contains a good deal of humor. And humor, I believe, is not opposed to religious feelings, as Etienne Gilson has shown (1924). When he speaks of the Parisian theologians and of their arguing of faith, he resembles Erasmus, his religious father, as he suggests, but the dose or overdose of satire and irony is bigger and fiercer than that of the Dutch humanist. The boundaries between Roman Catholicism and Lutheran or Calvinist Reformation are nearly crossed.

In the same chapter about Gargantua's birth, Rabelais writes, "Pourquoy ne le croyriez vous? Pour ce (dictes vous) qu'il n'y a nulle apparence. Je vous dictz que pour ceste seule cause vous le debvez croire en foy parfaicte. Car les Sorbonistes disent que foy est argument des choses de nulle apparence" (1:31–32) [Why shouldn't you believe what I tell you? Because, you reply, there is no evidence. And I reply in turn that for just that very reason, you should believe with perfect faith. For the gentlemen of the Sorbonne say that faith is the argument of non-evident truth (Le Clercq, 23)].[19] The text is derived directly from the Epistle to the Hebrews (11:1).

The comedy of Rabelais is a comedy of circumstances. It depends on the enunciator, on his aim, and on the effects the comedy produces on the mind of the reader, on his knowledge or ignorance of the Bible and its exegesis, on his attitude towards the Doctors of Theology of the Faculty of Paris. In short, for Rabelais as for Erasmus, writing is a matter of decorum and polysemia: the good orator, not unlike the good writer, has to persuade his listeners or readers of the rightness of his cause and of his own intelligence. Saint Paul and his commentators know that this paradoxical definition of faith is meaningful, but the mocker of the Sorbonists pretends not to have understood the significance. If we stay at a literal level, we talk but we say nothing, because to speak about nothing is the same as not to speak at all.

What we can say concerning the serious problem of faith in Erasmus and in Rabelais is that, for both of them, faith is different from the traditional Christian practices, pilgrimages, cult of saints, even prayers and confession.[20] We have already noted that the Erasmian and Rabelaisian mockery of ecclesiastical institutions, ritual practices, and even the Holy Scripture are not, as thought by Abel Lefranc, signs of their Lucianism, in the sense of the theologians and the censors of the sixteenth century.[21] In *Rabelais franciscain*, Etienne Gilson rightly noted that the mockery was fully integrated into medieval traditions and philosophies and was an old clerical tradition.

Rabelais's giants continuously praise the Gospels and are full of enthusiasm when speaking of God's goodness. We find out the same true devotion in Erasmus not only at the end of Moria's sermon but in all his works. Neither author liked imposed or self-interested prayers (see, for instance, the satiric and audacious colloquy *Shipwreck* (ASD I-3 1972, 325–32), which we can compare with the chapters on the mighty tempest in the *Quart livre*). Erasmus did compose prayers of his own to Christ, the Holy Virgin, Saint Genevieve, and so on. The Rabelaisian giants summon the people to simplicity and humbleness as does Erasmus. In this sense, we can think of both authors as evangelists, that is, two Christians convinced of the human value of the evangelistic message.

I have not enough space to comment on the noticeable differences between Erasmus's and Rabelais's faith. Some interpreters have seen in the latter a Lutheran or a quasi-Lutheran, because of the high praise of faith in comparison with deeds.[22] We know that Erasmus, in his controversial tract against Luther on free will and the bondage of the will, did not try to mitigate or belittle faith against deeds, but to associate good deeds and true faith in a cooperation between man and God for his salvation.[23] Rabelais did not express his theological ideas on this topic, other than by allusions in *Gargantua* and *Pantagruel* and in his "Pantagruelique prognostication." But the reference is too little to determine whether he might have been a Lutheran or a Calvinist.

Having briefly examined a few different themes or ideas in Erasmus and in Rabelais, we should now recall that they were and remain two of the greatest writers of the sixteenth century and perhaps of all time. Let us therefore contemplate the style of their writing, first what humanists call the *varietas* or the *copia verborum*, and then its opposite, *brevitas*. We shall try to see how, in spite of the differences between their personalities and their works, the Latino-Dutch humanist's language and style of writing may have contributed to shaping Rabelais's style and literary invention.

It seems very difficult to establish a common standard between works so dissimilar as Erasmus's books and Rabelais's novel. Erasmus wrote pedagogical tracts, theological essays, commentaries on Psalms, annotations to the New Testament, paraphrases upon the Gospels, vivid dialogues, prayers, commentaries on classical proverbs, apophthegms, apologues imitated from Greek and Latin authors, and so on. Rabelais's most important work, and for many, his only work, is his gigantic novel. We have already noted one feature common to both writers: the sense and spirit of humor and a paradoxical way of thinking and writing. Humor and paradoxes, in my opinion, are characteristic of more than thought and writing; they overflow a person's entire personality, they express a way of living, a way of being. Both authors are fond of language and words; they make love to them, to borrow a phrase from Louis Aragon. They play on words, even in the most serious passages, even in the titles of their books or chapters. In *Les langages de Rabelais*, François Rigolot demonstrated the value of wordplay in persuading and triumphing over others, whether friend or enemy. Although Rabelais did not develop theories about language, Erasmus did a little in his important though poorly known tract *Lingua* (ASD IV–1A 1979). When Erasmus writes his *Enchiridion militis Christiani*, he plays "jocoseriously" on the Greek word "enchiridion," the double meaning of which is dagger and handbook, or in French "manuel" and "poignard," itself derived from "poing," the "poignard" being "une arme de poing."[24] But this symbolic arm, a book which one keeps carefully in one's hand, is not aggressive or harmful; it is an arm for self-defense against the assaults of Satan, the synthesis of all bad passions.

Another Erasmian feature of his seriocomic way of writing and acting in his dialogue with the honest (and clever) reader is linked to the name he gives to the figures of his colloquies, such as Antronius, the stupid, rude abbot whose name reminds us of an ancient land of asses, or Bonifacius and Beatus, whose faces denounce the discrepancy, if not the opposition, between words and things (*vocabula* and *res*), because Beatus is not happy and Bonifacius still looks sad.[25]

But the differences between the two writers are great. Terence Cave, in *The Cornucopian Text* (1979), has written a fine chapter on Rabelais's style and writing. He rightly notes that the French novelist has followed the classical pattern of the text seen as a cornucopia, a universal source full of *"doctrina, ratio* and *natura"* (Cave 1979, 177).[26] On Erasmus and his *copia verborum ac rerum* (Cave 1979, 178), we discover rules of theorization that Rabelais, with his inventive genius, puts into practice more or less unconsciously.[27] However, one cannot consider Erasmus either a philosopher of langauge or a theoretician of rhetoric devices or the production of a text. His best approach is to produce examples, classical references, or his own devices, sometimes inventing or recalling little stories and fables to make the reader sensitive to the idea or event or saying that he wants to implant in our brain. Erasmus takes an original approach to teaching, in direct opposition to the long, austere, and boring arguments of the Scholastics. He wants to illustrate his thought with all the techniques used by rhetoricians. Rabelais is not teaching, but as he tells his pleasant story, he pours into our head, mind, heart, and the secret recesses of our flesh a mixture of ideas, dreams, fantasy, and pleasure.

The French of Rabelais, the pleasure he took in writing, his genial power of imagination, his creation of new words and new languages, must be considered his own ability. He admired the ease of expression of Erasmian Latin, and he was able to appreciate Cicero's style. On language, however, he cannot be considered and did not consider himself a disciple or heir to Erasmus. Although he was a humanist, faithful to the unwritten rules of humanism, a lover of Greek and Latin classical authors, he discovered by his own means the power of inspiration, at the *vis mentis* of the pagan authors, and the *spiritus* or breath of the biblical prophets. Hence the style and the way of speaking, laughing, or crying of his giants, those paradoxical images of the prophets of the Old Testament.

To come back to Erasmus's Latin style and Rabelais's French narrative writing, we could say at first that the *varietas* of the former is more significant than the unified tone of Rabelais's prose. Erasmus uses several registers according to the genre, the circumstances, the audience, or the destination of his written work. By contrast, in spite of his skill at making characters speak or think in accordance with their nature, Rabelais remains the great master of the language. Even though he mingles with the characters he has shaped, the narrator keeps his own verbal flow. But we must not be misled by Erasmus's *varietas* and Rabelais's *copia verborum*. After reading Erasmus's works and letters, we discover his predilection for the brevity, purity, and brightness of style. But this kind of atticism, to speak as old rhetoricians do, or this taste for *brevitas* is not at all contrary to the *copia verborum*. For Erasmus, as well for Rabelais, *copia* is not abundance in itself, but the intellectual potentiality of choosing, among the cornucopia of words, those which are particularly fitting for the orator's or the writer's purpose.[28] Even though some dialogues in Erasmus's *Colloquies* often look like scenes from *Gargantua* or *Pantagruel*, we must not be amazed at Erasmus using more often a *brevitas* taken from his reading of Seneca and from his *ingenium* and Rabelais a luxuriant vocabulary drawn from the tradition of the French rhetoricians and his own genius.

In conclusion, it seems to me impossible not to associate these two great personalities and writers of the sixteenth century. Rabelais broke with the ecclesiastical life, and Erasmus cuts all links of dependence to live a secular life. Erasmus was a scholar and writer of universal fame, and Rabelais, a scholar and physician, but above all a writer of genius. Both rebelled against a corrupt society, both civil and religious. Both wrote in different ways, from the funniest satire to the most serious style impregnated with deep feelings. They forged a committed literature with astonishing, imaginative constructions: Folly on one side, Gargantua and Pantagruel on the other side. Both were condemned by the Church, both were finally hostile to the Reformation after playing their part in the search for a reformation of society and the Roman church.

Erasmus was both older than Rabelais and in a way, his master: "My most humane Father" (Frame, 746). Rabelais, by recognizing his moral status of follower or disciple of Erasmus, does not behave, in my opinion, as a courtier paying his respect to a world-famous thinker and writer. The tribute seems sincere and justified. Rabelais is not Erasmus's intellectual or religious heir simply because both of them were condemned by the "theologastres" of the Sorbonne or because Rabelais's Greek books were confiscated by the same people, alarmed by Erasmus's commentaries on Luke. Even if he is not "the last French Erasmian," as suggested by Raymond Lebègue, Rabelais can be seen as fully impregnated with the Erasmian spirit, as difficult to define as it is obvious to recognize, for it is neither a philosophical system nor a concept. It is a way of being, feeling, living, acting, and reacting, of fighting against any kind of dogmatism. It is also a way of exercising an indefinable sense of humor and of *festivitas*, to use the Latin word. But the Erasmian Rabelais is still primarily Rabelais. In spite of their great influence, neither Erasmus nor Rabelais have any disciples or heirs in the full sense of those words.

# Marc Bensimon

# Like Father, Like Son?

> *Divine nécessité de l'imperfection,*
> *Divine présence de l'imparfait, du*
> *vice et de la mort dans les écrits,*
> *apportez-moi aussi votre secours.*
>
> — Francis Ponge, *Dix courts sur la méthode*

> *Nostre bastiment, & public & privé, est plain*
> *d'imperfection.*
>
> — Montaigne, "De l'utile et de l'honeste"

Chapter 8 of *Pantagruel* is one of the best known by schoolchildren and scholars alike and certainly one of the most quoted, because it contains Gargantua's famous letter to his son, exhorting him to studiousness.

Despite its apparent clarity, this letter has lent itself to multiple interpretations that attribute radically differing religious opinions to its author. Are we to read it as a communication between two giants and, in its program, find parodic intent? In its mannered style, so totally different from the usual Rabelaisian verve, are we to see a parody of the then fashionable Ciceronian style in French and Latin? Or, on the contrary, are we to find a sort of "substantific marrow," an assertion of the author's ideas through the words of good old Gargantua, who, abandoning for a moment all scoffing, was communicating to his readers the enthusiasm of a humanist? Even the seriousness of tone, which contrasts sharply with the rest, has not ceased to disturb. Although my purpose here is not to reopen this long chapter of Rabelaisian criticism, a few points need to be made.

Since Gérard Brault's commentaries, much ink has flowed. Raymond La Charité, in his "Gargantua's letter" (1981) has temperately but surely ruled out the specious arguments and underlined the serious side of the letter by drawing attention to the fact that it is above all a fictive text, which is not addressed to the reader directly but rather is written by one of the characters to another, a father wishing to encourage his son to pursue his studies for very precise reasons. These reasons should not be lost sight of, and we shall examine them later.

It must also be noted that the reader swept up in the linguistic eddy, accustomed to the volutes, the puns, and the inexhaustible verve of the preceding text, is astonished by the sudden change of tone, especially since the first words of chapter 7 are almost identical to those of the letter: "Après que Pantagruel eut fort bien estudié . . ." (1:248) [After Pantagruel had studied very well . . . (152)]; and in chapter 8: "Pantagruel estudioit fort bien, comme assez entendez . . ." (1:256) [Pantagruel studied very well as you understand well enough . . . (158)]. The reader cannot help but look for some linguistic fireworks in this epistle, which is true in all points to the Ciceronian epistolary models. But in vain.

He does experience some surprise. However, it is the effect of the surprise that has changed since Rabelais's time. Rabelais's contemporary was accustomed to the surprises of a fictive universe in which disparate, bizarre elements were intertwined on the same plane, moving as in the bidimensional grotesques of the gallery at Fontaine-bleau, from the organic to the geometric, where the painting and the frame, the oeuvre and the hors-d'oeuvre, the *ergon* and the *parergon* (the latter often far from restrained) still maintained unbroken relations with the real world. Mythology and daily reality could then cohabitate. This reminds us also of Ronsard's manner of describing the poets' aesthetics: "They build a magnificent palace, that they enrich, gild and embellish on the outside with marble, jasper, and . . . friezes and capitals and on the inside with panels, tapestries raised and embossed with gold and silver, and the inside of the panels chiseled and carved, rough and difficult to hold in one's hands, because of the crude carvings of the characters seemingly living within. Later they add orchards and gardens etc."[1]

The relationship between the elements suggested by these aesthetics demonstrates that the problem of continuity does not exist for the contemporary reader. As a consequence, all narrative requisites should be apprehended much more carefully when reading Rabelais, and the whole problem of the relation between inside and outside should be reevaluated in this light. What is most important and what should also orient the reading of the prologue is the fact that inside and outside become one and the same in Rabelais's world, the meaning, ironic to be sure, of the metaphor of marrow and bone and consequently of the whole work, casting a clearer light on its significance. Louis Marin explains, in his excellent study on Rabelaisian utopian bodies, how Thélème functions as an allegory of the textual body, as a place of nonclosure and also as an orifice, the "text's mouth," well guarded, "Here enter not . . ." (Frame, 120). He also shows that in chapter 32 of *Pantagruel*, where the narrator is swallowed by his own creation, an equation is established between verbality and orality: "le lecteur va se trouver en présence d'un nouvel espace . . . nouvel espace ou plutôt espace autre — régressif et fantasmagorique . . . dans lequel le dedans est le dehors et le dehors, le dedans, le petit contient le grand et la partie, le tout, l'englobant se trouve englobé par son propre procès d'englobement" (Marin, 117).[2]

In any case, as François Rigolot said long ago, the letter is not "un météore tombé du ciel" (Rigolot 1972, 57); rather, it is part and parcel of the rest, of the very first and last paragraphs of the chapter, which, in the studied style of our author, describe the metamorphosis of young Pantagruel's gigantic receptacle[3] into an "esperit . . . infatigable et strident" (1:262) [tireless and shrill mind (my translation)] set ablaze by the father's well-calculated missive. Furthermore, this letter is otherwise intimately linked to the narrative structure of *Pantagruel*, as we shall see below.

Let us consider the letter by itself, as separate from these two narrative hinges. In spite of its style, which produces a pastiche of the Ciceronian epistle and is so very different from the habitual Rabelaisian verve, the body of the good giant's letter to his son represents still in the vernacular a somewhat simplified reflection of current humanist thinking, yet moving, as François Rigolot puts it, in its classic simplicity (Rigolot 1972, 59). But it should be repeated, it is not parodic, as Gérard Defaux said when he likened this discourse to others, such as that of the Limousin scholar (Defaux 1973, 203). Must all the characters in the book be alike? Rather, these considerations were shared by Rabelais's contemporaries; witness Budé's two Latin texts, also of 1532, the *De studio* dedicated to Francis I and the *De philologia*, a dialogue between this humanist and Francis I, in which there is almost the same discourse as Gargantua's concerning the education of the young princes Henri d'Orléans and Charles d'Angoulême.[4]

If there is comedy in this letter from the good giant to his son, it is not present because of the enthusiasm expressed for the humanistic program. Here, exaggeration would be more readily attributable to this enthusiasm or more precisely to the rhetorical function of the epistle destined to convince the young Pantagruel. It should therefore relate to the giant's immense capacity, gigantism being here a sign of perfection. So any irony would be present rather because of the negation of the traditional program, the satire of scholastic methods initiated in the two preceding chapters, as Edwin Duval has demonstrated in his comparison of the two programs (Duval 1986, 30–44). In all likelihood, the letter does express ideas conforming to those probably entertained by humanists and cultivated people at the court of Francis I or more precisely by a certain category of *bien-pensants*.

Also, this educational program should be replaced in its context. It would be useful to recall briefly the letter's content. At the beginning of the epistle, the ability to survive, thanks to seminal propagation, is singled out by the good king Gargantua from among the gifts invested by the Creator in humans, who are otherwise condemned after the original sin to mortality. Thus, the human species can be saved from nothingness; it acquires "a kind of immortality," the giant explains to his son, which allows man to "perpetuate his name and lineage, stemming from lawful marriage," until the Last Judgement, "when Jesus Christ will have restored to God the Father His kingdom, peaceful, out of all danger and contamination of sin" (159).

There is no need to return to the old discussion regarding marriage, which is fundamental, since it runs through the entire work. Our subject touches only lightly on that; the question dealing with the place of sexual desire and of the couple in the work has already been clarified by Françoise Charpentier in her essay on the subject, "Un Royaume qui perdure." No need, either, to go back over the religious ideas of Rabelais. Mentioned here are commonplaces, about which Gilson and, after him, Screech have given us the sources and which are consonant with the Thomist and Patristic traditions. The Gargantuan eschatology that stems from it evokes, as did Aristotle, "this monarch of modern doctrine," as Montaigne still called him, a dialectics of destruction and of regeneration with, at the time of the Last Judgement, the coming of Christ, the *parousie*, and with it the advent of perfection: "Car alors cesseront toutes generations et corruptions, et seront les elemens hors de leurs transmutations continues, veu que la paix tant desirée sera consumée et parfaicte, et que toutes choses seront reduites à leur fin et periode" (1:257) [For then will cease all generations and corruptions, and the elements will be through with their continual transmutations, seeing that peace, so greatly desired, will be consummate and perfected, and that all things will be reduced to their end and period (159)].

This discourse is also, as Screech has noted (1979b, 65), close to St. Paul's words (1 Cor. 15:24), which evoke, with the coming of Christ, the abolition of corruption and of generation and, with the resurrection of the body, death's defeat.[5]

Let us also remember with Telle (215) that in Matthew 22:30, the reign of the angelic Virginity comes to pass after the Resurrection and that marriage is then no longer necessary: "Nihil enim illic opus coitu, ubi mors non erit" [There indeed, in Heaven, there shall be no work resulting from intercourse; there, there shall be no death], said Erasmus paraphrasing Matthew.[6]

That said, however much Gargantua alludes to the coming of Christ's and God's peace in a preened and perfect universe — that is, where all things have come to their end and perfection — we must wonder that Rabelais, this disciple of Erasmus, could have subscribed without any detachment to such a discourse. Erasmus abhorred the notion of perfection in that it implies limits and finiteness. According to him, as well as to Ficino, Cuse, and other contemporary philosophers, this could be applicable neither to God, infinitely incomprehensible, nor to man: "nihil in rebus humanis vere perfectum" will he say.[7] In any case, what is missing in this discourse is the enthusiasm, the religious fervour that energizes St. Paul's gospel, such as that famous apostrophe, "O Death, where is thy Sting?" (1 Cor. 15:54). There is something else missing from this discourse about immortality and sin, during which, in a parenthesis, Gargantua "confesses" that "nous pechons tous, et continuellement requerons à Dieu qu'il efface noz pechez" (1:257) [we all sin, and summon God to forgive us our sins (my translation)]. Such a parenthesis constitutes a form of concession, because it is parenthetical. What is missing here is an evocation of the Eucharistic mystery, of the identification to Christ by the embodiment of his flesh and blood, which allows the sinner to recover, along with pardon and innocence, the assurance of his immortality. Gargantua is far from these thoughts, and the future immortality that he evokes here without lingering over it is not his principal concern. He aspires to a more immediate satisfaction, and it is this aspiration that steers his whole discourse. Indeed, what he demands of his son, if his knowledge is to become abysmal and if he is to attain higher things ("plus hault tendre"), just as his father Grandgousier had demanded from him, is that the son, the heir, become an object of perfection, identical to him, the father, so that once dead, the father will be able to gaze at himself in his son and find his own image in this mirror.[8] It is the narcissistic desire of the father to find himself in his son's traits that motivates him to compose this letter. That is to say that the goal of the educational program is dependent upon this intention, a fact which we have tended to forget. Gargantua will remind his son "that he hasn't spared anything to help him perfect himself," "comme si je n'eusse aultre thesor en ce monde que de te veoir . . . absolu et parfaict, tant en vertu, honesteté et preudhommie, comme en tout sçavoir liberal et honeste, et tel te laisser après ma mort comme un mirouoir representant la personne de moy ton pere" (1:258) [as if I had no other treasure in this world but to see you . . . absolute and perfect, both in virtue, honor, and valor, and in every liberal and praiseworthy branch of learning, and to leave you so, after my death, as a mirror representing the person of myself your father (160)].

Pantagruel will then be in body and soul the mirror in which Gargantua will be able to enjoy contemplating his otherness.[9] He will be an image of perfection, just like the androgyne that adorned young Gargantua's gigantic bonnet, but then he will be as curious as his coin pouch made from a Libyan elephant's testicle or as exotic as the bonnet's plume taken from a pelican from the faraway land of Hyrcania (*G* 8).

Contrary to what is put forth in the critical editions of Lefranc, Jourda, and Demerson, Gargantua's androgyne differs from Plato's. As early as 1911, Sainéan denounced the parody in "Rabelaisiana," but this went subsequently unnoticed.[10] Yet Aristophane's fable does mention in the *Symposium* that the androgyne had "on a circular neck . . . a single head for the two faces, which looked in opposite directions" (Plato 1989, 189–90), whereas Rabelais, modifying his Plato, ascribes to his androgyne's body "deux testes, l'une virée vers l'autre, quatre bras, quatre piedz et deux culz" (1:38) ["two heads, one turning towards the other, four arms, four feet, and two arses" (my translation)]. Hence the legend, borrowed from St. Paul (1 Cor. 13:5).

"Charity seeketh not its own," is surely then only a simple sally, or, what is even more serious, St. Paul's agape is irremediably contaminated by this materialistic eros, and not in the manner which would have pleased Neoplatonists. Indeed, what remains of the gospel's dramatic, lyrical hymn exhorting one to charitable love in this quotation? The androgyne — a curiously visible figure and as ridiculous as Plato's painted ideas in the painting bought by Epistemon on the island of Medamothi — becomes an avatar of the Platonic myth in this facetious context.[11]

According to Pico della Mirandola who fuses the two myths, the two faces of the androgyne, outwardly facing like those of Janus, symbolize the two souls that simultaneously face the spiritual and the material, whereas, in the *Commentary on the Symposium* by Ficino, only the soul aspiring to find divine light is dealt with. This is not the case, though, with another Neoplatonist, Léon Hébreu (Leone Ebreo). In his 1503 *Dialoghi d'amore* published in Rome in 1535, a year after *Gargantua*, he makes a distinction between an androgyne with two faces diametrically opposed. Drawing on a Talmudic tradition, he presents these faces as similar to Adam, the primordial man, who is both masculine and feminine, until divided later by God, as it is said in the Bible. I quote Léon Hébreu from the 1551 French translation, *Dialogues d'amour*:

> L'homme fut creé en estat de beatitude et logé au Paradis terrestre, combien qu'il fust masle et femelle . . . ce néantmoins ces deux moitiez, ou *sexes en deux personnes et* parties d'homme, estoient . . . attachez et *conjoints* ensemble par les espaules en contreface, c'estasavoir que leur circonference n'estoit inclinée à la copulation charnelle ny generation, ny le visage de l'un se dressoit en front devers l'autre visage . . . [Après la faute], leur donnant Dieu, comme pour remede contre la mortalité, la solicitude de la procreation et generation des enfans, [il permit] la division comme pour luy laisser le pouvoir de s'incliner, face vers face, facilement à la copule charnelle, l'inclination ainsi se divertissant des choses spirituelles aux corporelles. (248–49)[12]

> [Man was created in a state of beatitude and accommodated in earthly Paradise, notwithstanding that he was male and female, however, these two halves, or sexes in two persons and parts of man were attached and conjoined together at the shoulder, facing out, it is to be known that their circumference was not inclined towards carnal copulation or generation, nor did the face of one stand before the other. [After the fall], giving them God as a remedy against mortality the charge of procreating and generating children, [he allowed] the division as if to leave him the possibility of permitting, by a face to face, carnal copulation; this inclination thus diverting from spiritual things to corporal ones. (my translation)]

Even in Léon Hébreu, the situation is clear; it is only after having been split that the androgyne can have had two faces turned toward each other.

Recall in passing that one of our contemporaries, Michel Tournier, relies on this last version of the myth in his work. Here we see an interesting evolution from a state of plenitude and self-sufficiency in the first narratives, through one of solitude, then onto an unmatched duality. "Le Paradis Perdu n'est-il pas empoisonné?" Tournier is to have said (Bouloumié 1990, 69), echoing the bitter situation in which Robert Musil's characters find themselves after the incest in *The Man Without Qualities*. Marguerite Duras's brother and sister in *Agatha* experience a similar anguish and also identify with Musil's characters. These considerations and these characters, yearning for an absolute which they can only find in transgression, have taken us far afield from the merry games of abstracting quintessence. Or have they?

Since 1536, the androgyne was fashionable in France. Antoine Héroët dedicates to Francis I, that same monarch of whom we have an androgyne portrait (Waddington 1991, 100), a poem entitled *L'Androgyne*. It is an adaptation of the Ficinian commentary that later ends up along with the *Parfaicte amye* and the *Contr'amie* in the whirlwind of the *querelle des femmes* at the royal court.

Was Rabelais thinking about copula, about the practice of the "gentle androgyne," that is, the double-backed beast practice ("la pratique de la beste a deux dos"), as the author of *Le Moyen de parvenir* would say later? Yes, certainly, but did he see, as did his mentor Erasmus, the symbol of the Incarnation, the union of the earthly and the divine in the androgyne and the union of two beings like that of the soul to Christ in marriage? Despite the importance that Gargantua attaches to legitimate seminal propagation in this chapter and despite the fact that marriage, a most topical question, with all the meanings that one would like to accord it, remains the core of the work, to accept this reading leads to serious misinterpretation.[13] Be that as it may, our author was well aware of everything that the androgyne suggests and, in our opinion, he never ceases to mock it. The androgyne and its legend, inviting a mutual turning towards one another, express symbolically the work's entire narrative development.

To return to our chapter, we should note that Gargantua's quest is circular and that this specular contemplation to which he aspires only offers him the discovery of an Other, identical to himself and set in his perfection or quasi-perfection, which, as I have already quoted, Erasmus abhorred. But as to seeing an allegorical character in the immoderate love that this all-powerful king avows when he looks upon the progeny who is to continue his lineage, a legitimate and harrowing consideration for any monarch, especially in the sixteenth century, this is doubtful. In fact, Erasmus's main argument is aimed at showing that man, in his quest for happiness, which he defines in part as the desire to be whoever one is, finds himself in a paradoxical situation in that he cannot opt for self-love or for self-hatred, preoccupations that have little to do with Gargantua's. In addition, the latter is far from being caricatural. The caricature of the monarch occurs with the character of Picrochole, for example, and not with our dear giant, whose sentiments, such as he expresses them in his epistle, conform completely with a social and religious orthodoxy.

The fundamental concepts of this letter, which ultimately determine its structure, are seminal propagation and its ensuing result, specularity. The study program itself is therefore subordinated to resemblance; any quest for perfection through knowledge must lead the young Pantagruel to resemble his father more.

This is in line with sixteenth-century views. For Rabelais's contemporaries, the principle of resemblance and analogy governs all epistemes. Any explanation of the world or humanity called upon this notion of splitting, of symmetry, as if an imperious irrational necessity required it. For example, Charles Bovelle (Carolus Bovellus), whom Cassirer called "one of the most curious and characteristic products of Renaissance philosophy," explains in his *De Sapiente* (1509) that, whereas reason is the power that nature uses to return cyclically to itself once severance has occurred, true unity of self can only be achieved schizogenetically, that is, when the ego divides itself into two parts to reconstitute itself in a subsequent unity (Cassirer 1963, 88).

In the sixteenth century, all reality, microcosmic and macrocosmic, is only a mirror image in a world in which resemblance excludes even the notions of temporality and space. The ubiquity, conferred by the contemplation of perfection, plays a primordial role in Ficino's works, for example, where the world is symmetrically and hierarchically ordered into a network of correspondences. Ficino, in a surprising text, suggests that his disciple ascend to heaven through the power of his imagination and, shedding arms and legs, that he metamorphose his body into a gigantic eye able to take in all things at a glance, thus permitting him to see everything without moving, like

God, omniscient and omnipresent (Ficino I:vi 1970, 227). Just like Montaigne, who rails against these systems that take in the wind, Rabelaisian humor, while using it, dissolves the principle of resemblance and the demiurgical illusion that it implies. Does he not have one of his characters say, "le grand Dieu feist les planettes et nous faisons les platz netz" (1:27) [the Good God made the planets, and we ourselves make our plates neat (my translation)]? The least one can say about this extraordinary equation is that it is disquieting because of the author's distancing, which can invite a pun of this nature. Yet the backdrop is unmistakenly analogical and so it goes with the whole Rabelaisian enterprise.

Let us here recall what Foucault says in *Les mots et les choses*. According to him, the sixteenth century superimposed semiology and hermeneutics (Foucault 1966, 44). In fact, the whole quest for knowledge aimed at bringing to light a likeness of that which was invisible or hidden. Reality, like its split image, says Foucault, constitutes "une sorte de gémellité naturelle des choses; elle naît d'une pliure de l'être dont les deux côtés, immédiatement, se font face" (Foucault 1966, 35).

Even Ronsard, or at least the one of the first book of the *Amours*, speaks no differently about the loved object, the Other, who functions like the image of another him. He calls this, as in sonnet 20, *entelechie* (from the Greek *entelechia*), signifying that which has its end in itself, therefore that which is completed, perfect.

On this subject and purely as an aside, I take the liberty of recalling the tenor of chapter 18 in the *Cinquième livre* when the travelers arrive in Lady Quint Essence's kingdom, Entelechia. A satire follows ridiculing the famous quarrel on the meaning of the two words, *entelechia* and *endelechia*, that divided the humanists during the 1550s. The author concludes that the Aristotelian term should be retained, since it is the most appropriate to the Queen of Quintessence. Let us note that the idea of perfection is here translated by that of greatness, of size. Indeed, the giant Pantagruel suddenly sees himself lilliputized as against the towering Captain with whom, because of this, he cannot communicate. Resigning himself, he remarks on his imperfection: " 'Baste! si nostre dame Royne vouloit, nous se-

rions aussi grans comme vous. Ce sera quant il luy plaira'" (2:349)
[Who cares! if our lady Queen wanted it, we would be as tall as you.
Oh, Well! It will occur whenever it is her pleasure (my translation)].
These words are far removed from those that a Pantagruel as
perfect as his father Gargantua would have uttered. Without taking
into account this Pantagruel of the *Cinquième livre*, whose attitude
better reflects, in our opinion, the spirit of the entire work, and to
come back to Gargantua's letter and to what it represents, there is
subversion, but one much more profound in that it topples the edi-
fice of the Renaissance. The disquieting conviction that Rabelais is
jeering at his character or rather at what he represents only emerges
later and insidiously in the following chapters, in fact only after
having read the entire text, thus in a way negating Gargantua's desire. Despite what Screech says, nowhere in the work do we see
Pantagruel and his companion following the path leading to perfection, to the three theological virtues, in accordance with the father's
wish expressed in Paulinian terms at the end of the letter: "il te
convient [de] mettre [en Dieu] toutes tes pensées et tout ton espoir; et
par foy formee de charité, estre à luy adjoinct, en sorte que jamais
n'en soys desamparé par peché (1:262) [it behooves you to serve,
love, and fear God, and in Him put all your thoughts and all your
hope; and by faith formed of charity, be adjoined to Him, in such
wise that you shall never be sundered from Him by sin (162)].

After the initial five chapters, in which all that is spoken of is paternity and genealogy — completely whimsically, by the way — denying
the relationship to the origin rather than cultivating it and after
the chapter of the letter, Gargantua the character disappears. He is
briefly mentioned in chapter 23, in which we learn that he has been
kidnapped by Morgan and "translaté au pays des Phées" (1:335)
[translated to Fairyland (209)], then he makes a brief and last appearance towards the end of the *Tiers livre* to approve the voyage
that Panurge is undertaking in his quest for the answer to the marriage question. This will preoccupy Panurge for many chapters, even
though the question is never raised for Grandgousier and Gargantua.
Gargantua approves the voyage, requiring, however, that his son,
like Panurge, also feel the desire to get married.

At the close of chapter 8, on the following page, Pantagruel, still ablaze with the desire to perfect himself through study and God's cult and following his father's instructions, goes about devising and philosophizing when he falls upon Panurge at the bend in the path. Henceforth, the narrative drifts off, as we well know.

Pantagruel no longer walks in his father's footsteps to act as his reflection and to repeat the father-son relationship. He forgets his father's recommendations to steer clear of dubious company: "Fuis les compaignies de gens esquelz tu ne veulx point resembler" (262) [flee the company of those whom you do not care to resemble (162)]. Instead, he teams up with Panurge for life. A sudden, unconditional, irrational love is provoked by the perception of a Panurge "handsome [in] stature and elegant in every bodily feature," suggesting to Pantagruel that he is born "of rich and noble line" (163), even though his rags and his wounds betray mysterious reversals of fortune, described by the latter as "accidents that happen to the adventurous" (163), that seem completely contrary to the existence already programmed by the image of the father.

What could be more seductive to the young Pantagruel? Especially since his unanswered questions, "Who are you? Where do you come from? Where are you going? What are you after? What is your name?" strengthen the bond that solders him forever to this mysterious alter ego. He, the giant from Utopia, devoted to a specular, bidimensional perfection will seek his *mauvais génie*, this bad character, this imperfect being, whose complexity, anxiety, and all too human qualities, "crafty, deceitful, cruel, timorous, obscene, otherwise the best brat in the world" (1:301, my translation), allow him to sense another dimension, which completes him. What does it matter if, a few chapters later, we come across this rather unappealing portrait of our scoundrel, no longer the handsome and brilliant scholar in command of all languages, but instead portrayed as being of "average stature" with a "nose fashioned after a razor's handle" and with a mind as sharp as "a lead dagger" (1:300, my translation)?

Panurge is a problematic and shifty character, and his relationship with Pantagruel is much the same. Clever is the one who can untangle the threads and identify the roles: Pantagruel imitates Panurge, the latter apes Pantagruel; Pantagruel steps back to let Panurge take front stage, but Panurge is never more than a rather pitiful character. The significance of this problematic relationship stems from the very ambiguity of its aspect and perhaps from the drawing together of opposite attitudes. Be that as it may, it creates situations in which a requestioning of all sixteenth-century religious, moral, and institutional values asserted by the letter can occur. In a way, this new orientation, which will be spearheaded by the famous quest, mirrors the double revolt against the national model of the tenebrous epoch of the Goths as well as against the narcissistic model, thirsty for perfection, that Gargantua proposes. Raymond La Charité has justly underlined the importance of the letter as a fictional dramatic device with metatextual functions reflecting Rabelais's concern with his own creative paternity, which in content and form expresses "the family of man and its place in the universe" and summarizes the fundamental drive of the book (La Charité 1981, 36). This is certainly very well put, but then creativity and the triumph of an artistic idiom must be viewed in the book as an ever-changing dynamic process that will seek to incorporate imperfection, rejecting any form of restraint and inviting even perversion and other regressive libidinal drives. Thus, at the conclusion of *Pantagruel*, as the giant swallows his narrator, the entire discourse grows in the very spot where it is being enunciated so that, as Louis Marin and other critics have remarked, to speak and to eat or be eaten become synonymous. Further, when the narrator respectfully narrates to his giant his activities, he concludes with no aggressive intention by answering the inquisitive giant, who is delighted with the answer, that he shit in the latter's throat.[14]

With the creation of the couple Pantagruel-Panurge, Rabelais expresses the beginnings of a rejection of the ideal quest at the expense of a quest for a more real, albeit imperfect nature of man. In this new project, however, the narrator still identifies with the fictional character who swallows him up, yet he points the way to the similarly ambiguous relationship that Montaigne maintains with the model as well as with the past. It is obvious, but it should still be said, I think, that without the new *énoncé* set forth by the couple Panurge-

Pantagruel, the very possibility of a discourse in search of a new and problematic model — and of what his entire autobiographical enterprise stands for — would have been unthinkable.

For Montaigne, the son will attempt to catch the monstrous, ever-changing, and problematic image of a being as unstable and diverse as his fellow men, by inviting him, this other Narcissus, to gaze at himself not in the stillness of the old mirror that throws back perfect images of the self but in a tumultuous torrent. But this son will no longer be of flesh and bone. Montaigne has elaborated extensively on the subject of the father's inability to entrust his progeny with the care of perpetuating his image, his person. Any seed, Montaigne says, proves to be a priori poisoned, just like knowledge, which he compares to poisoned meat.[15] So he entrusts himself to his spiritual son, to his work, as monstrous as it is.[16] And let us remember he compares it to the hors d'oeuvre (framing), to the grotesques surrounding the "gaping hole" corresponding to the "father's letter," to speak like Lacan.[17] This very particular mirror will have to testify, once Montaigne is dead, and give an account of his moods and affections with the greatest probity, and woe betide whoever exhibits another image of him: "I would willingly come back from the other world to give the lie to any man who portrayed me other than I was," he says in "Of Vanity" [Montaigne, 961 (my translation)]. We also learn in the same breath that if he "describes himself so curiously in his *Essais*, it is because his companion, who was the only one to enjoy the possession of his real image, had taken it with him to the tomb" [961, n. 3 (my translation)]. There is no need here to bring up the subject of La Boetie's relation to Montaigne's *Essais*. Richard Regosin dealt with it extensively in his superb book, *The Matter of My Book*, but it is not inappropriate to recall that Pantagruel, like Montaigne, is drawn to his alter ego by an equally inexplicable and irrational movement. Neither is it irrelevant to mention that he describes the relation as that of two souls (*volontés*) yearning to plunge and get lost in one another with great hunger (187).

Perhaps Gargantua's letter in form and content represents the triumph of a certain artistic paternity (La Charité 1981, 36–37), but it is the discourse that Pantagruel pronounces that constitutes, in my opinion, the flower of the artistic process of our author. François Rigolot has given an excellent account of this in great detail in his book on Rabelais's language. He has shown both the reasons for the grammatical coherence of the discourse and the impossibility of making sense out of it (Rigolot 1972, 41–47). Very simply, this marvelous orgy of extraordinary signifiers which gains for the young giant the admiration of the doctors who remain in "a swoon of ecstasy for quite three hours, so impressed are they with his wisdom which they compare to Solomon's," crowns the liberation of all dependence of the Rabelaisian discourse upon the father's letter. As Louis Marin said about Thélème's language and more particularly about chapter 32 of *Pantagruel*, the text expresses "une régression du discours au signifiant et précisément au signifiant pulsionel qui s'y trouve libéré de son enchaînement au signifié . . . bestialité heureuse du langage ramené . . . au narcissisme primaire et sans entraves du principe de plaisir" (Marin 118–19).[18]

This pleasure illustrates, may we submit by way of conclusion, what Rabelais means in his introductory poem to *Gargantua*, when he says that in this text,

> . . . perfection may be hard to find,
> Unless in point of laughter and good cheer;
> No other subject can my heart hold dear,
> Seeing the grief that robs you of your rest:
> Better a laugh to write of than a tear,
> For it is laughter that becomes man best.
> (Frame, 2)

# Michael J. B. Allen

# De Libro Sexto
# Cum Commento

To renew our knowledge of the *Gargantua*'s genealogy and its antiquity, we must refer to the Pantagrueline chronicle found in the very first chapter by ditch cleaners in a field near the Arch Gualeau, below the Olive on the way to Narsay, in a buried bronze tomb of immeasurable extent. "Un gros, gras, grand, gris, joly, petit, moisy livret" (1:13) [a huge, stout, big, gray, pretty little mouldy little book (8)], it was hidden under the middle flagon of nine, arranged "en tel ordre qu'on assiet les quilles en Guascoigne" (1:13) [in the order in which they put nine-pins in Gascony (8)]. The "moisy livret" I shall open here addresses the familiar topic of Rabelais's debt to Platonic hermeneutics, but I shall return to the order of the skittles.

One of the enduring questions raised by the Platonic dialogues is the problem of reading Socrates. "Beuveurs tres illustres, et vous, Verolez tres precieux . . . Alcibiades, ou dialogue de Platon intitulé *Le Bancquet*, louant son precepteur Socrates, sans controverse prince des philosophes, entre aultres parolles le dict estre semblable es Silenes" (1:5) [Most illustrious topers, and you, most precious poxies . . . Alcibiades, in Plato's dialogue entitled *The Symposium*, praising his master Socrates, incontrovertibly the prince of philosophers, among other things says he is like the Sileni (3)]. The boon companion and foster-father of Bacchus, Silenus himself was older, wiser, and usually drunker than the satyrs who also flocked in Bacchus's train and whom he physically resembled. He and his Sileni were expert musicians given to prophecy when captured, even though in the plaguy plays of the comic dramatists they appeared as cowards and boasters. It is the Silenus boxes, however, as the prologue declares, with their paintings of "harpies, satyres, oysons bridez, lievres cornuz, canes bastées, boucqs volans, cerfz limonniers" (1:5) [harpies, satyrs, bridled goslings, (horned hares,) saddled ducks, flying goats, harnessed stags (3)], that contained such rare drugs as "balm, ambergris, amomum, musk, civet, precious stones," [i.e., mineral essences] (Frame, 3), and the other mysteries of the apothecary's trade. Had you opened the box of the Silenus Socrates, with his pointed nose, bovine expression, and idiotic face, always laughing, always drinking, always fooling, always concealing his divine wisdom, you would have found inside "une celeste et impreciable drogue" (1:6) [a heavenly drug beyond price (3)]: a superhuman understanding, miraculous virtue, invincible courage, matchless sobriety, unfailing contentment, perfect assurance, and an incredible contempt for the things men strive for in this world. Inside Silenus is Apollo, Jove, Cronos, Ouranos, the theogonic succession of later Neoplatonic theology that leads back to the beauty that is the splendor of absolute truth, to the Socrates who rises like Aphrodite from the sea of contemplation.[1] If Rabelais is the intellectual heir of Erasmus, as Professor Margolin and others have persuasively argued, he is the heir preeminently of Erasmus's lifelong struggle with the problems of interpretation, of determining what is and what is not a painted box.[2]

Raising the issue of interpretation is not just a preambulatory flourish. It is central to the fabric of Rabelais's complex design, as the prologue advises us. In the *Tiers livre*, Panurge's misinterpretations of his own dreams, of the Virgilian lots, of the leafy predictions of the Sibyl of Panzoust, of Nazdecabre (Goatsnose), of Herr Trippa and the rest are not just the folly of the wise man. "Vous entendez autant (respondit Panurge) en exposition de ces recentes propheties comme faict truye en espices. . . . La vieille dict: ainsi comme la febve n'est veue se elle ne est esgoussée, aussi ma vertus et ma perfection jamais ne seroit mise en renom si marié je n'estoys . . . l'allegorie me plaist, mais non à vostre sens" (1:475–76) [You understand as much . . . in the expounding of these recent prophecies [he counters Pantagruel] as does a sow in spices. . . . The old woman says: Even as the bean is not seen if it is not shucked, so my virtue and my perfection would never be brought to renown if I were not married. . . . I like the allegory, but not in your sense (308–9)]. In the following chapter Pantagruel retorts, " 'L'esprit maling vous seduyt; mais escoutez. J'ai leu qu'on temps passé. . . . [m]ainctes foys y ont faict erreur ceulx voyre qui estoient estimez fins et ingenieux, tant à cause des amphibologies, equivocques et obscuritez des motz, que de la breifveté des sentences; pourtant, feut Apollo, dieu de vaticination, surnommé Λοξίας' " (1:479) ['The malicious spirit is leading you astray, but listen. I've read that in times past . . . many times mistakes were made even by those who were esteemed subtle and ingenious (in the interpretation of written or oral prophecies), both because of the uncertainties, ambiguities, and obscurities of the words and because of the brevity of the pronouncements; therefore was Apollo, god of vaticination, surnamed [*Loxias*] (311)], meaning the Ambiguous or Indirect. He proposes instead that they take counsel of some dumb person who might prophecy, like Thaumaste, by mute gestures and signs.

Let us examine for a moment the acknowledged lord of gestures and signs, loxiastic Apollo who presides over the spiced lozenges of Socratic and Platonic discourse. One of the more remarkable of Marsilio Ficino's decisions in presenting Plato as a second scripture to the century preceding Rabelais's own was to reject the principle of a fixed interpretation, even the multiple fixity of the standard medieval fourfold interpretation.[3] Of course, Plato had composed different kinds of dialogues for different occasions and purposes and therefore deployed different rhetorical strategies in them. Moreover, in any one work, as a methodological principle, he had always committed himself to mixing intentions, subjects, moods, levels of play and seriousness. For Ficino, however, it was not these objective variables in the text so much as the varying states of mind, the receptivity, the preparedness, the spiritual preparedness of the interpreter himself that must necessarily determine the "truth" behind an evolving or at least an ever changing discursive surface.

In a late commentary written in the early 1490s only a few years before his death in 1499, the Florentine summoned up his speculative energies in order to address what the ancient Neoplatonists had come to regard, after a long debate about its structure and its correct interpretation, as the "innermost sanctuary" of the dialogues, the *Parmenides*.[4] This dialogue had been named after the venerable Parmenides of Elea, the greatest of the monists and, from Ficino's viewpoint at least, the transmitter to Plato via his subtle disciples Zeno and Melissus of an inherited Pythagorean wisdom.[5] Like Panurge, though, Ficino had to contend with someone — ironically a distinguished *complatonicus* — who did not understand the gestures, the *loxotês*, of Apollonian prophecy in this, the capstone of Plato's metaphysical achievements. The story, I will contend, has some bearing, at least in its implications, on our understanding of Rabelais's wayward, loxiastic allegiance to Platonism.

In his *De Ente et Uno* of 1491, Pico della Mirandola, Count of Concordia, had embarked on a surprisingly unconcordant attack on one of the fundamental postulates of Neoplatonism. Its declared aim was to reconcile Plato's ideas with Aristotle's, but its effect was to portray Plato as the proponent of an essentially Aristotelian position over the question of whether the One is identical with Being, to identify him, that is, with Aristotle's position in his *Metaphysics* 12 that the two are one and the same.[6] Such a view was anathema to Ficino, who subscribed to the Plotinian distinction, like all the authentic *Platonici*, between the supreme hypostasis, the One, and the second hypostasis, Mind, the first being and therefore absolute Being. Pico polemicizes, indeed, in this polemical treatise specifically against the metaphysics of *Platonici* who had attacked Aristotle's immanentist view of the One.

By his own testimony, the springboards for Pico's unplatonic ontology were certain passages in the *Parmenides* and its companion dialogue, the *Sophist*. In chapter 2 of the *De Ente*, he declares that these passages have been misinterpreted by the *Platonici*, and it would appear also by his older friend Ficino. They had all taken the dialogue too seriously as the presentation of *doctrina*, whereas it was in his view only a dialectical exercise in which nothing is positively asserted. To nail home his challenge to the Plotinian position, he observes dismissively, "there are no more arbitrary or forced commentaries upon this dialogue than those introduced by people who want to interpret Plato's *Parmenides* in any other sense."[7] At the very heart of this unexpected and far-reaching controversy between Pico and Ficino, the twin stars traditionally of Medicean Platonism, lies the question of interpretation.

Despite Raymond Klibansky's claim for the revolutionary nature of Pico's account of the dialogue (Klibansky 1943, 316–25), Pico was in fact reviving a Middle Platonic position, espoused, for instance, by Albinus and fully described (before being dismissed) by Proclus in his *In Parmenidem* (Proclus 1864, 630.37–35.27).[8] While it testifies perhaps to the variety of dissenting or competing views explored in Florentine philosophical circles, many of whose members were educated as and remained Aristotelians, it had the immediate effect of goading the Neoplatonic Ficino into undertaking a full-scale analysis of the *Parmenides* and its monism.[9] In the process, inevitably, he had to confront the dialogue's hermeneutical challenges. "If only that wonderful youth [*mirandus ille*]," he writes in chapter 49 of his own *In Parmenidem* and punning on Pico's aristocratic title, "had diligently considered the disagreements and discussions I have just dealt with [in the preceding chapters] before he had the temerity to confront his teacher and to openly declare an opinion so at odds with that of all the *Platonici*! For he asserts that the *Parmenides* is merely a work of logic, and that Plato, like Aristotle, had identified the One and the Good with Being."[10] If this personal rebuke is effectively buried in the heart of Ficino's commentary, the contention that the *Parmenides* is not merely an exercise in logical analysis and cannot be approached, let alone understood, solely in discursive terms preoccupied Ficino from the onset of his career as a Plato scholar and interpreter.

In the *argumentum* he had penned in the 1460s for his translation of the dialogue, Ficino had written that Plato "at last seems to have excelled even himself" in bringing the work forth from "the sanctuaries of the divine mind" (1576, 1136). Accordingly, it requires a special and corresponding grace in the interpreter, not simply what Plato's own *Meno* had called a "correct opinion" but, says Ficino, the state of inward clarity and interpretive confidence that we arrive at only after a course of discipline: "whoever is about to undertake the reading of this sacred text must prepare himself first by sobriety of soul and liberty of intellect before he takes up the mysteries of this heavenly work."[11] By liberty of intellect, he appears to mean the constant exercising of interpretive choice and the freeing of oneself from formulaic responses, from hermeneutical rigidity; but a freeing that is itself free from any kind of emotional undercurrents and derives from sobriety, from temperance of soul. This combination of daring and balance is necessary because the mysteries of the work have been presented by Plato in a most subtle series of arguments, where the nine hypotheses of Plato's second part are divided up into five positive hypotheses concerning the five ontological hypostases and four negative hypotheses concerning the consequences of not supposing the primacy of the One. The four negative hypotheses mirror the last four of the positive ones.[12] Unless one understands this complex dialectical structure, thought to have been intended by Plato but rediscovered by the later *Platonici*, then the mysteries remain completely hidden; unless, that is, one can grasp the details of the Silenus boxes and their outward designs, then the miraculous balm or ambergris within remains unsuspected. To do so, however, requires the intuition that only comes to the wholly tempered, the chastened soul.

By contrast, to assume with Pico that the work is merely an exercise in logic is to succumb to what Panurge sees in the *Tiers livre* as the failing of all women, namely that "quelques choses qu'elles voyent, elles se representent en leurs espritz, elles pensent, elles imaginent que soit l'entrée du sacre Ithyphalle. . . . [E]lles les interpretent et referent à l'acte mouvent de belutaige" (1:481) [whatever things they see or represent to themselves in their minds, or think they imagine it's the entry of the sacred Ithyphalus *[sic]*, . . . and (they) refer them to the moving act of bolting (312)]. In this regard, Plato's inveterate foes, the Sophists, were ithyphallic; they reduced everything to a matter of words and usage, ignoring the realm of meaning and thus of essences and ideas. Therefore, in order to advance his Aristotelian thesis concerning the identity of Being and the One, Pico had been forced to argue unbecomingly like a Sophist or at least to adopt a Sophist's perspective on the *Parmenides*, the work which stood as a bastion ironically to Plato's and to Parmenides's essentialist metaphysics.

For us, Freud is the analyst par excellence of the self's inner sophistries of concealment and displacement while Rabelais is a household word because of his flagrant refusals to conceal so many of our oral and anal, our phallic and yonic energies, and because of his monstrous appetite for exposure and overexposure. If Freud's world is the world of the bishop, then Rabelais's obviously is that of the choirboys and of carnival. But the two, as we all realize, are interdependent: the act of Rabelais's exposure is rarely, perhaps never, a simple act of closure, because exposure itself is one of the most effective strategies for ensuring ever more intricate concealments. The yielding of Venus Pandemos is the wafting of the Anadyomene to shore; the temple prostitutes at the porch speak to the awesome power of the chastity of the presiding goddess whose chryselephantine statue looms within the sacred cella. "It was the custom," Ficino writes in the little proem he prepared for his *Parmenides* Commentary, "of Pythagoras, of Socrates, of Plato to conceal the divine mysteries everywhere in figures and veils" to protect them from the prying eyes, the bold *iactantia* of the Sophists.[13] The veils or rind around the sapiential fruit, to use another hallowed image, is the ultimate challenge to the commentator: Can he, should he strip it away?

Plato's style, his complex structuring of the dialogues, his dramatic and eristic interludes, his deployment of myth and story, all constitute a playing in seriousness and a jesting in earnest, a *iocari serio* and *studiosissime ludere* that enables the philosopher to outwit the philodoxers, the lovers of mere opinion, usually their own. It aligns him, moreover, with the gods. For the *Laws* 7.803C had declared that gods are playful beings whose toys and puppets are men made in their playful image. This ludic conviction had inspired Ficino in his youth to embrace Lucretius and a newly interpreted Epicureanism and to formulate a Christian-Platonic hedonism that emphasized the primacy of joy over knowledge, of the erected will over the erected wit, to draw on Sidney's famous dichotomy. The motto in his study at Careggi was the Horatian *Laetus in praesens*, the fleeing of *excessus* and *negotia*, though Ficino's life was the life of a workaholic, of intellectual and scholarly *negotium*.[14] However unexpected a dimension to Renaissance Platonism, the result indirectly of Ficino's liberation from the censorious views on Epicurus of the Stoic Cicero, this noetic hedonism led eventually to the elevation of Apuleius and Lucian, two of Rabelais's most obvious antique masters, into the company of the philosophers as serious jesters, as morosophers, who had echoed the contentious, rallying wit of the silenian Socrates, the midwife's son.

Epicurus was the master of an intellectual garden, because the games that delight us most as intellectual beings, as *ingeniosi*, are intellectual ones. For all the *Platonici*, the most intricate of such games is the *Parmenides* with its aporias, its distinctions, its antithetical progressions, its deliberately poised dilemmas. If we can be drawn into its games, writes Ficino, then our mood will become heightened, our intuitive intelligences exhilarated by the argumentative play (Ficino 1576, 1136–37, the *argumentum*), and in such a heightened mental alertness, in a kind of inner *gaudium* or *laetitia*, the mysteries will eventually be apprehended if not comprehended, glimpsed if not fully seen. Whereas the ordinary person has found nothing there but empty caviling, the wise man has found a treasure-house of theological negations and affirmations, monistic paradoxes. Marrow, says Rabelais in his great prologue, "est aliment elabouré à perfection de nature" (1:7) [is the food elaborated to perfection by nature (4)], which is sucked out by careful reading and frequent meditation. The trouble lies, of course, with the sucking crocodile who lied when he declared he always lied. How does one determine the times, the many times in Plato and in Rabelais, when there is no theological significance in what is being said, no mystery behind the veil, no serious doctrine in a punning rejoinder; when the philosopher is simply at play, Panurge expatiating on the ithyphallus?

Unexpectedly perhaps, Ficino carefully divorces himself from the unrelenting allegorical rigour and therefore the interpretive folly of the later *Platonici* and above all of Proclus, the fifth-century Suc-

cessor, even though he espouses their basic sense of Plato's Pythagorean masterpiece and its monistic core. Plato is the crocodile sacred
to Isis; he neither always lies like the logocentric sophists nor always
tells the truth like the essentialist Proclus. Paradoxically, he evades
paradox. In an internal preface to his analysis of the second part of
the *Parmenides*, Ficino argues that, if Plato had wanted to reveal all
the divine mysteries and to reveal them continuously throughout the
dialogue, he would not have deliberately introduced the sections of
exacting logical play, nor would he have selected the young Socrates
as the instructee (Ficino 1576, 1153–54).[15] Indeed, a commitment
to maintaining, first, that "individual mysteries lie hidden in every
single word" and, second, that the number of individual proposi-
tions in the dialogue corresponds exactly and consistently to the
number of divine realms and their spiritual beings had led Syrianus
into error along with his pupil Proclus and those who followed
them. It is the error of reading too literally, of assuming, for instance,
that everything being denied of the One as a hypostasis in the dialogue's first hypothesis is secretly being predicated of the second
hypostasis Mind, the subject of the second hypothesis. "But I have
trod the middle path," writes the judicious Florentine, "I think there
is an underlying theology in the *Parmenides* but only so much as the
dialectical artifice permits. Plato's views on divine matters are not
therefore wholly or continuously or ubiquitously present; rather,
they are scattered about here and there."[16]

   This principle of sapiential or mysterial intermittency — the logical consequence of Plato's decision, in Ficino's view, to weave theological and logical concerns together in what he calls "a serious and
businesslike game" [ludum serium negociosumque] — shifts attention away from the work and onto the interpreter. It is the interpreter's spiritual and mental preparedness, his state of Platonic grace,
that will determine intuitively at what level he will interpret and
with what consistency. This is not so much a milestone on the road
to establishing the autonomy of the reader over what is being read as
it is the result of imagining God as a player, not at dice with an
atomic world in the Democritean tradition, but with human puppets
into whom he breathes life and to whom, as the divine ventriloquist,

he gives voice.[17] Plato, Lucian, Apuleius, Rabelais, poets and dialec-
ticians equally, were all made in the image of this ventriloquist.
"What do a dialectician and a poet share in common?" asks Ficino in
yet another internal preface, this time to his analysis of the four
negative hypotheses that conclude the second part of the *Parmenides*, "*certe quam plurimum*" [indeed, almost everything] is the reply.
"For the dialectician and poet alone among men busy themselves
with their own conceits and their own devices; and both are thought
of as divine and both possess something of madness."[18]

This is an arresting and unusual pairing, given that in other works
like the *Republic* poets are carefully distinguished from philosophers, and that the bad, in the sense of immoral or passion-arousing
ones, are banished from the commonwealth. But Plato had always
distinguished between divine poets and others.[19] For Ficino and the
*Platonici*, at the fountainhead of Greek poetry were not the errant
Homer or Hesiod with their anthropomorphic tales of lust among
the gods, of Hephaestus and Aphrodite caught in the trochaic net of
hexameters for all to see, but rather the Thracian Orpheus and his
hymns and his great prefatory palinode, Orpheus whom Ficino and
others thought of as a gentile counterpart to David the Psalmist.[20]
These were the poets whom Plato and his followers had woven into
the fabric of their philosophy as *prisci theologi* and whose lines
enshrined the *prisca theologia*, the gentile wisdom that had prepared
the non-Hebrews for the coming of Christ as assuredly as Moses and
the Prophets had prepared the Hebrews. Furthermore, Parmenides
himself had been a poet and the surviving fragments of his *Poema*
are cast in the form of a visionary narrative of a chariot ascent in
ecstasy, accompanied by the daughters of the sun, into the presence
of the goddess of wisdom.[21]

As we have already seen, Rabelais was wholly familiar with the
theory of the divine ecstasies or furies, derived as it was from Plato's
*Phaedrus* and *Ion*.[22] But to suppose that the dialectician too is pos-
sessed by a divine fury as he winds his way through aporias, dilemmas, and negations is to extend the concept of inspiration to the
intellectual life in general. It is to set the ecstatic Platonist over and
against the static Aristotelian, the philosopher-poet over and against

the scholastic, who is the enduring object of Rabelais's love and hate, his derision and celebration. For such ecstatic fury is the intoxicating draft of wisdom that mocks the wrangling sobriety of the schools. In Rabelais's intoxicated verbalism, however, even the schools are metamorphosed and brought into the corybantic dance of the nine Muses of the *Parmenides*' hypotheses about Apollo, the One. And justly so. In the ultimate vision of redemption or inner transformation, the unredeemable itself is finally redeemed, the graceless porcine Gryll transformed into a gracious Thelemite, and all words, in Milton's haunting phrase in *Lycidas*, turn out to be lucky, to favor the urns of men's star-crossed destinies.

In chapter 18 of the *Tiers livre*, however, Panurge is urged by his companions not to rely on words at all, lucky or unlucky, because of the difficulty in interpreting them: "Vous exposez allegoricquement ce lieu, et l'interpretez à larrecin et furt. Je loue l'exposition, l'allegorie me plaist, mais non à vostre sens. . . . [F]urt, en ce paissaige comme en tant d'aultres des scripteurs latins et antiques, signifie le doulx fruict de amourettes; lequel veult Venus estre secretement et furtivement cuilly" (1:476) [You explain this bit allegorically and interpret it as robbery and theft, I praise the explanation, I like the allegory, but not in your sense. . . . [T]heft, in this passage, as in many other ancient Latin writers, means the sweet fruit of amourettes, which Venus wills to be secretly and furtively plucked (309)]. This observation may be correct in some contexts, but not in this one. Pantagruel accordingly exhorts him in chapter 19 to take counsel of some mute by using signs and not speaking at all. Having rejected a female mute on the aforementioned ithyphallic grounds, they turn to Goatsnose, deaf and dumb from the cradle.

We have already witnessed Thaumaste's gymnastical discourse with Panurge, who had filled in for the inexperienced Pantagruel, but this earlier *disputatio* had never raised the issue of numbers, the supreme language of signs. In chapter 20 of the *Tiers livre*, by contrast, Goatsnose, having looked curiously at Panurge's performance in gestural interrogation, replied by raising his left hand in the air and keeping all the fingers clenched except the thumb and index finger "des quels il acoubla mollement les deux ongles ensemble"

(1:483) [which he joined gently by the two nails (314)]. Pantagruel immediately takes this to be signifying a gamma and declares it incorrectly both to be the Pythagorean sign for marriage (*gamos*) and the numerical sign for his own age of thirty, which would be the gamma upside down, that is, the lambda. Goatsnose then extends all five fingers of the same left hand: "Icy (dist Pantagruel) plus ample-ment nous insinue, par signification du nombre quinaire, que serez marié" (1:484) [Here, said Pantagruel, he insinuates to us more fully, by signifying the quinary number, that you will be married (314)]. He boldly asserts, again incorrectly, that Pythagoras had thought of five as the nuptial number because it is composed of the three and two, the first odd and the first even numbers, added together and representing the coupling of male with female.[23] Thereafter, Goats-nose sneezes to the left and, by doing so, foretells Panurge's hapless destiny: he is to be cuckolded, beaten, and robbed. "Le mariage (dist Panurge) je concede, je nie le demourant" (1:487) [The marriage [says Panurge] I concede; I deny the rest (316)]. Panurge plays the part, in other words, of the selective Platonic interpreter, but of one who has never been prepared by sufficient "sobriety" of soul to be able to exercise the "liberty" of correct understanding. In particular, he has got the numbers wrong.

Platonic sobriety and Platonic liberty are still the issue when we come to the end of the fifth book, even if it is not authentic, with its climactic vision of Bacchus and the Bottle and its accompanying burlesquing of cult, mystery, initiation, and rites. The burlesquing nonetheless is half in love with its object, as the great parodic storm-at-sea description in the *Quart livre* speaks to Rabelais's love affair with nautical terms. Here, in the mosaic work of the temple in chap-ter 38 of the *Cinquième livre* with its detailed renderings of episodes in the myth of Bacchus's victory over the Indians, we again encoun-ter our old friend Silenus of the boxes. He leads the vanguard of bacchantes on a jackass as the man whom Bacchus trusted for his great courage and prudence, "un petit vieillard tremblant, courbé, gras, ventru à plain basts; et les aureilles avoit grandes et droictes, le nez pointu et aquilin et les sourcilles rudes et grandes" (2:432) [a tremulous little old man, bowed, fat, gorbellied, and he had straight ears, a pointed aquiline nose, and big unkempt eyebrows (695)]. But Silenus is now dressed like a woman in a yellow robe surrounded by young countrymen with goatlike horns, naked, and singing continuously as they dance the cordax — 85,133 tityri and satyrs. Pan brings up the rearguard, Pan the son of Mercury, lord of interpretation, with 78,114 of his own followers. Finally they are told in chapter 45 that man distinguishes himself by drinking cool delicious wine: "ils disent en Grec *oinos* estre comme *vis*, force, puissance. Car pouvoir il a d'emplir l'ame de toute verité, tout savoir et philosophie" (2:454) [they say that *oinos* in Greek is like *vis*, strength, power. For power it has to fill the soul with all truth, all knowledge and philosophy (710)]. This is the ambrosia and nectar of Plato's great myth in the *Phaedrus* of the charioteer.[24] It is the wine that flows at the gods' symposium, the wine that Ficino himself advocated, following Plato in the *Laws*, as the best remedy for melancholy and not necessarily in decorously unrabelaisian quantities.[25] It is this Bacchic wine that paradoxically gives us the sobriety of soul to interpret Apollonian mysteries, the nine hypotheses of the *Parmenides*.

I agree with those who believe it is the myth of Bacchus, or rather of a hybrid Bacchus-Apollo, that Rabelais chooses to erect as the master myth of wisdom over and against the sophistry of the schools.[26] Ironically, this myth speaks not only to the world of the wandering scholars and their taverns, but to the other more austere world of the Platonists as well. Rabelais points indeed to the ecstatic, the mythopoeic, the demonic, the arithmological, and what contemporary Aristotelians might call the irrational dimensions of Renaissance Platonism, with which he was more profoundly in tune than most of his contemporaries and which formed some of the most prominent features of his intellectual landscape. Above all, it was Platonism, as I have tried to suggest by way of my brief remarks on Ficino's analysis of the *Parmenides* and its hermeneutical challenges, that revived and metamorphosed contemporary interest in the problems of interpretation and of the interpreter, the *alphestes*. Had he done no more, the abstractor of the quintessence, by evoking the myth of Silenus-Socrates, signaled a relationship to the theme that has cleverly anticipated already a denial of that relationship: "Croiez vous," he quips in

the prologue, "en vostre foy qu'oncques Homere, escrivent *l'Iliade*
et *Odyssée*, pensast es allegories lesquelles de luy ont calfreté Plu-
tarche, Heraclides Ponticq, [etc.] . . . [quand] icelles aussi peu avoir
esté songées d'Homere que d'Ovide en ses *Metamorphoses* les sacremens de l'Evangile" (1:8) [Do you believe in all good faith that
Homer, writing the *Iliad* and *Odyssey*, ever thought of all the allegories with which he has been calked by Plutarch, Heraclides Ponti-
cus . . . (when) these were as little thought of by Homer as were the
sacraments of the Gospel by Ovid in his *Metamorphoses* (4–5)]. This
is, after all, the position, in part at least, of Ficino with regard to
Proclus's *ad unguem* analysis of the Plato text. And yet Alcofribas
concludes his oration, "pour tant, interpretez tous mes faictz et mes
dictz en la perfectissime partie" (1:9) [Therefore interpret all my
deeds and words in the most perfect sense (5)].

Rabelais's debts to the most perfect sense of Plato, of the Neoplatonists including the Pseudo-Areopagite, and of Ficino and Pico
will doubtless continue to surface as an issue. We are indebted to the
earlier studies of Abel Lefranc, Lucien Febvre, Robert Marichal, and
François Rigolot, to name only a tetraktys of savants who have been
drawn to the problems.[27] But I hope I have intimated within the
narrow limits of this article that the Platonism of Ficino at least is a
great deal more complicated and independent than has hitherto been
assumed. Scholars should no longer turn exclusively, as they have
been tempted to in the past, to his youthful *Symposium* commentary
as if it were an epitome of his views when it is only a partial and
nearly always a preliminary statement of those views. Rather, if
Rabelais's engagement, however dialogic or parodic or intermittent,
with Florentine Platonism is to continue at times to engage our attention, then we must deepen our understanding of that Platonism
and, I might add, of the refined Epicureanism that was one of its
principal strands. The *Parmenides* is not everyone's gayest dialogue,
in the sense of most ebullient, but we should bear in mind that in
order to interpret it Ficino sought to be *laetus in praesens*, invoking
the tag from the Epicurean Horace. He sought, that is, for the bacchic *hilaritas* that had animated Plotinus in the mystical dances of
the *Enneads*. It is my suggestion here that Rabelais's great work is

continually wrestling with some of the paradoxes, the *morosophia*, that such an *hilaritas* entails.

To conclude on an appropriately vinous and at the same time enneadic note, let us return to the nine flagons arranged after the fashion of Gascon skittles, meaning presumably in a triangular formation thus:

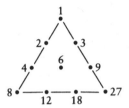

The most famous triangle in Plato derives from the so-called lambda formation, created by the two quaternary sequences 1–2–4–8 and 1–3–9–27 in the *Timaeus*'s description of the harmonic structure of the soul and of the cosmos. These quaternaries provide us with a key to the understanding of all reality, and they are pointedly invoked in chapter 35 of the *Cinquième livre* by the Princess Bacbuc, lady-in-waiting to the Bottle and priestess of all the mysteries, perhaps because she is alluding to Panurge's lambdal or skittlish age of thirty and not yet married, not yet a *genitor*. But Rabelais had already wittily suggested in the prologue to *Gargantua* that the lambda formation of the skittles is also the key to the Pantagrueline genealogy and thus to his own great book of giants and to the "mouldy, pretty, little book" within it of its Platonism.[28]

Later commentators on the *Timaeus* had filled in the lambda's geometric means, putting 6 between 4 and 9, and 12 and 18 between 8 and 27, in effect transforming the lambda into a delta of ten numbers, a delta signifying four, the Pythagoreans' tetrad, that is, the first four numbers that added together make up ten.[29] With and without these means, we can establish the products of the lambda's three horizontal steps thus: $2 \times 3 = 6$, $4 \times 9 = 36$, $4 \times 6 \times 9 = 216$, $8 \times 27 = 216$, and $8 \times 12 \times 18 \times 27 = 46,656$. The products are all powers of 6, 216 being the cube of 6 and the number of years assigned by the Pythagoreans to the intervals between successive incarnations and 46,656 being the square of 216 and thus 6 to the sixth or 36 cubed.[30]

From the point of view of Pythagorean mathematics, 6 is the first perfect number, being the first number that is the sum of its parts, even as it is the first nuptial number, being the product of the first odd and the first even number, that is, of 3 and 2.[31] It was traditionally assigned to Jupiter as the philosopher-king and father of gods and men. The ratio governing 2:3, 4:6:9 and 8:12:18:27 is 2:3, which, in terms of Plato's Pythagorean harmonics, is musically the perfect fifth, the *diapente*.[32] The 6 is thus tied to the primary, the jovian harmony of the *diapente*.

The middle flagon of nine above the book of Pantagruel's genealogy must therefore occupy the position of the first mean in the lambda, the 6, the jovian number at the heart both of the lambda's and of the Pantagrueline generations, of the skittles played by the giant's *progenitores* with his *progenitrices*. Or did the Gascons arrange their skittles unplatonically after all? Was Rabelais boozily hinting as much when he made room for only one mean instead of two means for the base of the lambda? He thus effectively took the Pythagoreans' decad of numbers constituting the lambda and rejected it for the ennead, which is sacred to the muses of literary inspiration and to the heavenly choirs of Christian belief, and is, moreover, the Apollonian number governing the hypotheses of the second, the supremely mysterious part of the *Parmenides*. Of the sixth book of his Platonism, Rabelais deliberately left us it would seem just a few mouldy pretty pages under a flagon, itself under the sign of a goblet with the inscription HIC BIBITUR in Etruscan letters, and all under the mud of a drainage ditch that entered the Vienne.

# Notes

## Introduction   *Jean-Claude Carron*

1. Unless otherwise indicated, all quotations from Rabelais are taken from the *Œuvres complètes*, ed. Pierre Jourda, 2 vols. (Paris: Garnier, 1962). The accompanying translations are by Donald M. Frame from his *Complete Works of François Rabelais* (Berkeley: University of California Press, 1991). The volume and page numbers of each citation will be given in parentheses immediately following the quoted passage. Arabic numbers immediately following Rabelais's book titles indicate chapters. For all other citations, please see the bibliography.

2. With the exceptions of Defaux's, Duval's, and Rigolot's articles; close, but different versions of their papers are also being published separately. We have decided to include them in this collection as part of an overall project meant to bring together representatives of Rabelais's different schools of criticism through a common publication. All three contributions assume new, full meaning when read with the other contributions to the collection, as this introduction shows.

3. See Berrong and Lachman, but also Kristeva who, already in 1967, insisted on the political context of Bakhtin's language of contestation. I owe this bibliographical remark to M. A. Wiesmann.

4. See however Bauschatz, Charpentier, Weinberg, and Chesney Zegura.

5. Raffel, *Gargantua and Pantagruel* (New York: Norton, 1990).

In the name of the UCLA Department of French, under the auspices of which this publication is placed, I would like to thank here all the participants in the symposium and all who contributed to its success. I would like to acknowledge especially the UCLA Division of the Humanities and its former dean, Professor Herbert Morris, as well as the Borchard Foundation and its director, Dr. William Beling, for their support and their generous financial contributions. Marc-André Wiesmann was involved since the beginning in this project. I am indebted to him for countless hours of bibliographical research, reading reports, and immeasurable contribution, including the suggestions for the titles of the three parts of this collection. A number of other colleagues (Marc Silberman, Eric Gans, Shuhsi Kao) and research assistants (Guy Bennett, Diane Duffrin, Markus Müller, and Marcella Munson) were pressed into service at various stages of this publication. This colloquium would not have been possible without the dedication of Mary Pottala, administrative head of the department, and Anne Chapman, our research assistant. My deepest appreciation to all.

## The Framing of Rabelais's *Gargantua*    Raymond La Charité

1. On *Pantagruel* and the *Grandes Chronicques* as intertextual anti-model, see Gray, "Rabelais' First Readers."

2. My discussion of narrative situation owes a great deal to Ross Chambers's seminal work, *Story and Situation: Narrative Seduction and the Power of Fiction.* For studies of how Rabelais situates his text "in terms of a literary or discursive context that serves as the interpretant, or criterion of relevance and determines the selective process of reading" (Chambers, 31), see La Charité 1985 and 1986.

3. Floyd Gray points out that "le prologue [all of them], contrairement au texte continu qui le suit, semble procéder plus immédiatement de ce qui appartient au monde de la vue" (Gray 1974, 32). See Duval's use of the same reference below and Regosin.

4. A fuller discussion of the workings of reversibility in the prologue can be found in Rigolot 1977 and La Charité 1985.

5. Cf. Cave 1979, 99: "The Janus-faced character of this prologue controverts any attempt to extract a theoretical model which may then be used to 'explicate' the book as a whole." But see Duval 1985 and Defaux 1985.

6. To mention but a few examples. For Barry Lydgate, however, the "Fanfreluches antidotées" episode, in spite of its "symmetry of position" and its discovery "in a similar manner" is not a text of analogous character: "The 'Fanfreluches' are in the book but outside the contextualizing story. The 'Enigme,' on the other hand, is incorporated into the larger fiction. It is read out loud by Gargantua, and its interpretation is the subject of an animated discussion between the hero and Frère Jean" (Lydgate, 372).

7. For a "iocari serio" interpretation of the little book and the Gascon skittles, see M. J. B. Allen below.

8. See Defaux 1974.

9. Glauser, 104, regarding Gargantua's letter to Pantagruel in *Pantagruel* (8). Gray suggests that, in *Pantagruel*, "le livre ne renvoie qu'au livre" (Gray 1974, 63), a remark that is equally pertinent for *Gargantua*.

10. François Rigolot explains the discrepancy a reader might feel between the expression of beauty and freedom expressed monotonously and heavy-handedly in the following way: "C'est qu'elle [l'Abbaye] était 'fondée' sur une *énigme*, c'est-à-dire sur une déception" (Rigolot 1972, 97).

11. "à la base d'un édifice voué à l'existence harmonieuse, on se heurte à la nécessité du déchiffrement des textes" (Demerson 1986, 139).

12. In his "Notes sur l'abbaye de Thélème," Jean-Yves Pouilloux shows incisively how the voices of Gargantua, Frère Jean, and the narrator function as one in ch. 52.

13. Terence Cave presents an excellent discussion of the "thematization in Renaissance texts of the act of reading" (1982, 152).

14. See Defaux's use of this same passage in the present volume.

15. I am borrowing here François Rigolot's astute distinction in Rigolot 1986.

## Rabelais's Realism, Again   *Gérard Defaux*

1. For a parallel reading, see J. C. Margolin's essay below.

2. For Gorgias and the Sophists, see M. J. B. Allen's article below.

3. Desiderius Erasmus, "Prefatory Letter to Thomas More" (p. 4) in *The Praise of Folly.* Translations are mine.

4. See La Charité's interpretation of this passage in the present volume.

5. See reference to passage I, 171 in Cave's contribution below.

6. In his contribution to the present volume, J.-C. Margolin arrives at a similar conclusion.

7. See Cave's article below.

8. See the concept of dialectical connection in Cave below.

9. La Ramée, 76. Aristotle 1961, ch. X ("De oppositis"). See also Aristotle's *Rhetoric*, III, 2.

10. See J.-C. Margolin below for the same subjective dimension of the text.

11. See Defaux 1987, mainly 11–54.

12. Duval 1985. See also, on *Gargantua*'s prologue, Defaux 1985; Cave, Jeanneret, and Rigolot; and my reply, Defaux 1986.

## Travelers and Others   *Terence Cave*

1. The nature and limitations of this role are clear as soon as one notes that, in Lucian, the stranger whom the narrator meets is himself exiled in an alien world; he is also not planting cabbages, with all that that connotes in terms of a reassuring familiarity and rootedness.

2. Cf. M. A. Screech's brief reference to this episode in Screech 1979b, 101. After the serious episode recounting Pantagruel's prayer before battle (*Pantagruel* 29), "we are whisked away again into a world of laughter."

3. On this episode, see also Antonioli 1980.

4. It is clear that Rabelais has only a vague idea of where, say, Greenland

is; Megiser will again classify Greenland and even Iceland, with Madagascar, as new-world territories.

5. Pantagruel's teeth are like the "monts des Dannoys" (presumably the mountains of Norway), etc. See Auerbach, 235; Lestringant, 47–48.

6. See Lestringant 44–47. The episode recounting Epistémon's descent into Hell (*Pantagruel* 30) is also mentioned by Lestringant in this context and should indeed be grouped with the travel episodes in any more detailed study. Many of these themes, particularly those concerning pilgrimage, have been analyzed in the 1994 Oxford D. Phil. dissertation of C. W. C. Williams. Dr. Williams's reflections have at several points nourished my own.

7. For the parallel homily to the pilgrims, see Rabelais (Jourda) 1:169–70. See the same episode in Defaux's article.

8. Rabelais 1962, 2:95 (*Quart livre* 18). Cf. Montaigne, 87: "que la mort me treuve plantant mes chous, mais nonchalant d'elle, et encore plus de mon jardin imparfait."

9. In discussing this double episode, I shall in the main assume the reader's familiarity with the text; page references within these chapters will not be provided. Recent studies include Tournon, Demerson 1981, and Kotin. I shall frequently allude here to aspects of the episode that I have treated in greater detail in Cave 1990, 1982, and 1979 111–15. Also relevant are chapters 1 and 2 of Defaux 1982. Demonet's brilliant analysis (1992, 176–87) appeared after this essay was written.

10. In Lucian's *True History* as in many scenes of the *Odyssey*, the old man the narrator meets in the whale's belly observes an ethic of hospitality according to which a stranger is given sustenance before he is asked to recount his adventures or identify himself.

11. It is perhaps not insignificant that the Utopian subtext that nourishes Rabelais's apodemic episodes throughout the first two books reinforces these connections. For example, Panurge speaks Utopian, a journey to Utopia is represented in *Pantagruel* 24, and Picrochole's imperial plan, together with the homily of *Gargantua* 46, is foreshadowed in a passage of Book I of More's *Utopia* in which such ambitions are attributed to the French king.

12. The reference is to the unsuccessful French siege of Mytilene in 1502. The Turkish episode is analyzed in ample detail by Timothy Hampton in Hampton 1993.

13. Panurge's second language is identified by Epistémon as "langaige des Antipodes." After the sixth, Epistémon comments, "Parlez vous christian, mon amy, ou langaige Patelinoys? Non, c'est langaige Lanternois" (1:266) [Are you speaking Christian, my friend, or Pathelin language. No, that's Lanternese talk (164)].

14. Cf. the phrase "les adventures des gens curieulx," used by Pantagruel

to indicate the probable motivation for Panurge's journey, and Panurge's reference to the six thousand florins he pocketed on his crusading venture in *Pantagruel* 17 (1:309).

15. André Tournon seems to take for granted that the perspective from which Panurge's languages are viewed is that of a "lettré" or humanist (Tournon, 111, 114), see also Kotin, 695.

16. For a bibliography of this family of manuals, see Bart; a useful bibliography of modern language pedagogy in this period is provided in Bingen. See also Simonin.

17. Tournon claims that his deduction is "aussi vaine que douteuse" (Tournon, 119). It seems, on the contrary, quite plausible that Panurge should have lived for a while in Greece while on his travels.

18. See, for example, *Sex linguarum....*, fol. B[i]r; de Mesmes fols. A iii–iv; Meurier fols. A ii ff.; Barlaimont, quadrilingual preface to reader (not paginated); Nicolay 45–46. On the topos of the deceitful interpreter, see Gomez-Géraud.

19. *Les Navigations, Quatrième livre* 16 (1989, 233–34).

20. See among many others Rigolot 1972, 34–37 and Screech 1979b, 29–33. Tournon discusses the compensation of Babel by Pentecost (Tournon, 126–27, 132–33); see also Céard 1980. On myths of language in the sixteenth century, Dubois remains a standard point of reference.

21. After the nine modern languages, the three ancient languages are arranged in their traditional chronological order; the interpolation of Utopian interrupts the sequence, but does not affect this diachronic axis. Besides, the mythology of Utopia suggests that its language might well have an antiquity located between Greek and Latin. The etymology of More's Utopian, though admittedly not Rabelais's, has Greek but not Latin affinities.

22. For a recent account of this topic, see Smith.

23. See *Gargantua* 52 and the inscription on the gate of Thélème (54).

24. See the contribution of Edwin Duval to the present volume.

25. This point is cogently made in Duval 1991, 137. The view that Rabelais's work reflects a marked change in attitudes to popular culture in the sixteenth century is defended in Berrong; Stephen Greenblatt sees the Rabelaisian shift not as a rejection of popular materials but the translation of those materials into a different and more learned context, where they are already marked as the popular, thus heralding an eventual hierarchization (Greenblatt 64–69). On the relation fiction/ideology, see also Defaux's article below.

26. On money in Rabelais, see my forthcoming article "'Or donné par don': Échanges matériels et métaphoriques chez Rabelais," to be published in the proceedings of an international colloquium entitled, *Or, monnaie, échange dans la culture de la Renaissance* held at Lyon in September 1991.

27. This question is excellently treated in Freccero 1991.

28. On this shift from the threatening giant of tradition to the benevolent Rabelaisian giant and many other related matters, see Stephens.

29. See Lestringant, 43 and 45. Cf. also Mikhail Bakhtin's account of the way the "grotesque body" is confronted in Bakhtin 1968, esp. 337–41.

30. See a parallel remark in Rigolot's article on Rabelais's medieval background.

## Signs Gone Wild    *Michel Jeanneret*

1. See Jeanneret 1992.

2. See La Charité's reading of this passage, as well as M. J. B. Allen's use of the same episode in their essays in the present volume.

3. These same questions are posed by M. J. B. Allen in his essay included here.

4. The summary which follows on medieval hermeneutics is simplified to the extent of being a distortion. My only apology is that it reflects the way the humanists themselves saw it.

5. On hermeneutics and semiology in the Middle Ages, see Lubac, Seznec, Chydenius, and Strubel.

6. On Renaissance semiology, see Waswo.

7. In his contribution to the present volume, M. J. B. Allen presents a discussion on the humanist debate on the question of Neoplatonist interpretation.

8. See Eco 1990.

9. See the parallel with the Ficinian concept of "preparedness" in M. J. B. Allen's article below.

10. This break with scholastic hermeneutics does not mean that Rabelais severed all links with the Middle Ages. His work is saturated with such vestiges of medieval literature as comic devices and word play, the marvelous and the chivalric. Rabelais's culture is heterogeneous and unstable; it mixes the old and the new (see Cave's contribution to this collection), a strong dislike for "gothic" epistemology and an obvious sympathy for traditional narrative.

11. See Margolin's and Defaux's essays in this collection.

12. This is part of the trouble with the *Cinquième livre*, which in several ways takes a step back to allegorical structures.

13. See Cave's parallel treatment of the unfamiliar in this volume.

## Feminism, Rabelais, and the Hill/Thomas Hearings
*Carla Freccero*

1. See also Freccero 1985 and 1986.

2. I am referring, of course, to the second night of the Senate confirmation hearings.

3. If we want to remain within the terms of the oedipal, we might argue that Booth here undercuts the homosocial in his identification with the mother. Identification with the mother constitutes the undoing of the oedipal triangle. The submission to the Law of the Father requires that the primal identification with the mother, an identification that lies beneath, so to speak, both homosociality and homosexuality, be suppressed. I thank Helene Moglen for providing me with these observations. See also Kaja Silverman.

4. See Sedgwick and Rubin.

## The Three Temptations of Panurge  *François Rigolot*

I wish to thank Howard Bloch and Florence Weinberg for their careful reading of this paper and many invaluable suggestions.

1. To quote one of Edwin M. Duval's compelling statements from his *The Design of Rabelais' Pantagruel*: "Only to the degree that we are able to enter the community of intended readers by bringing to the *Pantagruel* the Christian humanist culture it presupposes in us will we be successful in making sense of its design" (Duval 1991, xvii).

Recontextualizing the literary text, however, always remains problematic. As Samuel Kinser remarks, "Context is the bane of criticism. Everyone uses it; no one knows how to encompass it. Context cannot be connoted or defined because its boundaries themselves depend on context" (Kinser, 265).

2. Like Bakhtin, Saulnier also insisted on Rabelais's down-to-earth humor in the vein of the Goliard tradition (1946, xxxv).

3. See, for instance, the studies of Peter Burke (quoted in Berrong, 14), Natalie Z. Davis, and Robert Muchambled.

4. Rabelais writes, "Quand je diz femme [dist Rondibilis], je diz un sexe tant fragil, tant variable, tant muable, tant inconstant et imperfaict, que Nature me semble (parlant en tout honneur et reverence) s'estre esguarée de ce bon sens par lequel elle avait créé et formé toutes choses, quand elle a basty la femme" (1:539) [When I say woman [said Rodibilis], I mean a sex so fragile, so variable, so mutable, so inconstant and imperfect, that Nature (speaking in all honor and reverence) seems to me to have strayed from that good sense by which she had created and formed all things, when she built woman (356)].

5. Quoted from Saulnier's edition of *Pantagruel* (Saulnier, 177). In subsequent editions, Rabelais replaced this expression with a less provocative one: "Ce sont belles besoignes" (1:385) [These are fine works (*my translation*)].

6. This episode can be found in chapters 21–24 of the definitive edition of the book. In the *editio princeps*, the episode is recorded in chapters 14–15 (Rabelais 1946, 115–32).

7. All translations are my own except when Frame's version is noted with a page reference.

8. Gargantua had used the same expression in the context of his praise for educated women: "Que diray je? Les femmes et les filles ont aspiré à ceste louange et *manne celeste* de bonne doctrine" (1:260; my emphasis) [What am I to say next? Women and girls have aspired to this praise and *celestial manna* of good learning].

9. In the passage quoted by Jesus from Deuteronomy, Moses, who has just revealed the Ten Commandments to the children of Israel, exhorts his people to keep God's covenant. Transposed in Rabelais's text, the exhortation to keep the Commandments may correspond to the lady's willingness to let Panurge keep her *patenostres*. When Panurge begs her to part with her rosary beads, she answers, "Tenez, et ne me tabustez plus" (1:329) [Here you are, and do not pester me any more].

10. The Vulgate text simply gives "Vade Satana" (Matt. 4:10) 955.

11. "Et ce dict, s'en fouit le grand pas, de peur des coups, lesquelz il craignoit naturellement" (1:331) [And, that said, he ran away at a good pace, for fear of blows, of which by nature he was afraid].

12. Several parallels between Panurge's seductive language and the narrator's *captatio benevolentiae* can be found especially in the first two books. The tempter's alluring display of precious objects in front of the lady's eyes is echoed in the implied author's praise of his own book in the Prologue: "Trouvez moy livre . . . qui ayt telles vertus, proprietés et prerogatives, et je poieray chopine de trippes. Non, Messieurs, non. Il est sans pair, incomparable et sans parragon" (1:217) [Find me a book . . . that has such virtues, properties, and prerogatives, and I shall treat you to a pint of tripes. No, gentlemen, no. It is peerless, incomparable, and beyond comparison].

13. "But," said he, "play inversions with *A creek rises for a handsome punt* [A Beaumont le Vicomte]."

"I couldn't do that," said she.

"That," said he, "makes *A prick rises for a handsome cunt* [A beau con le vit monte]." (205)

14. Frame ingeniously translates: "so much that he tried to give her come-uppance to one of the great ladies" (203) and notes, "*venir au dessus de* means 'get the better of, dominate,' but literally 'come over' or 'come on top of,' as is clearly meant here" (note 2, 833).

15. See Jean Bouchet's expression: "Ilz ont le sacre en leur eglise," quoted in Huguet under "sacre."

Emile Littré mentions examples ranging from Froissart: "Ceux de la cité de Reims doivent le sacre du roi," to Marot: "De son bon gré ta gent bien disposée / Au jour très sainct de ton sacre courra" (Littré 6: 1807).

16. Bynum 1982, 110–69 and 1987, 246; Sturtz, 42 ff. Rabelais also

knew that Christ's humanity was symbolized by the hen who, as a good mother seeks to protect her offspring: "quemadmodum *gallina* congregat pullos suos sub alas" (Matt. 23:37, my emphasis). In *Pantagruel* 32, the eponymous hero puts his tongue out to cover his troops from the rain "comme une *geline* faict ses poulletz" (1:378) [as a hen does her chickens (239 my emphasis)].

17. Psalm 21(22) "Petitio et laudatio Christi," 21:8, 17, 21.

18. Such deciphering is, of course, made clear by the address on the letter sent to Pantagruel: "Au plus aymé des belles, et moins loyal des preux, P.N.T.G.R.L." (1:337) [To the best beloved of the fair, and the least faithful of the valiant, P.N.T.G.R.L. (210)].

19. J. M. Cohen incorrectly translates: "And he would have embraced her, had she not *struggled* to get to the window" (Rabelais 1955, 240).

20. One can find numerous examples of this usage in Marguerite de Navarre's *Heptaméron*.

21. See Cave's similar conclusions on Rabelais's use of the "old," above.

22. See Freccero's paper on Booth's laugh above.

## Rabelais and the Language of Malediction   *Thomas Greene*

1. Quoted in Drogin, 89.

2. This would seem to be the meaning of an old Irish legend. In interpreting it, we need to remember the association of Irish bards with invective, which made them feared by king and peasant from the dimmest prehistory at least until the time of Spenser. The legend describes the metamorphosis of a "foul-faced gillie" whose aspect was "unbelievably hideous." But the repulsive gillie overcomes a recognized bard in a poetic contest and is abruptly transformed: he appears as a "young hero with golden-yellow hair . . . royal raiment he wore, and his form was the noblest that hath been seen on a human being. . . . It is not . . . doubtful that he was the Spirit of Poetry." Quoted in Elliott, 22–23. I wish to acknowledge my indebtedness to Elliott's important book.

3. May the next thinge thou stoop'st to reach containe
   Poyson, whose nimble fume rot thy moist braine,
   Or libells, or some interdicted thinge,
   Which negligently kept thy ruine bringe.
   Lust-bred diseases rot thee' and dwell with thee
   Itchy desire and no abilitie.
   May all the hurt which ever Gold hath wrought,
   All mischiefes which all devills ever thought,
   Want after plenty, poore and gouty age,
   The plagues of travellers, love and marriage

Afflict thee; and at thy lifes last moment
May thy swolne sins themselves to thee present.
(Donne, 4)

4. The curse against a reader's incredulity appears to have been traditional and by no means always playful. Gregory of Tours writes in his *Vita S. Abbadi* that, if any one doubts his veracity, "et hic et in aeternum per virtutes sancti et beati domini Martini sit excommunicatus et anathematizatus, et veniat illa maledictio, quam psalmus CVIII continet in Judam Scariotis." M. S. L. 71, 1149. Quoted in Archer, 251. For Psalm 108 (109), which was believed to anticipate the story of Judas, see below.

5. Spitzer 1988. For Rabelais, see especially 18–30.

6. Archer in "The Judas Curse" reports that a curse was incorporated in the papal bull of 1035, proclaiming the Peace of God, as doubtless in many other bulls. This particular bull was promulgated from the pulpit as tapers were being extinguished. It read in part, "May they who refuse to obey be accursed, and have their portion with Cain the first murderer, with Judas the archtraitor, and with Dathan and Abiram, who went down alive into the pit. May they be accursed in the life that now is; and may their hope of salvation be put out, as the light of these candles is extinguished from their sight." See Archer, 235–36 and 236, note 6.

7. See Rigolot 1976, especially 125: "Tout se passe . . . comme si l'accord des éléments sonores du langage, et leur rassemblement par le poète, pouvait devenir licite, et même recommandé, lorsqu'il a essentiellement pour but de *sceller*, de figurer symboliquement, un accord préexistant des composantes sémantiques du discours."

8. See Defaux 1987, 26 and 30. See also Norton, 267.

9. See Defaux 1987, 47 for a discussion of "le Cratylisme radical du siècle."

## History, Epic, and the Design of Rabelais's *Tiers Livre*
### Edwin M. Duval

1. See the essays by La Charité and Regosin in the present collection for a similar reference.

2. See Regosin's article below for the same reference. *How to Write History* had been included in all of the eight Greek editions of Lucian's complete works published before the *Tiers Livre* first appeared. It had also been published as a separate work in two different Latin translations (one by Cataneus in 1507, another by Pirkheimer in 1515) before being translated yet a third time by Iacobus Micyllus and included in the latter's standard Latin edition of Lucian's complete works, published in Frankfurt in 1538 and 1543 and in Paris in 1546. See Lauvergnat-Gagnière 352–53 (#1001–11), 394 (#2104), 395 (#2110), and 378–79 (#2038–40).

3. English translations of Lucian in these pages are my own. Parenthetical references are to the standard paragraph numbers in all editions. Bracketed references are to page numbers in the modern Loeb edition.

4. As a detailed continuation of Froissard's chronicle that begins precisely where Froissard had left off (on Easter Sunday, 1400), Monstrelet's chronicle was of considerable interest to readers of Rabelais's generation, for whom the Hundred Years' War was still a recent crisis. Monstrelet's chronicle was also quite accessible, having been published at least four times in Paris before the *Tiers livre* appeared. Two editions were published by Antoine Vérard circa 1500 and 1503, one by Jean Petit and Michel Lenoir in 1512, and one by Francois Regnault in 1518. See Tchemerzine.

5. I quote the text of the second Vérard edition (ca. 1503), fol. v$^v$. Earlier manuscripts read "finalement, quant au fait, rien n'en fut exécuté, ne mis à effect." See Monstrelet 1:31.

6. Cf. "Cum olim quidam rudes atque agrestes homines viderent in monte terram intumescere moverique, concurrunt undique ad tam horrendum spectaculum, exspectantes, ut terra novum aliquod ac magnum portentum ederet, monte nimirum parturiente, foreque, ut Titanes rursum erumperent, bellum cum Diis redintegraturi. Tandem ubi multum diuque suspensis attonitisque animis exspectassent, mus prorepsit e terra, moxque risus omnium ingens exortus." Erasmus 1961–62, 2:339c–e. English translations of Erasmus are my own.

7. "Utitur hoc adagio Lucianus in libello, cui titulus, *Quemadmodum oporteat Historias conscribere. . . .* Utitur et Horatius in *Arte Poetica.*"

8. For the formal and ideological coherence and the teleological perfection of Rabelais's first Pantagrueline epic, see my *Design of Rabelais's Pantagruel* (New Haven: Yale University Press, 1991).

9. Nec gemino bellum Troianum orditur ab ovo;
   semper ad eventum festinat et in medias res
   non secus ac notas auditorem rapit, et quae
   desperat tractata nitescere posse, relinquit,
   atque ita mentitur, sic veris falsa remiscet,
   primo ne medium, medio ne discrepet imum.
   (1970, 462, lines 147–52)

10. Micyllus's Latin translation of this passage is especially clear in its implications: "[Dicamus] quibus rebus utendo *non aberraverit a recta via, et eo quo tendit, ducente:* nempe *quo exordio* incipiendum sit, *quo ordine* res quaeque iungendae inter se et componendae sint, *quis modus* singulis adhibendus, quae silentio praetereunda, quibus immorandum, et quae cursu praetervehi satius sit, quomodo exponenda eadem et coaptanda sint" (my emphasis).

11. Humano capiti cervicem pictor equinam
iungere si velit, et varias inducere plumas
undique collatis membris, ut turpiter atrum
desinat in piscem mulier formosa superne,
spectatum admissi risum teneatis, amici?
credite, Pisones, isti tabulae fore librum
persimilem, cuius, velut aegri somnia, vanae
fingentur species, ut nec pes nec caput uni
reddatur formae. (1970, 457, lines 1–9)

12. I am currently working out the consequences of such questions in a book to be titled *The Design of Rabelais's* Tiers livre.

## Opening Discourse    *Richard Regosin*

1. For the prologues to the first two books see Gray 1965 and 1986, Regosin, and La Charité 1986. See also Glauser, Cave 1979, and Greene 1970.

2. For a general discussion of the problematic nature of opening, see the opening chapters of Said.

3. See Duval's article above for Rabelais's use of the same treatise.

4. See, for example, Screech 1979b and, for a reading from a different perspective, Berry.

5. On the relationship of the bacchic and the apollonian in Rabelais, see Berry.

6. "De ce poinct expedié, à mon tonneau je retourne. Sus à ce vin, compaings! Enfans, beuvez à plains guodetz" (1:401) [With that point expedited, I return to my barrel. Up and at this time, mates! Fill up your mugs, lads! (259)].

7. See Cave's excellent pages on Rabelais and the *Tiers livre* in Cave 1979, 171–72 and 189–94.

## Rabelais, Erasmus's Intellectual Heir?    *Jean-Claude Margolin*

1. For instance, Delaruelle, Thuasne, Plattard, W. F. Smith, L. Febvre. See also Lebègue, Screech 1972 a and b, and Dresden. See also Screech 1979 and La Charité 1986.

2. See Rummel 1986a and Rummel 1986b, 41–57.

3. See Rabelais 1532. About Rabelais and medicine, see Antonioli 1976. For Erasmus's translation, see "Galeni exhortatio ad bonas artes; de optimo docendi genere; quod optimus medicus sit etiam philosophus, Erasmo interprete," in Galenus.

4. For individual nature, see our critical edition of the *De pueris statim ac*

*liberaliter instituendis* (Basel: Froben, 1529) in Erasmus, *Opera omnia Desiderii Erasmi* (referred to as ASD) I–2 1971, 1–78. Also see the *De libero arbitrio* in Erasmus 1703–6, X, col. 1215.

5. See especially Bené.

6. For Erasmus's poetry, see Reedijk. His poems seem artificial and rhetorical. They are good Horatian, Ovidian, or Ausonian poems, but not truly Erasmian.

7. See Miller's translation (Erasmus 1979) as well as his critical edition of this work in ASD III 1979.

8. *Complete Work of Erasmus*. See also Erasmus 1933, 3–135.

9. See Kay. Cf. the Ficinian *iocari serio* and *studiosi* in M. J. B. Allen's essay and Defaux's insistence on the marriage of opposites in their respective contributions to the present work.

10. The *declamatio* in itself is a rhetoric or literary genre based on paradoxes. See Thompson and Margolin 1986.

11. See Blum.

12. See Calogero and Chomarat 1987.

13. Erasmus 1961–62 II, 770c–782c (n. 2201). For an English translation, see Mann Phillips 269–96.

14. See Rummel 1989 and Winkler.

15. See Reeve 1986 and Erasmus CWE 1984, vol. 42 ("Paraphrases on Roman and Galatians"), 1991, vol. 46 ("Paraphrase on John"), and 1988, vol. 49 ("Paraphrase on Mark").

16. See Margolin's edition of *De pueris*, (ASD I–2 1971, 1–78 and Margolin 1973.

17. See *Playne and Godly Exposition or Declaration of the Commune Crede* (Devereux, 182–85; original Latin text: *Symbolum sive catechismus*, ASD V–1 1977, 205–320); *Preparation to Deathe* (Devereux, 100–101; original Latin text: *De praeparatione ad mortem*, ASD V–1 1977, 321–92); *An Epistle Concerning the Verytie of the Sacrament of Christes Body and Bloude* (Devereux, 125–27; original Latin text: *Epistola ad Balthasarem episc. Hildesheimensem sive De veritate corporis et sanguinis Dominici in Eucharistia*); *De sarcienda ecclesiae concordia* (ASD V–3 1986, 245–313), a commentary on the psalm *Quam dilecta tabernaclula tua*, showing the Church as the house of the Lord in which all factions should seek peace (Devereux, 78); and his sermon *Of the Excedynge Great Mercy of God* (original Latin text: *De immensa Dei misericordia concio*).

18. For one of the latest identifications, see Rigolot's contribution to the present volume.

19. This passage appears in a footnote; the text was reprinted in 1537 and suppressed in 1542.

20. For Erasmus, see especially his *Colloquies*. It is almost certain that

Erasmus did not have a Catholic priest at his death bed. See, among others, Garcia Villoslada.

21. See Lauvergnat-Gagnière, especially ch. 6 (Erasme, "Lucien batave") and 7 (Rabelais, "Lucien français"). See also Mayer.

22. On this point, see Demerson 1991.

23. *De libero arbitrio diatribe* (Basle, 1524); Luther, *De servo arbitrio* (Wittenberg, 1525).

24. Antwerp, 1503. See Erasmus, CWE 1988, 66.

25. *Abbas et erudita* (ASD I–3 1972, 463–68) and *De rebus ac vocabulis* (ASD I–3 1972, 566–71).

26. See also *De pueris instituendis* (ASD I–2 1971, 1–78).

27. *De duplici copia verborum ac rerum* (ASD I–6 1988).

28. See Chomarat 1981, 711–61.

## Like Father, Like Son?   *Marc Bensimon*

1. My translation. "[Ils] font un magnifique Palais, qu'ils enrichissent, dorent et embellisent par le dehors de marbre, Jaspe et . . . frises et chapiteaux et par dedans de Tableaux, tapisseries eslevees et bossees d'or et d'argent, et le dedans des tableaux cizelez et burinez, raboteux et difficiles a tenir és mains, à cause de la rude engraveure des personnages qui semblent vivre dedans. Apres ils adjoustent vergers et jardins." "Au lecteur apprentif," *La Franciade*, Laumonier ed. XVI, 340.

2. See further Marin 89–120. For further discussion of the bidimensional, see my essay "Modes of Perception," my edition of Ronsard's *Amours*, Choay, Derrida 1978, the first page of the present essay, and the reference to Foucault below.

3. "entendement à double rebras, et capacité de memoire à la mesure de douze oyres et botes d'olif" (1:256) [understanding enough for two, and a memory with a capacity of twelve skins and bottles of oil (158)].

4. M.-M. de La Garanderie, 5, quoted by Jerome Schwartz in his excellent and thorough study, *Irony and Ideology*, 21–22. Although Schwartz believes that Rabelais mirrors the humanists, I attempt to demonstrate in the following pages that the Rabelaisian venture undermines their position.

5. Screech chooses to see in this evocation a "useful corrective to any misunderstanding of Rabelais's enthusiasm for the 'species of immortality' that God has granted man through his children," I prefer to read here that, after lip service to that distant immortality, Rabelais will concentrate on having his Gargantua perpetuate his image for narcissistic reasons.

6. *Tomus primus Paraphaseon D. Erasmi Roterdami in novum Testamentum*, Froben, 1524, in–4, 143 quoted by Telle, 215, note 2 (my translation).

7. *Ratio verae theologiae*, quoted by Telle, 217, note 2. Telle also reminds

the reader of Erasmus's absolute rejection of the notion that the soul could unite to God in contemplative ecstasy or of the possibility for anyone to reach, during his lifetime, a state of perfection — utopian and inaccessible to mortals.

8. Re: "plus hault tendre": This is one of the very rare anagogical signs in Rabelais's work where one is not immediately reminded of the genital or the scatological, as at the end of *Gargantua* 7 — wine/ecstasy/farting — or in *Gargantua* 13 and 14 — marvelous, divine understanding/ass-wipe. In fact, a case could also be made in this example; there is a direct relation between seminal propagation and the goal to be achieved by the young giant if he soars to greater heights. Even the androgyne, a myth used to evoke the aspiration of the soul towards unity, is twisted in its iconic representation from its anagogical meaning, as we shall see below. "L'androgyne occupe les deux pôles du sacré. Pur concept, pure vision de l'esprit, elle [sa représentation] apparaît chargée des plus hautes valeurs. Actualisée en un être de chair et de sang, elle est une monstruosité, et rien de plus." Delcourt, *Hermaphrodite*, 68, quoted by Freccero in her excellent article "The Other and the Same."

9. That is the meaning, as has often been said, of the term *personne* according to religious orthodoxy.

10. Cf. also Cook Carpenter. For a long discussion of the possible meanings of Gargantua's *image*, see Jerome Schwartz's seminal article (1972) and his references in his more recent book, *Irony and Ideology* (1990, 56–65) to Pico della Mirandola's allusions and their relation to Leone Ebreo's (Léon Hébreu) famous description of the androgyne. I am indebted to him for these references. I choose, however, to retain only the antiplatonic meaning, and I arrive at a very different conclusion. Freccero also opposes a syncretic reading of the Rabelaisian androgyne (1986a, 149). For the place of the androgyne in the Renaissance, see Bensimon 1974, 221–72. See also Yavneh.

11. "Epistémon bought another one [painting], on which were portrayed to the life Plato's Ideas and Epicurus's atoms. Rhizotome bought another, showing Echo in her natural form" (Frame, 440).

12. Note also how Hébreu describes the androgyne: "Cest Androgyne, donq, estoit grand et terrible, pource qu'il avoit deux corps humains liez *et attachez* l'un à l'autre par la partie de l'estomac, et deux visages conjoints par le col en une teste, l'un d'un costé, l'autre de l'autre. Il avoit quatre yeux, quatre oreilles, et deux langues, et double partie genitale. Il avoit quatre bras avec les mains, et quatre jambes avec les piedz, tellement qu'il venoit quasi en forme *ronde et* circulaire. Il s'esmouvoit en treslegere vistesse, non seulement en l'une et l'autre partie, mais encor en mouvement circulaire, en grande legereté et vehemence avec quatre piedz et quatre mains" (*Dialogues d'amour* 1974, 243, translator's emphasis). This description coincides with the figure on Marcantonio Passeri's medal (Wind, *Pagan Mysteries*, 1968, plate 68).

13. As J. Schwartz proposes in 1990, 64–65. See also from the same author, "Aspects of Androgyny" (1978).

14. "Régression narcissique aux pulsions primitives mais que *le texte met en liberté dans un ordre symbolique renversé qui se joue de la loi . . .*" (Marin, 119, the author's emphasis).

15. "L'emploite [de la science] en est bien plus hasardeuse que de toute autre viande . . . ce que nous avons achetté, nous l'emportons au logis en quelque vaisseau. . . . Mais les sciences, nous ne les pouvons d'arrivée mettre en autre vaisseau qu'en nostre ame: nous les avallons en les achettans, et sortons de marché ou infects desjà, ou amendez. Il y en a qui ne font que nous empescher et charger au lieu de nourrir, et telles encore qui, sous tiltre de nous guerir, nous empoisonnent" (3:xii, 1015).

16. "De l'Affection des peres aux enfans," 2:viii, 380–83.

17. "De L'Amitié," 1:xxviii, 180–81. Cf. F. Rigolot, "Montaigne's Purloined Letters."

18. Marin continues to describe the anarchical condition of intense pleasure (*jouissance*): "jouissance dans le texte de langage d'un bouleversement des valeurs instituées de la langue, du discours, de la société, 'hors de toute finalité imaginable . . . rien ne reconstitue, rien ne se récupère. Le texte de jouissance est absolument intransitif . . . extrême toujours déplacé, extrême vide, mobile, imprévisible.' " (Marin, 120, quoting Barthes, 82–83).

## De Libro Sexto Cum Commento    *Michael J. B. Allen*

1. See M. J. B. Allen 1984, ch. 5, with further references.

2. See Margolin and Defaux in the present volume.

3. See Hankins, 1:337–39 and 1:344–45.

4. See the *argumentum* in *Opera Omnia* (1576), 1136–37. In general, see M. J. B. Allen 1986.

5. Plato's Pythagoreanism was an ancient topos. See, for example, Diogenes Laertius, *Lives of Eminent Philosophers* 1.21, and Proclus, *In Parmenidem* 1:619.4. It was repeated by Ficino in his *Platonic Theology* 17.4 (ed. Marcel, 3:168); in his own *In Parmenidem* proem and ch. 1, 16, and 21; and in the *argumentum* for his translation of the *Parmenides* (in his *Opera Omnia* [Basle, 1576] 1137, 1138, 1142, 1144).

6. See Garin 1937, parts 2 and 3.

7. *De Ente et Uno*: "totus [liber] nihil aliud est quam dialectica quaedam excitatio . . . ut nullae exstent magis et arbitrariae et violentae enarrationes quam quae ab his allatae sunt qui alio sensu interpretari *Parmenidem* Platonis voluerunt" (Garin 1942, 390).

8. ["Klibansky"] This essay has been reprinted in Klibansky 1981.

9. ["Aristotelians"] See Garin 1961, 60–71, 102–8.

10. "Utinam mirandus ille iuvenis disputationes discussionesque superi-

ores diligenter consideravisset antequam tam confidenter tangeret praeceptorem ac tam secure contra Platonicorum omnium sententiam divulgaret et divinum *Parmenidem* simpliciter esse logicum et Platonem una cum Aristotele ipsum cum ente unum et bonum adaequavisse" (Ficino 1576, 1164).

11. "Ad cuius sacram lectionem quisquis accedet, prius sobrietate animi mentisque libertate se praeparet quam attrectare mysteria coelestis operis audeat" (Ficino 1576, 1136–37).

12. See M. J. B. Allen 1982, 19–44, especially 28–41.

13. "Pythagorae Socratisque et Platonis mos erat ubique divina mysteria figuris involucrisque obtegere, sapientiam suam contra Sophistarum iactantiam modeste dissimulare, iocari serio et studiosissime ludere" (Ficino 1576, 1137).

14. See the letter to Francesco Musano of Iesi in Ficino's first book of *Letters*: "A bono in bonum omnia diriguntur. Letus in presens. Neque censum aestimes, neque appetas dignitatem. Fuge excessum, fuge negotia. Letus in presens." (Ficino 1990, 92–93 as No. 47; in Ficino 1576, it appears as No. 5 on p. 609.2). The Horatian reference is to the *Odes* 2.16.25.

15. See M. J. B. Allen 1986, 440–44.

16. "Ego vero mediam secutus viam; arbitror tantum saltem theologiae subesse quantum admittit artificium ut communiter dicitur dialecticum; ideoque non ubique omnino continuatas sed quandoque divulsas de divinis inesse sententias" (Ficino 1576, 1154).

17. For the puppet metaphor, see Plato's *Laws* 1.644D, 7.804B.

18. "Verum quidnam dialectico cum poeta commertii? Certe quam plurimum. Utrique enim atque soli circa suos, ut aiunt, conceptus et propria machinamenta versantur; habentur utrique divini et habent nescio quid furoris" (Ficino 1576, 1199verso). See M. J. B. Allen 1986, 444–48.

19. *Republic* 2.377B–382D, 3.387B–398B, 10.607A; *Laws* 10:890A, etc.

20. See Walker 1958, ch. 1; Walker 1972, 22–29 and 36–37; and Warden. For Ficino and the Orphic hymns, see Klutstein. In general, see Buck.

21. Ficino makes a number of references to this *Poema* throughout his *Parmenides* Commentary; see, for example, Ficino 1576, 1138.3, 1169.1,2, 1176.2, 1177.2, 1180.1, 1199recto-verso, etc.

22. See, for example, Tigerstedt. For Ficino and the *furor poeticus*, see M. J. B. Allen 1984, ch. 2.

23. The truly nuptial number is 6, not 5, since it is the product of 3 × 2 and not the sum of 3 + 2. Aristotle apparently claimed that the Pythagoreans thought of 5 as the nuptial number *apud* Alexander of Aphrodisias, *In Metaphysicam* 39.8 (fr. 203); but see Theon of Smyrna's *Expositio* 2.45 (ed. Hiller, 102.4–6).

24. *Phaedrus* 247E. For Ficino's analyses, see my *Platonism*, 163, 207, 210–13, 221, 224–25.

25. *Laws* 2.671A–674C (the "discourse about drink" and its regulation).

For Ficino's praise of Dionysiac feasts, see two letters in his third book of *Letters*, Nos. 15 and 42 (Ficino 1576, 728.2–729, 739.2–740.4).

26. See for example, Weinberg 1972, with the reviews in Coleman 1976; and Rigolot 1974.

27. See Marichal 1953, for further references; also Rigolot 1976.

28. See La Charité's reading of the "Fanfreluches antidotées" in the present volume.

29. Following Plato's own argument in the *Timaeus* 32AB that there is one mean between two square numbers, but there are two means between cubes.

30. See Dillon. 216 is also the reincarnational interval, because it is the sum of the cubes of the three numbers in the right triangle made famous by the Pythagoreans with sides of 3, 4, and 5, and because it is the product of the two feet of the Platonic lambda, that is, of $8 \times 27$.

31. See, for instance, Theon of Smyrna's *Expositio* 2.45 (ed. Hiller, 102. 4–6), and Ficino's *Timaeus* Commentary 12 (Ficino 1576, 1443.2).

32. For disquisitions on the consonances and the proportions that generate them and on the harmonic composition of the soul, in both of which "the Venerean grace" of the diapente plays a signal role, see Ficino's *Timaeus* Commentary 32 and 33 (Ficino 1576, 1456.2–1460).

# Bibliography

Allen, M. J. B. "Ficino's Theory of the Five Substances and the Neoplatonists' *Parmenides*." *Journal of Medieval and Renaissance Studies* 12, no. 1 (1982): 19–44.

———. *The Platonism of Marsilio Ficino*. Berkeley: University of California Press, 1984.

———. "The Second Ficino-Pico Controversy: Parmenidean Poetry, Eristic, and the One." *Marsilio Ficino e il ritorno di Platone. Studi e Documenti*. Edited by Gian Carlo Garfagnini. 2 vols. Florence: L. S. Olschki, 1986. 417–55.

Antonioli, Roland. *Rabelais et la médecine*. Etudes Rabelaisiennes 12. Geneva: Droz, 1976.

———. "Le motif de l'avalage dans les 'Chroniques gargantuines'." *Etudes seizièmistes offertes à M. le Professeur V.-L. Saulnier*, 77–85. Geneva: Droz, 1980.

Archer, Winston. "The Judas Curse." *American Journal of Philology* 42 (1921): 234–51.

Aristotle. *Aristoteles Latinus, Categoriae vel Praedicamenta*. Edited by Laurentius Minio-Palluelo. Paris: Desclée de Brouwer, 1961.

———. *The Complete Works*. The Revised Oxford Translation. Edited by Jonathan Barnes. Princeton: Princeton University Press, 1984.

Auerbach, Erich. *Mimesis: The Representation of Reality in Western Literature*. Translated by Willard Trask. New York: Doubleday, 1957.

Bakhtin, Mikhail. *Rabelais and His World*. Translated by Hélène Iswolsky. Cambridge: MIT Press, 1968.

———. *L'Œuvre de François Rabelais et la culture populaire au Moyen Age et sous la Renaissance*. Translated by A. Robel. Paris: Gallimard, 1970.

———. *The Dialogic Imagination*. Translated by Caryl Emerson and Michael Holquist. Austin: University of Texas Press, 1981.

Barlaimont, Noâl de. *Vocabulario, colloquios o dialogos en quatro lenguas, Flamengo, Frances, Espanol, y Italiana*. Antwerp: Jan Verwithagen, 1558.

Bart, A. Rossebastiano. *Antichi vocabolari plurilingui d'uso populare: la tradizione del "Solenissimo Vocabolista."* Alessandria: Edizione dell'Orso, 1984.

Barthes, Roland. *Le plaisir du texte*. Paris: Editions du Seuil, 1973.

# Bibliography

Bauschatz, Cathleen M. "Une description du jeu de paulme soubz obscures parolles: the portrayal of reading in *Pantagruel* and *Gargantua*." *Etudes Rabelaisiennes* 22 (1988): 57–76.

Beaujour, Michel. *Le jeu du Rabelais*. Paris: L'Herne, 1969.

Bené, Charles. *Rabelais et l'éducation: Rabelais, disciple d'Erasme?* Dissertation, Sorbonne, Paris: 1970.

Bensimon, Marc, ed. Pierre de Ronsard, *Les amours*. Paris: Garnier Flammarion, 1981.

———. "Modes of Perception of Reality in the Renaissance." *The Darker Vision of the Renaissance: Beyond the Field of Reason*. Edited by R. Kinsman. Berkeley: University of California Press, 1974. 221–72.

Berrong, Richard M. *Rabelais and Bakhtin. Popular Culture in* Gargantua *and* Pantagruel. Lincoln: University of Nebraska Press, 1986.

Berry, Alice. *Rabelais: Homo Logos*. Chapel Hill: University of North Carolina Press, 1979.

*The Holy Bible, Authorized King James Version*. New York: The Modern Library, 1943.

*Biblia Sacra* [*Vulgate Edition*]. Edited by P. Michael Hetzenauer. Ratisbon: F. Pustet, 1929.

Bingen, Nicole. *Le maître italien (1510–1660): bibliographie des ouvrages d'enseignement de la langue italienne destinés au public de langue française, suivie d'un répertoire des ouvrages bilingues imprimés dans les pays de langue française*. Brussels: Van Balberghe, 1987.

Bloch, R. Howard. *Medieval Misogyny and the Invention of Western Romantic Love*. Chicago: University of Chicago Press, 1991.

Blum, Claude. "Le fou, la folie et la mort à la fin du XVe siècle et au début du XVIe siècle." *La représentation de la mort dans la littérature française de la Renaissance*, 1: 85–160. Paris: Champion, 1989.

Booth, Wayne. "Freedom of Interpretation: Bakhtin and the Challenge of Feminist Criticism." *Critical Inquiry* 9 (1982): 45–76.

Bouloumié, Arlette. "Le mythe de l'androgyne dans l'oeuvre de Michel Tournier." *L'androgyne dans la littérature*, 63–79. Edited by F. Monneyron. Paris: Albin Michel, 1990.

Briçonnet, Guillaume, and Marguerite d'Angoulème. *Correspondance (1521–1524)*. Edited by Ch. Martineau, M. Veissière, and H. Heller. 2 vols. Vol. I Geneva: Droz, 1975, Vol. II 1979.

Buck, August. *Der Orpheus-Mythos in der italienischen Renaissance*. Krefeld: Sherpe, 1961.

Burke, Peter. *Popular Culture in Early Modern Europe*. New York: New York University Press, 1978.

Bynum, Caroline Walker. *Jesus as Mother: Studies in the Spirituality of the High Middle Ages*. Berkeley: University of California Press, 1982.

———. *Holy Feast and Holy Fast: The Religious Significance of Food to Medieval Women*. Berkeley: University of California Press, 1987.

Calogero, Guido. "Erasmo, Socrate e il Nuovo Testamento." *La Cultura* (Roma) 12 (1974): 1–22.

Cassirer, Ernst. Translated by Mario Damandi. *The Individual and the Cosmos in Renaissance Philosophy*. Oxford: Blackwell, 1963.

Cave, Terence. *The Cornucopian Text. Problems of Writing in the French Renaissance*. Oxford: Clarendon Press, 1979.

———. "The Mimesis of Reading in the Renaissance." *Mimesis: From Mirror to Method, Augustine to Descartes*, 149–65. Edited by John D. Lyons and Stephen G. Nichols, Jr. Hanover, N.H.: University Press of New England, 1982.

———. "Panurge and Odysseus." *Myth and Legend in French Literature*, 47–59. Edited by Keith Aspley, David Bellos and Peter Sharratt. London: Modern Humanities Research Association, 1982.

———, with Michel Jeanneret and François Rigolot. "Sur la prétendue transparence de Rabelais." *Revue d'Histoire Littéraire de la France* 86 (1986): 709–16.

———. "Panurge, Pathelin and Other Polyglots." *Lapidary Inscriptions: Renaissance Essays for Donald A. Stone, Jr.*, 171–82. Edited by Barbara C. Bowen and Jerry C. Nash. Lexington, Ky.: French Forum, 1990.

Céard, Jean. "De Babel à la Pentecôte: la transformation du mythe de la confusion des langues au XVIe siècle." *Bibliothèque d'Humanisme et Renaissance* 42 (1980): 577–94.

———, and Jean-Claude Margolin, eds. *Rabelais en son demi-millénaire. Actes du colloque international de Tours, 24–29 Septembre 1984*. Geneva: Droz, 1988.

Chambers, Ross. *Story and Situation: Narrative Seduction and the Power of Fiction*. Minneapolis: University of Minnesota Press, 1984.

Charpentier, Françoise. "Un royaume qui perdure sans femmes." *Rabelais' Incomparable Book*, 195–209. Edited by Raymond C. La Charité. Lexington, Ky.: French Forum, 1986.

Chesney Zegura, Elizabeth. "Toward a Feminist Reading of Rabelais." *Journal of Medieval and Renaissance Studies* 15, no. 1 (1985): 125–34.

Choay, F. "Le dehors et le dedans." *Nouvelle Revue de Psychanalyse* 9 (1974): 239–51.

Chomarat, Jacques. *Grammaire et rhétorique chez Erasme*. Paris: Société d'Editions Les Belles Lettres, 1981.

———. "Erasme et Platon." *Bulletin de l'Association G. Budé* 1 (1987): 25–48.

Chydenius, Johan. "La théorie du symbolisme médiéval." *Poétique* 23 (1975): 322–41.

Clark, Hilary A. "Encyclopedic Discourse." *SubStance* 67 (1992): 95–110.

Cohen, J. M. Introduction and Translation. *The Histories of Gargantua and Pantagruel*, by François Rabelais. London: Penguin Books, 1955.

Coleman, Dorothy. *Rabelais: A Critical Study in Prose Fiction.* Cambridge: Cambridge University Press, 1971.

———. Review of *The Wine and the Will: Rabelais's Bacchic Christianity*, by Florence Weinberg. *French Studies* 30 (1976): 60–61.

Conley, Tom. "Hiéroglyphes de Rabelais." *Hors Cadre* 1. Publications de l'Université de Paris 8 (1983): 95–117.

Cook Carpenter, Nan. "Rabelais and the Androgyne." *Modern Language Notes* 68 (1953): 452–57.

Cotgrave, Randle. *A Dictionarie of the French and English Tongues.* London, 1611. Reprint with an Introduction by William S. Woods: Columbia: University of South Carolina Press, 1950.

Crahay, Roland. "L'evangélisme d'Erasme. Eléments d'un dossier." *Réforme et Humanisme: Actes du IVe Colloque*, 71–101. Montpellier: Centre d'Histoire de la Réforme et du Protestantisme, Université Paul Valéry, 1977.

de Mesmes, J.-P. *La grammaire italienne, composée en Françoys.* Paris: Estienne Groulleau, 1548.

Defaux, Gérard. *Pantagruel et les sophistes. Contribution à l'histoire de l'humanisme chrétien au seizième siècle.* The Hague: Nijhoff, 1973.

———. "Rabelais et son masque comique: *sophista loquitur.*" *Etudes Rabelaisiennes* 11 (1974): 89–136.

———. *Le curieux, le glorieux et la sagesse du monde dans la première moitié du XVIe siècle: l'exemple de Panurge.* Lexington, Ky.: French Forum, 1982.

———. "D'un problème à l'autre: herméneutique de *l'altior sensus* et *captatio lectoris* dans le Prologue de *Gargantua.*" *Revue d'Histoire Littéraire de la France* 85 (1985): 195–216.

———. "Sur la prétendue pluralité du Prologue de *Gargantua.*" *Revue d'Histoire Littéraire de la France* 86 (1986): 716–22.

———. *Marot, Rabelais, Montaigne: l'écriture comme présence.* Paris: Champion-Slatkine, 1987.

Delcourt, Marie. *Hermaphrodite: mythes et rites de la bisexualité dans l'antiquité classique.* Paris: Presses Universitaires de France, 1958.

Demerson, Guy. "Le plurilinguisme chez Rabelais." *Réforme, Humanisme, Renaissance* 14 (1981): 3–19.

———. *Rabelais: Une vie, une oeuvre, une époque.* Paris: Balland, 1986.

———. *François Rabelais.* Paris: Fayard, 1991.

Demonet, Marie-Luce. *Les voix du signe. Nature et origine du langage à la Renaissance (1480–1580).* Paris: Champion, 1992.

Derrida, Jacques. *De la grammatologie*. Paris: Minuit, 1967.

———. *La dissémination*. Paris: Editions du Seuil, 1972.

———. *La vérité en peinture*. Paris: Flammarion, 1978.

Desonay, Fernand. "En relisant l'Abbaye de Thélème. . . ." *François Rabelais: Ouvrage publié pour le quatrième centenaire de sa mort, 1553–1953, 93–103.* Geneva: Droz; Lille: Giard, 1953.

Devereux, E. J. *Renaissance English Translations of Erasmus*. Toronto: Toronto University Press, 1983.

Dillon, John M. "A date for the death of Nicomachus of Gerasa." *Classical Review* 19 (83 old series) (1969): 274–75.

Donne, John. *The Elegies and the Songs and Sonnets*. Edited by Helen Gardner. Oxford: Clarendon Press, 1965.

Dresden, Sem. "Erasme, Rabelais et la "festivitas" humaniste." *Colloquia Erasmiana Turonensia*, 1:463–78. Edited by J.-C. Margolin. Paris: Vrin, 1972.

Drogin, Marc. *Anathema: Medieval Scribes and the History of Book Curses*. Montclair, N.J.: Allanheld and Schram, 1983.

Dubois, C.-G. *Mythe et langage au seizième siècle*. Bordeaux: Ducros, 1970.

Duras, Marguerite. *Agatha*. Paris: Editions de Minuit, 1981.

Duval, Edwin M. "Interpretation and the 'Doctrine plus Absconce' of Rabelais' Prologue to *Gargantua*." *Etudes Rabelaisiennes* 18 (1985): 1–17.

———. "The Medieval Curriculum, the Scholastic University, and Gargantua's Program of Studies." *Rabelais' Incomparable Book*, 30–44. Edited by Raymond C. La Charité. Lexington, Ky.: French Forum, 1986.

———. *The Design of Rabelais'* Pantagruel. New Haven: Yale University Press, 1991.

Eco, Umberto. *The Name of the Rose*. Translated by William Weaver. New York: Warner Books, 1984.

———. *The Limits of Interpretation*. Bloomington: Indiana University Press, 1990.

Elliott, Robert C. *The Power of Satire: Magic, Ritual, Art*. Princeton: University of Princeton Press, 1960.

Erasmus, Desiderius. *Opera omnia*. Edited by J. Clericus. 11 vols. 1703–1706. Hildesheim: Georg Olms, 1961–62.

———. *Opus Epistolarum Des. Erasmi Roterdami*. Edited by P. S. Allen, H. M. Allen, and H. W. Garrod. Oxford: Clarendon Press, 1906–1958.

———. *Desiderius Erasmus Roterodamus, Ausgewählte Werke*. Munich, 1933.

———. *Opera omnia Desiderii Erasmi Roterodami* (ASD). Amsterdam: North Holland Publishing Company, 1969–.

———. *Collected Works of Erasmus* (CWE). Toronto: University of Toronto Press, 1974–.

———. *The Praise of Folly.* Translated by Clarence H. Miller. New Haven: Yale University Press, 1979.

———. *Erasmus' Annotations on the New Testament: The Gospels.* Edited by A. Reeve. London: Duckworth, 1986.

Febvre, Lucien. *Le problème de l'incroyance au XVIe siècle: la religion de Rabelais.* Paris: A. Michel, 1942.

Ficino, Marsilio. "Marsilii Ficini in commentaria suum in Parmenidem." *Opera omnia,* vol. 2 (1576): 1137–1206.

———. *Opera omnia.* Basle, 1576. Photographic reproduction (P. O. Kristeller and M. Sancipriano). Torino: Bottega d'Erasmo, 1959.

———. *Théologie platonicienne de l'immortalité des âmes.* Critical Edition and French Translation by Raymond Marcel. Paris: Société d'Edition Les Belles Lettres, 1964–70.

———. *Marsilio Ficino: Lettere.* Edited by Sebastiano Gentile. Florence: L. S. Olschki, 1990.

Fish, Stanley E. *Self-Consuming Artifacts: The Experience of Seventeenth-Century Literature.* Berkeley: University of California Press, 1972.

Foucault, Michel. *Les mots et les choses.* Paris: Gallimard, 1966.

Frame, Donald M., trans. *The Complete Works of François Rabelais.* Berkeley: University of California Press, 1991.

Freccero, Carla. "The Politics of Interpretation." *Critical Inquiry* 9, no. 1 (1982): 45–76.

———. "Damning Haughty Dames: Panurge and the Haulte dame de Paris (*Pantagruel,* 14)." *Journal of Medieval and Renaissance Studies* 15 (1985): 57–67.

———. "The Other and the Same: The Image of the Hermaphrodite in Rabelais." *Rewriting the Renaissance,* 145–58. Edited by M. Quilligan, M. Ferguson, and N. Vickers. Chicago: University of Chicago Press, 1986.

———. "The 'Instance' of the Letter: Woman in the text of Rabelais." *Rabelais' Incomparable Book,* 45–55. Edited by Raymond C. La Charité. Lexington, Ky.: French Forum, 1986.

———. *Father Figures. Genealogy and Narrative Structure in Rabelais.* Ithaca: Cornell University Press, 1991.

Freud, Sigmund. *Jokes and their Relation to the Unconscious.* The Standard Edition, Edited and Translated by James Strachey. New York: Norton, 1960.

Galenus. *Opera.* Basileae, 1529.

Gallop, Jane. "Why Does Freud Giggle When the Women Leave the Room?" *Thinking Through the Body,* 33–39. New York: Columbia University Press, 1988.

Garber, Marjorie. *Vested Interests: Cross-Dressing and Cultural Anxiety.* New York: Routledge, 1992.

Garcia Villoslada, Ricardo. "La muerte de Erasmo." *Miscellanea Giovanni Mercati* 4:381–406. Città del Vaticano: Biblioteca Apostolica Vaticana, 1947.

Garin, Eugenio. *Giovanni Pico della Mirandola: vita e dottrina.* Florence: F. Le Monnier, 1937.

———, ed. *Giovanni Pico della Mirandola: De hominis dignitate. Heptaplus, De ente et uno, e scritti vari.* Florence: Vallecchi, 1942.

———. *La cultura filosofica del Rinascimento italiano.* Florence: Sansoni, 1961.

Genette, Gérard. *Figures III.* Paris: Editions du Seuil, 1972.

Gilson, Etienne. *Rabelais franciscain.* Paris, 1924.

Glauser, Alfred. *Rabelais créateur.* Paris: Nizet, 1966.

Gomez-Géraud, Marie-Christine. "La figure de l'interprète dans quelques récits de voyage français à la Renaissance." *Voyager à la Renaissance,* 319–35. Edited by Jean Céard and Jean-Claude Margolin. Paris: Maisonneuve et Larose, 1987.

Gray, Floyd. "Structure and Meaning in the Prologue to the *Tiers livre.*" *L'Esprit Créateur* 3, no. 2 (1963): 57–62.

———. "Ambiguity and Point of View in the Prologue to *Gargantua.*" *Romanic Review* 56 (1965): 13–21.

———. *Rabelais et l'écriture.* Paris: Nizet, 1974.

———. "Rabelais' First Readers." *Rabelais' Incomparable Book,* 15–29. Edited by Raymond C. La Charité. Lexington, Ky.: French Forum, 1986.

Greenblatt, Stephen. "Filthy rites." *Learning to Curse: Essays in Modern Culture,* 59–78. New York: Routledge, 1990.

Greene, Thomas M. *Rabelais: A Study in Comic Courage.* Englewood Cliffs, N.J.: Prentice-Hall, 1970.

———. *The Light in Troy. Imitation and Discovery in Renaissance Poetry.* New Haven: Yale University Press, 1982.

Halkin, Léon F. "Un pamphlet religieux au XVI^e siècle: L'Eloge de la Folie." *Actes du Colloque International Erasme* (THR 239), 109–25. Geneva: Droz, 1990.

Hampton, Timothy. *Writing from History.* Ithaca: Cornell University Press, 1990.

———. " 'Turkish Dogs': Rabelais, Erasmus, and the Rhetoric of Alterity." *Representations* 41 (1993): 58–82.

Hankins, James. *Plato in the Italian Renaissance.* 2 vols. Leiden: E. J. Brill, 1990.

Héberu, Léon (Leone Ebreo). *Dialogues d'amour.* Edited by A. Perry. Chapel Hill: University of North Carolina Press, 1974.

Héroët, Antoine. "L'androgyne." *La parfaicte amye.* Edited by F. Gohin. Paris: Didier, 1909.

Horace. *Satires, Epistles and Ars Poetica.* Translated by H. Rushton Fair-clough. Loeb Classical Library. Cambridge, Mass.: Harvard University Press, 1970.

Houston, John Porter. *The Traditions of French Prose Style. A Rhetorical Study.* Baton Rouge: Lousiana State University Press, 1981.

Huguet, Edmond. *Dictionnaire de la langue française du XVIe siècle.* Paris: Didier, 1925–67.

Hutcheon, Linda. "Ironie, satire, parodie. Une approche pragmatique de l'ironie." *Poétique* 46 (1981): 140–55.

Jeanneret, Michel. "Les paroles dégelées (Rabelais, *Quart Livre,* 48–65)." *Littérature* 17 (February 1975): 14–30. In *Le défi,* 113–29.

———. *Des mets et des mots: Banquets et propos de table à la Renaissance.* Paris: José Corti, 1987.

———. "Débordements rabelaisiens." *Nouvelle Revue de Psychanalyse* 43 (1991): 105–23. In *Le défi,* 183–201.

———. "Rabelais, les monstres et l'interprétation des signes (*Quart Livre* 18–42)." *Writing the Renaissance: Essays on Sixteenth-Century French Literature — Mélange in honor of Floyd Gray,* 65–76. Lexington, Ky.: French Forum, 1992. In *Le défi,* 101–112.

———. *Le défi des signes: Rabelais et la crise de l'interprétation à la Renaissance.* Orléans: Paradigme, 1994.

Kaiser, Walter. *Praisers of Folly: Erasmus, Rabelais, Shakespeare.* Cambridge, Mass.: Harvard University Press, 1963.

Kay, W. David. "Erasmus' Learned Joking: The Ironic Use of Classical Wisdom in *The Praise of Folly.*" *Texas Studies in Literature and Language* 19 (1977): 247–67.

Kelley, Donald R. *The Beginning of Ideology. Consciousness and Society in the French Reformation.* Cambridge: Cambridge University Press, 1981.

Kinser, Samuel. *Rabelais' Carnival: Text, Context, Metatext.* Berkeley: University of California Press, 1990.

Klein, Robert. "Le thème du fou et l'ironie humaniste." *Umanesimo e Ermeneutica, Archivi di Filosofia* 3 (1963): 11–25.

Klibansky, Raymond. "Plato's Parmenides in the Middle Ages and the Renaissance." *Medieval and Renaissance Studies* (1943): 281–330. Revised and reprinted in *The Continuity.*

———. *The Continuity of the Platonic Tradition During the Middle Ages.* Munich: Kraus International Publications, 1981.

Klutstein, Ilana. *Marsilio Ficino et la théologie ancienne: Oracles Chaldaïques, Hymnes Orphiques, Hymnes de Proclus.* Florence: L. S. Olschki, 1987.

Kosofsky Sedgwick, Eve. *Between Men: English Literature and Male Homosocial Desire.* New York: Columbia University Press, 1985.

Kotin, Armine. "*Pantagruel*: Language versus communication." *Modern Language Notes* 92 (1977); 691–709.

Kristeva, Julia. "Bakhtine, le mot le dialogue et le roman." *Critique* 239 (April 1967): 438–65.

——. "Du symbole au signe." *Tel Quel* 34 (Summer 1968): 34–41.

La Charité, Raymond C. "Gargantua's letter and *Pantagruel* as novel," *L'Esprit Créateur* 21, no. 1 (1981): 26–39.

——. "Lecteurs et lectures dans le prologue de *Gargantua*." *French Forum* 10 (1985): 261–70.

——. "Rabelais and the Silenic Text: The Prologue to *Gargantua*." *Rabelais' Incomparable Book*, 72–86. Edited by Raymond C. La Charité. Lexington, Ky.: French Forum, 1986.

——, ed. *Rabelais' Incomparable Book. Essays on His Art*. Lexington, Ky.: French Forum, 1986.

Lachmann, Renate. "Bakhtin and Carnival: Culture as Counter Culture." *Cultural Critique* 11 (1988–89): 115–52.

Laertius, Diogenes. *Lives of Eminent Philosophers*. Trans. R. D. Hicks. Cambridge, Mass.: Harvard University Press, 1964–65.

La Garanderie, Marie-Madeleine de. *Christianisme et lettres profanes (1515–1535)*. Paris: Champion, 1976.

La Ramée, Pierre de. *Dialectique*. Edited by Michel Dassonville. Geneva: Droz, 1964.

Lauvergnat-Gagnière, Christiane. *Lucien de Samosate et le lucianisme en France au XVIe siècle: Athéisme et polémique*. Geneva: Droz, 1988.

Lebègue, Raymond. "Rabelais, the Last of the French Erasmians." *Journal of the Warburg and Courtauld Institute* 12 (1949): 91–100.

Le Clercq, Jacques. *The Complete Works of Rabelais*. New York: The Modern Library, nd. (1936).

Lefèvre d'Etaples, Jacques. *Epistres et Evangiles pour les cinquante et deux dimanches de l'an*. Edited by Guy Bedouelle and Franco Giacone. Leiden: E. J. Brill, 1976.

Lefranc, Abel. Introduction. *Œuvres de François Rabelais*. Edited by Abel Lefranc et al. 6 vols. Vol. 1–5: Paris: Champion; vol. 6: Geneva: Droz, 1912–55.

Lestringant, Frank. "Dans la bouche des géants (*Pantagruel*, 32; *Gargantua*, 38)." *Cahiers textuels* 4, no. 5 (1989): 43–52.

Littré, Emile. *Dictionnaire de la langue française*. Paris: Gallimard-Hachette, 1961.

Lubac, Henri de. *Exégèse médiévale. Les quatre sens de l'Ecriture*. 4 vols. Paris: Aubier, 1959–64.

Lucian. *Luciani ... Opera, quae quidem extant, amnia, e graeco sermone in latinum, partim jam olim diversis autoribus, partim nunc demum per Jacobum Micyllum . . . translata. . . .* Frankfurt, 1538.

———. "How to Write History." *Lucian in Eight Volumes.* Vol. 6, 1–73. Translated by K. Kilburn. Loeb Classical Library. Cambridge, Mass.: Harvard University Press, 1968.

Lydgate, Barry. "Printing, Narrative and the Genesis of the Rabelaisian Novel." *Romanic Review* 71 (1980): 345–73.

Lyons, John D. "In the Folds of the Renaissance text." *Diacritics* 13, no. 3 (1983): 33–43.

———. *Exemplum: The Rhetoric of Example in Early Modern France and Italy.* Princeton: Princeton University Press, 1989.

Mallarmé, Stéphane. "Un Coup de dés jamais n'abolira le hasard." *Oeuvres complètes.* Edited by Henri Mondor and G. Jean-Aubry. Paris: Gallimard, 1945.

Mann Phillips, Margaret. *The Adages of Erasmus.* Cambridge: Cambridge University Press, 1964.

Margolin, J.-C., ed. *Colloquia Erasmiana Turonensia.* Paris: Vrin, 1972.

———. *Guerre et paix dans la pensée d'Erasme.* Paris: Aubier, 1973.

———. "Parodie et paradoxe dans 'L'Eloge de la Folie' d'Erasme." *Nouvelles de la République des Lettres* 2 (Naples): 27–57. (Republished in *Erasme, le prix des mots et des choses.* London: Variorum Reprints, 1986.)

Marichal, Robert. Introduction. Rabelais, *Le quart livre.* Geneva: Droz, 1947.

———. "L'attitude de Rabelais devant le néoplatonisme et l'italianisme. (*Quart livre*, ch. IX à XI)." *François Rabelais Quatrième Centenaire (1553–1953),* 181–209. Geneva: Droz, 1953.

Marin, Louis. *La parole mangée et autres essais théologico-politiques.* Paris: Klincksieck, 1986.

Mayer, C. A. *Lucien de Samosate et la Renaissance française.* Geneva: Slatkine, 1984.

Megiser, Hieronymus. *Warhafftige . . . Beschreibung, der . . . Insul MADAGASCAR.* Leipzig: Henning, 1623.

Mehlman, Jeffrey. "How to Read Freud on Jokes: The Critic as Schadchen." *New Literary History* 6, no. 2 (1975): 439–61.

Mendelson, Edward. "Encyclopedic Narrative: from Dante to Pynchon." *Modern Language Notes* 91 (1976): 1267–75.

Meurier, Gabriel. *Conjugaisons regles et instructions, moult propres et necessairement requises pour ceux qui desirent apprendre françois, italien, espagnol et flamen.* Antwerp: van Waesberghe, 1558.

Monstrelet, Enguerrand de. *Chronique.* Edited by L. Douet-d'Arcq. 6 vols. Paris: Jules Renouard, 1857–62.

Montaigne. *Œuvres complètes*. Edited by Albert Thibaudet and Maurice Rat. Paris: Gallimard, 1962.

Morçay, Raoul, ed. *L'Abbaye de Thélème*. Paris: Droz, 1934.

Musil, Robert. *The Man Without Qualities*. Translated by E. Wilkins and E. Kaiser. New York: Capricorn Books, 1965.

Navarre, Marguerite de. *Dialogue en forme de vision nocturne*. Paris: 1525.

———. *Heptaméron*. Edited by Michel François. Paris: Garnier, 1967.

Nicolay, Nicolas de. "Les navigations, pérégrinations et voyages faits en Turquie (1567–68)." *Dans l'empire de Soliman le Magnifique*. Edited by Marie-Christine Gomez-Géraud. Paris: Presses du CNRS, 1989.

Nichols, Fred J. "Generating the Unwritten Text: the Case of Rabelais." *L'Esprit Créateur* 28, no. 1 (1988): 7–17.

Norton, Glyn P. *The Ideology and Language of Translation in Renaissance France*. Geneva: Droz, 1984.

O'Rourke Boyle, M. *Erasmus on Language and Method in Theology*. Toronto: University of Toronto Press, 1977.

Paris, Jean. *Rabelais au futur*. Paris: Les Editions du Seuil, 1970.

Pico della Mirandola, Giovanni. *De Hominus Dignitate . . . De Ente et Uno*. Edited by Eugenio Garin. Florence: Valecchi, 1942.

Plato. *Plato in Twelve Volumes*. With an English Translation. Loeb Classical Library. Cambridge, Mass.: Harvard University Press, London: W. Heinemann, 1967–82.

———. *Symposium*. Translated by Tom Griffith. Berkeley: University of California Press, 1989.

Plattard, Jean. *L'Œuvre de Rabelais. Sources, invention, composition*. Paris: Honoré Champion, 1910.

Pouilloux, Jean-Yves. "Notes sur l'abbaye de Thélème." *Romantisme* I, no. 2 (1971): 200–204.

Proclus. *In Parmenidem*. Edited by Victor Cousin. Paris, 1864.

Rabelais, François. *Hippocratis ac Galeni libri aliquot, ex recognitione Francisci Rabelaesi*. Lyon: Gryphius, 1532.

———. *Œuvres de François Rabelais*. Edited by Abel Lefranc et al. 6 vols. Vols. 1–5: Paris: Champion; Vol. 6: Geneva: Droz, 1912–55.

———. *Pantagruel*. Edited by Verdun L. Saulnier. Paris: Droz, 1946.

———. *Le quart livre*. Edited by Robert Marichal. Geneva: Droz, 1947.

———. *Œuvres complètes*. Edited by Pierre Jourda. 2 vols. Paris: Garnier, 1962.

———. *Œuvres complètes*. Edited and translated by Guy Demerson. Paris: Seuil, 1973.

Raffel, Burton, trans. *Gargantua and Pantagruel*. New York: W. W. Norton, 1990.

Reedijk, C., ed. *The Poems of Desiderius Erasmus*. Leiden: Brill, 1956.

Reeve, A., ed. *Erasmus's Annotations on the New Testament: The Gospels.* London: Duckworth, 1986.

Regosin, Richard. *The Matter of My Book.* Berkeley: University of California Press, 1977.

———. "The Ins(ides) and Outs(ides) of Reading: Plural Discourse and the Question of Interpretation in Rabelais." *Rabelais' Incomparable Book,* 59–71. Edited by Raymond C. La Charité. Lexington, Ky.: French Forum, 1986.

Rigolot, François. *Les langages de Rabelais. Etudes Rabelaisiennes* 10. Geneva: Droz, 1972.

———. Review of *The Wine and the Will: Rabelais's Bacchic Christianity,* by Florence Weinberg. *Revue des Sciences Humaines* 154 (1974): 341–43.

———. "Cratylisme et Pantagruélisme: Rabelais et le statut du signe." *Etudes Rabelaisiennes* 13 (1976): 115–32.

———. "Sémiotique de la sentence et du proverbe chez Rabelais." *Etudes Rabelaisiennes* 14 (1977): 277–86.

———. *Le texte de la Renaissance. Des rhétoriqueurs à Montaigne.* Geneva: Droz, 1982.

———. "Montaigne's Purloined Letters." *Montaigne: Essays in Reading. Yale French Studies* 64 (1983): 144–66.

———. " 'Enigme' et 'Prophétie': les langages de l'hermétisme chez Rabelais." *Œuvres et Critiques* 11 (1986): 37–47.

Rossebastiano Bart, A. *Antichi vocabolari plurilingui d'uso populare: la tradizione del "Solenissimo Vocabolista."* Alessandria: Edizione dell'Orso, 1984.

Rubin, Gayle. "The Traffic in Women: Notes on the 'Political Economy' of Sex." *Toward an Anthropology of Women,* 157–210. Edited by Rayna Reiter. New York: Monthly Review Press, 1975.

Rummel, E. *Erasmus' Annotations on the New Testament: From Philologist to Theologian.* Toronto: University of Toronto Press, 1986a.

———. "Nameless Critics in Erasmus' Annotations on the New Testament." *Bibliothèque d'Humanisme et Renaissance* 48 (1986b): 41–57.

———. *Erasmus and his Catholic Critics.* 2 vols. Nieuwkoop: De Graaf, 1989.

Russell, Daniel. "Conception of self, conception of space and generic convention: an example from the *Heptaméron.*" *Sociocriticism* 4–5 (1987–88): 159–183.

Said, Edward. *Beginnings: Intention and Method.* Baltimore: The Johns Hopkins University Press, 1975.

Sainean, Lazare. "Rabelaisiana." *Revue d'Etudes de la Renaissance* 9 (1911): 249–94.

Sarocchi, J. *Rabelais et l'instance paternelle.* Paris: Nizet, 1986.

Saulnier, V.-L., ed. F. Rabelais, *Pantagruel*. Geneva: Droz, 1946.

Schwartz, Jerome. "Gargantua's Device and the Abbey of Thélème: A study in Rabelais' iconography." *Image and Symbol in the Renaissance. Yale French Studies* 47 (1972): 232–42.

———. "Aspects of Androgyny in the Renaissance." *Human Sexuality in the Middle Ages and the Renaissance*, 121–31. Edited by D. Radcliff-Umstead. Pittsburgh: Center for Medieval and Renaissance Studies, 1978.

———. *Irony and Ideology in Rabelais. Structures of Subversion.* Cambridge: Cambridge University Press, 1990.

Schwartz, Regina M. "Joseph's Bones and the Resurrection of the Text: Remembering in the Bible." *PMLA* 103 (1988): 114–24.

Screech, Michael A. *Marot évangélique.* Geneva: Droz, 1967.

———. "Some Reflexions on the Abbey of Thelema." *Etudes Rabelaisiennes* 8 (1969): 107–14.

———. Editor, introduction, commentaries. François Rabelais, *Gargantua.* Geneva: Droz, 1970.

———. "Comment Rabelais a exploité les travaux d'Erasme: Quelques détails." *Colloquia Erasmiana Turonensia*, I:453–61. Edited by J.-C. Margolin. Paris: Vrin, 1972a.

———. "Folie érasmienne et folie rabelaisienne." *Colloquia Erasmiana Turonensia*, 1:441–52. Edited by J.-C. Margolin. Paris: Vrin, 1972b.

———. *L'évangélisme de Rabelais.* Geneva: Droz, 1979a.

———. *Rabelais.* London: Duckworth, 1979b.

———. *Ecstasy and the Praise of Folly.* London: Duckworth, 1980.

Sedgwick, Eve Kosofsky. *Between Men: English Literature and Male Homosocial Desire.* New York: Columbia University Press, 1985.

*Sex linguarum dilucidissimus dictionarius / mirum quam utilis / nec dicam necessarius omnibus linguarum studiosis.* Venice: Marchio Sessa, 1541.

Seznec, Jean. *The Survival of the Pagan Gods: The Mythological Tradition and its Place in Renaissance Humanism and Art.* Translated by Barbara F. Sessions. New York: Harper Torchbooks, 1961.

Silverman, Kaja. *Male Subjectivity at the Margins.* New York: Routledge, 1992.

Simonin, Michel. "Des livres pour l'Europe? Réflexions sur quelques ouvrages polyglottes (XVIe siècle–début XVIIe siècle)." *La conscience européenne*, 384–94. Paris: Ecole Normale de Jeunes Filles, 1982.

Smith, Paul J. *Voyage et écriture: Étude sur le "Quart Livre" de Rabelais.* Geneva: Droz, 1987.

Spitzer, Leo. "Le prétendu réalisme de Rabelais." *Modern Philology* 37 (1939–40): 139–50.

———. "Rabelais et les 'rabelaisants'." *Studi Francesi* 12 (1960): 401–23.

———. "Linguistics and Literary History." *Leo Spitzer. Representative Es-*

*says*, 3–40. Edited by A. K. Forcione, H. Lindenberger, and M. Sutherland. Stanford: Stanford University Press, 1988.

Stephens, Walter. *Giants In Those Days*. Lincoln: University of Nebraska Press, 1989.

Stierle, Karlheinz. "L'histoire comme exemple, l'exemple comme histoire." Translated by J.-L. Lebrave. *Poétique* 10 (1972): 176–98.

Strubel, Armand. "*Allegoria in factis* et *Allegoria in verbis*." *Poétique* 23 (1975): 342–57.

Surtz, Ronald E. *The Guitar of God. Gender, Power and Authority in the Visionary World of Mother Juana de la Cruz (1481–1534)*. Philadelphia: University of Pennsylvania Press, 1990.

Tchemerzine, Avenir. *Bibliographie d'éditions originales et rares*. 8 vols. Paris: M. Plee, 1927–33.

Telle, E.-V. "A propos de la lettre de Gargantua à son fils." *Bibliothèque d'Humanisme et Renaissance* (1957): 208–33.

Tetel, Marcel. *Rabelais*. New York: Twayne, 1967.

Theon of Smyrna. *Expositio rerum mathematicarum*. Edited by Edward Hiller. Leipzig: Teubner, 1878.

Thompson, Sister Geraldine. "Erasmus and the Tradition of Paradox." *Studies in Philology* 51 (1964): 41–63.

Tigerstedt, E. N. "Plato's Idea of Poetical Inspiration." *Commentationes Humanarum Litterarum* 44, no. 2 (1969): 5–76.

Tournon, André. "Ce qui devait se dire en utopien (*Pantagruel* IX)." *Croisements culturels*, 115–35. Edited by André Tournon. Ann Arbor: University of Michigan Press, 1988.

Uitti, Karl D. "Women Saints, the Vernacular, and History in Early Medieval France." *Images of Sainthood in Medieval Europe*, 247–67. Edited by R. Blumenfield-Kosinski and T. Szell. Ithaca, N.Y.: Cornell University Press, 1991.

Verville, Béroalde de. *Le moyen de parvenir*. Edited by Hélène Moreau and André Tournon. Publication de l'Université de Provence. Marseille: J. Laffitte, 1984.

Virgil. *Georgics*. Translated by H. Rushton Fairclough. The Loeb Classical Library. Cambridge: Harvard University Press, 1974.

Waddington, Raymond. "The Bisexual Portrait of Francis I: Fontainebleau, Castiglione and the Tone of Courtly Mythology." *Playing with Gender*. 99–132. Edited by Jean A. Brink, Maryanne C. Horowitz, and Allison P. Coudert. Urbana: University of Illinois Press, 1991.

Walker, D. P. *Spiritual and Demonic Magic from Ficino to Campanella*. London: Warburg Institute, 1958.

———. *The Ancient Theology: Studies in Christian Platonism from the Fifteenth to the Eighteenth Century*. London: Duckworth, 1972.

Warden, John. "Orpheus and Ficino." *Orpheus: The Metamorphoses of a Myth*, 85–110. Edited by John Warden. Toronto, 1982.

Waswo, Richard. *Language and Meaning in the Renaissance*. Princeton: Princeton University Press, 1987.

Weinberg, Florence M. *The Wine and the Will, Rabelais' Bacchic Christianity*. Detroit: Wayne State University Press, 1972.

———. "Written on the Leaves: Rabelais and the Sibylline Tradition." *Renaissance Quarterly* 43, no. 4 (1990): 709–30.

Wind, Edgar. *Pagan Mysteries in the Renaissance*. New York: Barnes and Noble, 1968.

Winkler, G. B. *Erasmus von Rotterdam und die Einleitungsschriften zum Neuen Testament*. Münster: Aschendorff, 1974.

Yavneh, Naomi. "The Spiritual Eroticism of Leone's Hermaphrodite." *Playing with Gender*, 85–98. Edited by J. Brink, M. Horowitz, and A. Coudert. Urbana: University of Illinois Press, 1991.